THE CRITIC, POWER, AND THE PERFORMING ARTS

The Critic, Power, and the Performing Arts

A Twentieth Century Fund Essay

JOHN E. BOOTH

COLUMBIA UNIVERSITY PRESS
New York

COLUMBIA UNIVERSITY PRESS
New York   Oxford

Copyright © 1991 The Twentieth Century Fund
Printed in the United States of America

Library of Congress Cataloging-in-Publication Data

Booth, John E. (John Erlanger)
   The critic, power, and the performing arts / John E. Booth.
      p.   cm.
   "A Twentieth Century Fund essay."
   Includes bibliographical references and index.
   ISBN 0-231-07460-3
   1. Performing arts—United States.   2. Criticism.   3. Mass media
and the arts—United States.
I. Twentieth Century Fund.   II. Title.
PN2266.5.B66   1991   90-20506
791'.0973—dc20   CIP

Clothbound editions of Columbia University Press books are Smyth-sewn
and printed on permanent and durable acid-free paper.
c 10 9 8 7 6 5 4 3 2 1

To Douglas Booth and Oscar H. McPherson

The Twentieth Century Fund is a research foundation undertaking timely analyses of economic, political, and social issues. Not-for-profit and nonpartisan, the Fund was founded in 1919 and endowed by Edward A. Filene.

CONTENTS

FOREWORD

Quite a few of us, for quite a while, have known that John Booth was working on a study of criticism and the performing arts. His enthusiasm, his dedication to the project, made that fact evident! It is a pleasure now, on behalf of the Twentieth Century Fund and the small committee that guided the undertaking, to present the results to the public.

Books sponsored by the Fund are normally introduced by the Director, but the present holder of the office, Richard C. Leone, has kindly ceded to me the privilege of saying a few words. I have known Mr. Booth for almost forty years in connection with the Fund's work. When he retired as Associate Director in 1984, I was gratified that the trustees voted to support a study in the field of his choice. That field turned out to be, almost inevitably, the performing arts. Although a great many of the things that go on in the world engage his curiosity—and often his indignation—it is the performing arts that seem to stand first. He has already produced one excellent and long-running work on the subject. His involvement in the Theatre Development Fund, of which he has been a trustee since its inception, and his role in founding the Independent Committee on Arts Policy have helped to satisfy his interest, and to extend his influence.

I suppose that Mr. Booth is himself a critic at heart, which must account for his having launched on a quest so uncharted, toward a goal so seemingly elusive. It might have appeared (and indeed it did sometimes to the committee watching over the project) that criticism in the performing arts is so haphazard in today's cultural scene, that it is so often totally neglected, or is so perverted, or so concentrated in one seemingly all-powerful journalistic organ, that serious discussion of the critic's role must prove thankless. Mr. Booth, I think, has shown otherwise. His zeal, his optimism, his readiness to travel to cities far from Broadway, have paid rich dividends. Reading this book one cannot but be impressed by the number of men and women at work as critics, and by the importance of their task, and by the need to ensure that they are performing it well.

Mr. Booth, correctly I think, gives much emphasis to the press of this country. The newspapers nurture and give scope to effective critics, and if their editors and publishers are not enlightened, the most significant source of criticism dries up. He is aware of the problem editors face, in assigning space and funds to a kind of arcane and often sober writing that is in daily competition with news of sports, murders, and other more or less intriguing events. But he is insistent in maintaining that reviewers of the theater, dance, and music be men and women trained for the job and subject to conditions that let them perform it effectively. Competitive salaries, a reasonable chance to specialize, opportunities for travel and for discussion with their peers are among the essential prerequisites.

I have to confess that, editing a small daily, I once reviewed the local theater without any special qualifications for doing so. Once, also, I suggested to my publisher that we conduct a survey to see what percentage of our readers regularly perused such features as the book review. My publisher dissented. He said that a good newspaper should carry a good book review column, even if it had only a half dozen readers. He was right, of course, but I have to add that, in this case, the book reviews were written by the publisher's wife. Mr. Booth would undoubtedly disapprove of such practices. Yet we ran a pretty good paper—well-written, liberal, open to the best impulses of the community, and my only real complaint was that the moving picture advertisements, which ran on the editorial page, expanded on Thursdays to such disproportionate size that they practically crowded out my editorials.

In his extended and provocative essay, Mr. Booth looks at criticism from many angles and views it in many unexpected juxtapositions. He lets the critics speak about actors and producers, as indeed they are accustomed to do; he also lets the actors speak about the critics, which they have opportunity to do less frequently. The results are often surprising. How well they talk, these practitioners of the performing arts, skillfully interviewed and caught by Mr. Booth's attentive ear! He has sympathy for those who bear unfavorable or unjust criticism, as well as for those who wait in fear only to find they have been handsomely praised. He even has sympathy for the critics themselves. His chapter on the perils of being a critic should make all except the most hardy hesitate to adopt the profession. And yet, the world being what it is, it will perhaps only tempt more to enter the lists, for better or worse.

What makes this book irresistible above all, and what should give it wide attention, is Mr. Booth's unqualified love of the performing arts. He is interested in their diverse aspects, sympathetic to all who play a part in promoting and developing them, ardent in demanding for them their due place in the national life. In discussing them he is free from sentiment or pretentiousness. Making criticism his point of entry, he has got hold of a central factor in the performing arts and has made it a means for reminding us how lively, how adventurous, and in the end how all-important they are.

August Heckscher
Director Emeritus
The Twentieth Century Fund
September 1990

PREFACE

When in the course of writing this book I arrived for an interview with one of the most redoubtable figures in the arts in the United States, Lincoln Kirstein, president of the New York City Ballet, he gave me a frosty welcome that soon became glacial. A black mood that matched his black suit, black tie, black shoes, set off by a white shirt, was pervasive. In the few words he vouchsafed me, it became quickly evident that he held the world of criticism in low esteem, with two or three exceptions, and regretted the impulse that had led him to make this appointment with me in the first place. Nevertheless, wanting to tap his vast knowledge and his perceptions into the world of the arts that are so evident in his writings, I said that in the best of all possible worlds I was hoping I might make a positive contribution that would take into account some of the problems he indicated. With only a ghost of a smile, Kirstein said, "Best of all possible worlds? Mr. Booth, you have an excess of energy." My interview with Kirstein faltered to a halt, but I remembered his words. And there were times when I came to agree.

As I entered more deeply into my work I came to appreciate more fully the complexities of fairly and perceptively gauging the essential effect of criticism on performing and creative artists, on arts companies and institutions; and of ordering and analyzing the information I had gathered and how much energy would be required. I also recognized how idiosyncratic the world of criticism was, even at its best—often especially at its best.

The most compelling force in analyzing criticism in the performing arts is the knowledge that criticism shapes the arts in important ways throughout the country. Criticism, of course, is only one factor among many that determine the destiny of the arts. But, criticism helps to establish the texture and growth and place of the arts in our national life. While the power of the critic, save in very few instances, is not absolute and varies radically, critics can affect the survival and the destiny of arts institutions. They have power over the trajectory of a career, sometimes even over the professional survival of the creative or performing artist—the composer, playwright, choreographer, musician, dancer, actor. The critic can influence the funders of the arts and the audience for them.

But if critics do have power, then it is essential to ask how well qualified they are to shape the currents of the arts, what their differing criteria and philosophies are, how they have prepared for their jobs, and how they got them. This book attempts to answer some of these questions.

The wellspring of the critic's power is the editor and publisher of the publication for which he or she works or the producer or head of the news division in television. On newspapers the critic is chosen by an editor who in turn is chosen by a publisher. The critic works at the pleasure of that editor; the nature and the scope of the critic's activity are defined by that editor and the resources and opportunities to do the job are provided or withheld by that editor, who in turn faces the often immutable realities of the economics of the newspaper industry.

This book rests on what I regard as conclusive evidence that the critic has significant power, and that such power is a positive force IF the critic is well qualified, IF the editors and publishers understand the uses of that power and the place of the arts in our society, IF the audience develops the knowledge and independence to be guided rather than to be dominated by the critic. None of these conditions obtains with sufficient force to provide assurance that criticism is fulfilling its function adequately.

This book is also about reviewers. There are those who make a marked distinction between critics and reviewers, and I am sympathetic to this attitude. Generally, those making the distinction reserve the higher ground for the critic. But I have not made such a distinction, largely because I found it impossible to do so for each writer as I went along. This work deals largely with those writing for newspapers, and the fact is that most writers covering performance openings for newspapers write as critics, whether qualified or not, and do give their opinion and do evaluate the work, sometimes adequately, sometimes inadequately. They are therefore acting as critics. The specific issue here, then, is not what distinguishes a critic from a reviewer but rather what constitutes effective criticism.

The importance of criticism in the performing arts gains in dimension when set against the proliferation and scope of arts activity in the United States. The arts throughout the country are marked by a dynamism, a variety, and a creativity never before achieved on the present scale. John E. Frohnmayer, chairman, National Endowment for the Arts, in a statement before the House Subcommittee on Postsecondary Education in March 1990, pointed out that in 1965 (when the National Endowment for the Arts came into being) there were 56 professional nonprofit theaters in the United States; in 1990 there were over 400. Professional dance companies increased from 37 to over 250. There were about 60 professional orchestras in 1965. By 1988 there were 212. Audiences have kept pace with this growth. In dance alone attendance has swelled from an estimated one million in 1965 to 16 million in 1983.

John Adams, according to his wife Abigail, had a vision of the republic of the arts when in 1780 he predicted that the arts would become central to the lives of his descendants. He said that "he would study legislation and administration so that his sons—or daughters . . . might study mathematics and philosophy, natural history and naval architecture, navigation, commerce and agriculture in order to give their children a right to study painting, poetry, music, architecture, statuary, tapestry and porcelain."

Despite the growing importance of the arts and their often high artistic achievement and expanding audiences, they are still rarely a subject of study in schools or universities and are far from central to our national life. They are a frail plant compared to what we might expect them to be in so wealthy and privileged a country as ours, nor is their future secure. An attack was mounted on government support for the arts, and more subtly on the arts themselves, in 1989. The catalyst for the attack was photographs by Andres Serrano and Robert Mapplethorpe in museum exhibitions supported by federal funds. The attack spawned legislative proposals that could seriously threaten the awards system of the National Endowment for the Arts and in the long run the life of the agency itself. The incident provides striking evidence of the frailty of the arts and of our support for them. Some critics have risen to the attack and are in the forefront of efforts to save the federal support system, exposing the fatal result which censorship could have and defending the indispensability of freedom for the artist in a democratic society.

In general, the critic has a unique opportunity to forward the development of the arts by both positive and negative criticism. Taking note of this opportunity, and strikingly describing a particular gift of criticism, Arlene Croce, dance critic of *The New Yorker,* says of the late dance critic Edwin Denby: "With other critics you can agree or disagree. With Denby you undergo a form of conversion. You have new eyes, new ears, and a sensibility that lets you respond to meanings you hadn't dreamed were there."

In speaking of criticism at its best, Lloyd Richards, dean of the Yale School of Drama and artistic director of the Yale Repertory Theatre, as well as a highly prestigious director, said:

> Criticism promulgates standards and it provokes the artist to achieve those standards. It urges artists to do their most accomplished work. It supports their most daring explorations and understands their breaking new ground and appreciates their smallest efforts. The arts are a dangerous place to be.

If the arts are a dangerous place to be, so is the world of the critics. Because of their influence, the critics can play an often crucial role in the daring quest of the arts to achieve the high ground of artistic distinction. Critics need therefore to achieve as high a level of professionalism as the most gifted artist. This work is an exploration of that dangerous place and that dangerous world.

This enquiry into the realm of criticism in the performing arts—dance, music, and theater—is in large part based on interviews—with the critics who wield the power, with the editors and publishers who choose the critics and thereby essentially determine the scope and nature of criticism, with the creative and performing artists whose destinies may be shaped to a greater or lesser extent by the critic, and with the directors of performing arts companies and institutions whose destinies are influenced by criticism.

The critics include primarily those who work for the daily press, to a far lesser extent those in the electronic media and on weekly magazines. The focus is on newspaper critics, who have the most immediate and telling impact on the arts in their communities and nationally. Traditionally, some of the most important and distinguished criticism is carried in smaller publications or in books, and to a limited extent this is dealt with here. The fact is that some of the most distinguished of these critics have just about given up writing on the performing arts.

Some three hundred interviews were conducted in eleven cities across the country.* In most instances I interviewed also the editors in charge of the newspapers whose critics I had interviewed; the directors of arts institutions whose productions had been importantly affected by those critics; and performing and creative artists whose careers had in some cases been shaped by them. This cross-current of opinion, the counterpoint of impressions, of ambitions, biases, and insights, I believe, adds to the validity of the exploration.

There were others along the way whom I interviewed—board members of artistic institutions, teachers in journalism schools, foundation executives. The interviews were supplemented by extensive readings of criticism and the works about criticism that must be involved in any such endeavor, as well as by the experiences of the author.

For each of the three hundred persons I interviewed, there are five others from whom I also could have benefited by interviewing. Time and opportunity impose their limitations. Even among those I did interview, I could use only a fraction of the material. Yet all of the insights and information provided to me has informed this work and was indispensable in formulating my suggestions for raising the level of the art of criticism.

John E. Booth

*In Atlanta, Boston, Chicago, Los Angeles, New York, Minneapolis, St. Paul, San Francisco, Seattle, Washington, and Winston-Salem. Supporting documentation comes from a survey conducted for this work in twenty-seven cities that I did not visit personally. The results are discussed in Chapter 4. The Twentieth Century Fund will make the survey materials available to interested scholars.

ACKNOWLEDGMENTS

A work such as this must be in one sense supremely collaborative, depending as it does on the generosity in time and effort of those creative and performing artists, arts managers, editors and publishers, and critics whom I interviewed and whose testimony and insights must inform to so great an extent the author. I am most deeply grateful to them.

The Twentieth Century Fund supported the research and writing of this work with grace, generosity, and considerable wisdom along the way. I am grateful to the Board of Trustees of the Fund, headed by Brewster Denny, and especially to a small committee of the Board which oversaw this project. It was headed by David B. Truman, and its other members were Peter A. A. Berle, Charles Hamilton, and August Heckscher. They understood to near perfection the equation involving enough help but not too much help.

Without minimizing my own rather unremitting efforts to complete this work as satisfactorily as possible, it is simply impossible to imagine doing so without the selfless efforts of Beverly Goldberg, director of publications for the Twentieth Century Fund and its chief editor. She is an editor of consummate skill and unyielding professionalism. Adding to her value is an unnerving psychological insight into her authors. Carol Kahn, with the most admirably honed craft, assisted in the editing.

Stephen Benedict, president, Board of Directors, Theatre Development Fund, and Thomas Lask, formerly a staff writer and editor on cultural affairs for *The New York Times,* with their astonishingly original insights and their broad and deep knowledge of the arts, read the manuscript at different stages and made the most perceptive and helpful suggestions, probably including those I did not take and may well come to regret.

Hilda and William Baumol, pioneers in work on the economics

of the arts, gave me invaluable advice and guidance with the greatest generosity. Audrey E. McDonald of Audrey McDonald Associates designed and surpervised with great distinction the survey made for this work.

I called upon others for different kinds of assistance at different points along the way, and among those who helped most were John F. Breglio, Esq.; the staff of the Performing Arts Research Center of the New York Public Library at Lincoln Center, including Betty Corwin, director, Theater on Film and Tape; Jennifer Crewe, editor, Columbia University Press; Rhoda Gilinsky, contributor, Westchester edition, *The New York Times;* Howard Klein, consultant in the arts; Florence Manson; Ruth Mayleas, program officer, Education and Culture Program of the Ford Foundation; Barbara B. Millhouse, president, Reynolda House Museum of American Art; Nona Porter; Sally Sommer; Ana Steele, acting deputy chairman for program, National Endowment for the Arts; Geraldine Stutz, publisher, Panache Press; Daniel E. Troy, Esq.; George Wachtel, director of research, the League of American Theatres and Producers; George C. White, president, Eugene O'Neill Memorial Theater Center; and Eileen C. Conroy, an extraordinarily competent and gifted secretary-researcher.

PART I

The Impact of Criticism

★ THE PREMISE of this book rests on the broad and sometimes decisive influence that criticism can have on the performing arts in the United States, on its capability to influence if not determine the currents of the cultural life of the country. This power, responsibly and competently wielded, be the criticism positive or negative, can enhance the life of the arts and of cultural development.

This part of the book explores the testimony of actors, musicians, dancers, playwrights, choreographers, composers, directors, and producers on the effects of criticism. Sometimes the testimony is suffused with the exhilaration of an artist whose career has been launched by the critics; sometimes it is sober and despairing. Collectively, it offers indisputable proof of the important, often crucial, impact of criticism on the performing arts.

This book deals with the profit-making and nonprofit sectors of the performing arts, differentiated legally by the tax-exempt status of the nonprofit sector. This sector is composed of virtually all the symphony orchestras, chamber music ensembles, opera companies, ballet and dance companies, and a broad swath of theaters throughout the country. The profit sector is composed largely of Broadway and of those touring companies that are booked into commercial theaters around the country. The book does not deal with concerts by popular rock bands or singers largely because they represent a universe far outside the question of critical impact dealt with here.

1 ★ The Impact on the Performing and Creative Artist

The arts constitute a universe of anxiety for the performing and creative artist, a universe in which success or failure, professional survival or annihilation, are in an agonizingly precarious balance. The artist knows that his or her future depends on some combination of talent along with accident, luck, and the unpredictable forces of changing tastes or the tyranny of trends. For many performers that future depends on the uncertain toll of age and the mysterious fluctuations of talent itself. The state of the economy, particularly as it affects support for the arts, and international tensions, sometimes preventing a tour, for instance, also take their toll. A major element in shaping this universe of anxiety is the critic.

There have always been critics in the performing arts, in the fine arts, and in literature who have been in the vanguard of discovering, sustaining, and celebrating talent. One thinks of George Bernard Shaw's championing of Ibsen, of George Jean Nathan's support of Eugene O'Neill, of H. L. Mencken's defense of Theodore Dreiser, of John Ruskin's critical allegiance to Turner, of Harold Rosenberg's sympathetic analysis and understanding of the abstract impressionists. There was Robert Schumann, writing as a critic and hailing Brahms at the beginning of his career, virtually announcing the coming of a new age. Closer to our time, there was Olin Downes, music critic for *The New York Times*, championing Jean Sibelius. Recently, the chief theater critic of the *Times*, Frank Rich, gave a rave review to Martha Clarke's performance art production of *Vienna: Lusthaus* that endowed her with a galaxy of new opportunities.

The perceptivity and prescience of critics can bring the arts to new heights. Critics serving as guardians of the gates often bar those they consider misguided or meretricious. Some of their negative critiques emerge from their understanding and passion for the art they are writing about. But on other occasions critics have failed to understand, appreciate, or acknowledge the gifted and talented and have used their powers irresponsibly, perhaps driven by excesses of ambition or ego or ignorance.

The writer, choreographer, composer, actor, dancer, singer, and musician all know that criticism is part of their lives. Some artists have decided to ignore criticism or fortify themselves against it insofar as they can—perhaps as England's infinitely gifted and redoubtable actress Edith Evans did when she was introduced at a cocktail party in London to the city's reigning theater critic, the late Kenneth Tynan. Standing before her, he had started, in his stammering way, to express his admiration for her, when Miss Evans interrupted him and said in that imperious voice which had riveted the attention of audiences from the stages of the world, "I never talk to the enemy." With her perfect timing she returned to the conversation she had been engaged in.

The insights of men and women, performing artists and creative artists, whose lives have been touched, influenced, or sometimes shaped, for better or worse, by critics are worth hearing. What happens to the artist? What are the implications for the next performance, the next effort? How do artists assess and evaluate criticism? What do they consider the elements of professional competence for anyone judging their work, how do they see the interplay of the many forces that shape a critic's viewpoint? What elements in a critique might the artist find fair or constructive? Which cross the line to the destructive? Which critics are admired, which are unacceptable, and what are the criteria for the opinion?

These are some of the questions that surface in talking to artists about criticism and the fight for survival. True, all of us are subject to judgments in the workplace or at home. But neither doctor nor lawyer nor Indian chief, in fact very few of us, are subjected to critiques every time out, carried openly and publicly in the press and television.

In working on this chapter I have had to gauge the reliability of the testimony of the performing and creative artist. In the universe of anxiety their responses can hardly be counted on to be invariably reasonable and measured any more than the reviews of their work can always be counted on to be reasonable and measured. But it seems clear to me that the perceptive performing and creative artist drawing upon his or her unique experience can give us highly informed insights about the role and quality and effects of contemporary criticism.

Of Champions and Enemies

Not all performers and creative artists regard the critic as the enemy. Nevertheless, the relationship between artist and critic is bound to be marked by tension if not confrontation. This basic reality is usually recognized by both, but mainly by artists. There seems to be some immutable law of life which suggests that even the most gifted and highly praised talents are likely to be given their comeuppance eventually. So the tension is omnipresent. Even Michael Crawford, opening on Broadway in the title role of Andrew Lloyd Webber's *Phantom of the Opera,* a show whose mega-hit proportions in London paved the way for record advance sales in New York, guaranteeing hit status, panicked on the night he was told the critics were coming. "I think I had a breakdown on the spot. Frank Rich of *The New York Times* was going to be there."[1]

What Is a Fair Break?

Most performing and creative artists want to feel first and foremost that they will be given a "fair break." What a fair break means, of course, is as open to interpretation as any answer given by the Delphic Oracle. But, give or take a few interpretations, a fair break means being reviewed by a person with an excellent background in the art he or she is reviewing, and one who will put the particular performance or presentation into the context of its unique possibilities (that means not judging a newly organized symphony orchestra by the same criteria used in judging the New York Philharmonic). Nevertheless, while the actress playing Lady Macbeth need not be judged against every Lady Macbeth in history but only within the context of her own performance, the standards set by the great performances of the role inevitably become involved in a critic's judgment. A fair break also means that the intention and purposes of the performer or writer or choreographer be explored and that the work be criticized within that context; that momentary fashions and prejudices in the arts not dictate the review; and perhaps, above all, that the critic understand that, without releasing his most rigorous hold on standards, he is part of a process that can have a profound effect on the arts.

George Bernard Shaw made the point succinctly and eloquently in his advice to a young critic: "If you want to enjoy masterly acting twenty years hence, you must be very tender to the apprentices and journeymen of today."[2] Conversely, the artist who pleads for the critic's understanding in order to allow for certain deficiencies

5

or any number of special circumstances would do well to consider Samuel Johnson's response to a plea to soften his harsh opinion of an artist because of the amount of time and effort that had gone into the work and the difficulty of the effort. Johnson replied, "Difficult, do you call it, Sir? I wish it were impossible."[3]

Formulating a philosophy to deal with criticism is an only sometimes successful preoccupation of many performers and creative artists. William Schuman, the first composer to win a Pulitzer Prize, one of his many honors, and the first president of Lincoln Center for the Performing Arts, looked back at age seventy-five and recalled that

> Criticism affected me greatly when I was young. It had to do with damaged ego or swollen ego, depending on which side the critic spoke . . . whether it was flattering or not flattering, and when you are young that's very important. It no longer is to me. For the last twenty-five years I've never looked up an out-of-town newspaper. When I first started out I would race down to Times Square and get all the out-of-town newspapers when I had a performance. That was a growing up process. I soon learned that there are critics and critics. I formed a philosophy when I was very young. It was that I would steel myself so that I would feel no pleasure if I were praised from a source I didn't respect and I would feel no pain if I were lambasted from a source I didn't respect. Now, how did that philosophy work out in practice? Easy. I loved every good review, and hated every bad review—regardless of the source! But however aggravated one may become with the critics either at times, frequently, or always, they do create a certain excitement on the part of the general public which I think without them would not quite exist in the way it does.

The Critic's Effect—Long Range

Schuman is disinclined to think that critics can account for ultimate success or failure but believes that they can accelerate or retard the acceptance of a performer or a composer. Composers tend to have time on their side; for performers, on the other hand, immediate judgments are more consequential. Yet the immediacy and the force of criticism can also exert great influence on the life of a composer. The case of Samuel Barber as Schuman recounts it is haunting.

At the time that Schuman was president of Lincoln Center, he urged Rudolf Bing, general manager of the Metropolitan Opera, to commission an American composer to do a work for the opening of the new opera house at Lincoln Center. Schuman says that Bing chose Samuel Barber, both because he admired Barber and because he didn't know the name of any other American composer. The opera, *Antony and Cleopatra,* got devastating reviews. Schuman says:

> Sam was really crushed by this. He left the country by slow boat and I don't think he ever got over it. It was a mortal blow. You slave away at something for several years and it's all decided in one night. Was it decided fairly? Time will answer that. Many people think it was, others feel that the production was too lavish and hurt the work. It has been done in a revised version and hasn't had any greater success. Barber's first opera, *Vanessa,* which was widely admired, is no longer performed at the Met. So neither is performed—one was hailed, one was damned. But that may tell you more about the Met management than about the critics.

Despite the generalities in the impact of criticism running throughout the performing arts, there are distinct differences among dance, music, and theater artists about what kind of criticism is most important and in terms of the concerns that dominate their reactions. There are also differences in impact upon careers and the art form itself.

MUSIC

A distinguishing fact of life in music is the heavy reliance on classics of the eighteenth and nineteenth centuries and before and the rejection of new music by vast audiences in opera and concert halls across the country. The audiences make incontrovertible their argument at the box office. It is hard to say how many managers would plan more adventuresome programs if they were not faced with economic penalties for doing so. Composer Ezra Laderman says:

> What we demand in theater or books is what is new. But in music we demand what is known and loved. We don't like surprises. If at a traditional symphony concert Reich or Glass is presented,

7

half the audience walks out unless there are enough young people. What these composers do is hire Avery Fisher Hall and at $25 per ticket they fill the place.

Nevertheless, there are some managers who take risks to be contemporary and there are a number of critics who are in the forefront of those trying to reform the musical world, especially audiences, to accept today's music. But according to some composers, many critics are not prepared to deal with new music and are part of the problem. In fact, the music itself is all too often not dealt with. To an unusual extent, therefore, musical criticism is a matter of performance criticism. Just how much a critic can help a contemporary composer in a world not particularly attuned to new music is a question addressed by Ellen Taaffe Zwilich, the first woman to win a Pulitzer Prize for musical composition; her body of work includes symphonies, string quartets, and music for the New York City Ballet: "I write almost exclusively instrumental music. My first audience and my first critic is my performer and I honestly believe that word-of-mouth is the best review." But Zwilich acknowledged the boost she got from Michael Walsh's review in *Time*. He wrote: "For quite a while musicians have considered Zwilich to be an important composer and now the audiences are catching on."

Without discounting the power of the right review in the right place, Zwilich also believes that it is the cumulative effect that will gain acceptance for a composer: "One of the problems today even in a city like New York, where you essentially have only one major reviewing institution, *The New York Times* . . . you get only one person's opinion. I know that the people at the *Times* are very conscious of this and I think they take it very seriously." In Boston (at a festival sponsored by the International Society for Contemporary Music in 1976) a larger number of critics covered the event, which Zwilich believes was advantageous to her because a profile emerged between the ones who loved her work and the ones who thought it was, as Zwilich says, "O.K."

Zwilich is not inclined to believe that an arsenal of really good reviews is a prerequisite for moving ahead in the music world. "My impression," says Zwilich, "is that for composers it really doesn't matter on the reviewing level. I've gotten extraordinarily good reviews that didn't produce any measurable results. Where I think it makes a difference for a composer—and this may be so for a performer as well—is to get to a point where you're discussed and a body of your work is discussed and where you're important enough a figure to be talked about. The problem for the young artist is to get to that level, to get past the one shot, thumbs-up, thumbs-down business into the general arena."

Getting commissions is of great importance to composers, and in the early years prospects can be particularly chancy and difficult. Favorable critical attention helps.

> One of the reviewers, Richard Dyer of *The Boston Globe,* is quite knowledgeable, writes well, and has the courage to say what he thinks. He really came out and said some very nice things about my string quartet in spite of the fact that I was an unknown element and that really helped lead to an important commission in Boston. If you're trying to get money for something and you can use this as positive evidence—I'm sure it doesn't hurt . . . but I don't think in and of itself it does anything. I think specifically at the stage of looking at individual works it does almost nothing, but it can lend credence to someone.

One factor that has little to do with talent is charisma, yet it affects both critical and public reception. "You can play flawlessly," according to one agent, "but without charisma you are unlikely to have a major success. Artur Rubinstein was never famous for his accuracy, but something about him, his body language, catapulted him over others."

A Debut Doesn't Always Mean a Beginning

While in all the performing arts the problem of launching a career is involved with critical reception, it is particularly important to performers of classical music, whose debut carries with it the knowledge that its critical reception can frame an entire career. For pianists, violinists, indeed any instrumentalist or singer, a New York debut is essential. One of the major agents for music talent in the country, who wishes to remain anonymous, explained that such debuts must be made in New York because managers around the country read *The New York Times.* According to this agent, other important New York critics are Andrew Porter in *The New Yorker* and Peter G. Davis in *New York* magazine. Performing a semicritical role are such people as Charles Kuralt on the "Sunday Morning Show" and Morley Safer on "Sixty Minutes," both of CBS-TV, who give attention to new talent once in a while. On rare occasions *The New York Times Magazine* will do an article on a talented performer, which is the top of the possibilities for attention to a new or burgeoning career. While the agent considers Boston's Richard Dyer and Martin Bernheimer of the *Los Angeles Times* as particularly influential, this agent argues that recognition in New York is of far greater importance.

The importance of the debut (and the review) is underscored by the $12,000 to $20,000 necessary to finance it—a sum the artist or his supporters must come up with. The extent of the advertising is a chief variable, along with the choice of the hall and the day on which the recital is given. Alice Tully Hall is considered the prime New York location; Carnegie Hall, Weill Hall, Merkin Hall, and, to a far lesser extent today, Town Hall are also desirable.

An Ear Is an Ear Is an Ear—Maybe

In music the ear is master—the ear of the composer, of the performer, of the conductor—and of the critic. But performers and composers reading a review of a performance are sometimes perplexed by what the critic reports he heard.

Zwilich recalls that on listening to her Chamber Symphony, one reviewer said it was like Schoenberg, another compared it to minimalism, and both liked it. But she knew her piece was like neither Schoenberg nor minimalism, both of which are at opposite poles: "That's when you are ready to sit down and cry . . . the sense of addressing someone who is not hearing you."

Indeed, that situation haunts all artists—the sense of not being "heard" or "seen." Of course, the fault may lie in the failure of the artist to convey his meaning. But that is not necessarily so. Ezra Laderman puts it this way:

My Fourth Symphony was given in Los Angeles to nine reviews. . . . Four were raves, three were pans, and two mixed. If you read the reviews you would not believe it was the same work they were reviewing. It tells how they hear. They compared the music with so many composers it boggles the mind—Bartok, Stravinsky, Vaughan Williams. They were trying to let the audience know something about where I came from. Although I am eclectic there is nothing of Williams or Stravinsky in my music. [Something else] I don't understand is that five or six critics who cover music for *The New York Times* don't see eye-to-eye. They have very different aesthetic perceptions.

10

William Schuman says the worst offense is to thank a critic for a good review as though it were a favor. The second big offense—to damn somebody who reviews your work negatively:

They're trying to make their living and I try to give them the benefit of the doubt. I think they're trying to do the best and fairest job they can do. Now, having said that you will find sometimes that the most brilliant critics, such as Virgil Thomson during his years on *The New York Herald Tribune,* can be the most capricious, because as the record shows, Thomson, although he had some enthusiasm for the work of his colleagues, favored everything French. You can't say, however, that he didn't make a sizable contribution because that was his point of view. I rather suspect that he did . . . but it was not balanced. So I guess if you are looking for balance in criticism, you can just forget it. I don't think newspapers are interested in balance in their critical comments either.

Artists have an especially hard time being objective about a lack of "balance" in criticism when they are young. Isaac Stern, the violinist, considered giving up after an unfavorable review at the start of his career, according to Harold Schonberg, former chief music critic for *The New York Times.*[4] Recognized now as one of the great violinists of the century, Stern gives the following account:

When the reviews came out I was in a state of shock. I remember getting on one of those New York double-decker buses and riding around for five hours, thinking of my future. Should I take a safe job as a concertmaster of an orchestra? I had an offer. I didn't know what to do. Finally I said to myself, "Dammit, I want to play!" So I came back to New York the next year and got rave reviews and maybe I didn't even play as well.

The Frustrations of No Redress

Virtually all performers, creative artists, and directors of major arts institutions, as well as those who run the most modest performing arts companies, are frustrated by their lack of ability to successfully seek redress when they believe they have been unjustly dealt with by the critic. They may believe him to be incompetent, unqualified, or biased, but fear that if they create a fuss it will simply make an enemy of the critic. Sometimes their complaints are baseless, but sometimes they have a very good point. On rare occasions they do make a representation, and on even rarer occasions corrective action is taken by the critic.

To composer-lyricist Stephen Sondheim just about the worst thing about getting rotten reviews

> is that you never get a chance to tell critics how many of them are illiterate, how they don't know what they are talking about . . . how sneering and mean and unfunny and styleless they are. . . . They don't know the difference between [the function] of the director and the actor and the writer. . . . How can they? I don't. When I see a wonderful moment on stage, I don't know who's responsible for it. I wouldn't dare say [as they do], "Oh, that director's terrible, that actor saved the scene, or that writer is wonderful but that actress almost killed the line." The fact is they use space for the most part for their own purposes which has to do with sneering and showing off.

Franco Zeffirelli apparently had no qualms in expressing his distress over the highly negative review Donal Henahan, chief music critic of *The New York Times,* gave to the Metropolitan Opera production of *Turandot,* which Zeffirelli directed. (It became the Met's hottest ticket even though it received generally bad notices.) His letter to the *Times* is worth quoting, both because it is a robust example of an artist's attempt to fight back, and because it touches on questions of negativism and positivism that frequently crop up in conversations among creative and performing artists about critical assessments of their work.

Zeffirelli wrote the *Times* that Henahan's dismissal of his staging of *Turandot* caused such an outpouring of support for him and his colleagues that

> I feel compelled to suggest you seriously scrutinize the present policies and practices of your staff in an effort to rectify a situation that many people have come to regard as intolerable. . . . The fact that performances of my production invariably are sold out far in advance and receive extended ovations surely indicates that there is something, however slight, that is positive about them. . . . Long ago I stopped taking what most critics said seriously, for in general they are a destructive lot who can gain attention only by producing outrageously condescending affronts to the dignity of dedicated artists. Giuseppe Verdi, for example, was so crushed by the critical reception to *Aida* that he wrote nothing for the next seventeen years. Just think how many more works of the caliber of *La Traviata, Rigoletto* and *Il Trovatore*

we would have today if the reviewers had not imagined themselves in competition to see who could be the nastiest.[5]

Zeffirelli went on to note the injury felt by Georges Bizet over
the critics' notices when *Carmen* was first presented: "A sensitive
man was destroyed by amateurs whose resentment, jealousy and
soured ambition found an outlet in reviling the leader of an artistic
discipline otherwise closed to them."

An instance in which the artist did have the last word and did
get back at the critic occurred when Gerard Schwarz, music director of the Los Angeles Chamber Orchestra, principal conductor of
the Seattle Symphony Orchestra, and musical director of Lincoln
Center's "Mostly Mozart" concerts, went to the publisher of a particular newspaper, protesting the critic's incompetence. In Schwarz's
view, musical ignorance, a lack of integrity, and a bad ear are
among the major deficiencies of a bad critic, and a bad critic is a
destructive critic. He cited a case in which the critic had severely
criticized the trombonists in a movement of the Bartok *Concerto for
Orchestra,* "when the trombonists played three notes in the whole
movement!" The critic complained that the trombones played in a
rowdy fashion, when in fact that's exactly what the composer asked
for. The publisher told Schwarz he liked a little controversy. Schwarz
agreed that controversy was wonderful, but dishonesty wasn't. The
critic was removed from covering Schwarz's music—at least an
important partial victory in a game of power in which the prestige
and reputation of the artist making the complaint, the prestige and
reputation of the critic, and the relative strength of the journal all
came into play.

Of course, it is always possible to take the position that the critics
don't matter much anyway, a position the British composer Andrew Lloyd Webber is reported to have taken when he tried to
buck up the dispirited young cast of his *Song and Dance* following
generally poor reviews. He read them all the lukewarm notices that
attended his earlier superhits, *Jesus Christ Superstar, Evita,* and *Cats.*

Two artists who did not have the last word were the actress
Angela Paton and her director husband, Robert W. Goldsby, who
ran the Berkeley Stage Company in San Francisco's Bay Area. The
theater had made a reputation for mounting avant-garde works
and was slowly building an audience. But its directors felt they
were endlessly battling the critics. Finding the battle unequal, they
decided to close the theater. Some of the critics claimed the theater
simply did not do good enough work and that they were being
given the rap.

13

The breaking point for Goldsby and Paton came with the production of Lynn Siefert's play, *Coyote Ugly,* about a demon child. The work was challenging and, according to Goldsby, "came from one of the newest, most interesting voices I had heard. Remarkably alive. This play was in a sense a tragic farce." It went on to have a number of productions at other locales, including Chicago's Steppenwolf Theatre and the Kennedy Center in Washington, and was runner-up for the Susan Smith Blackburn Prize, a prestigious award given annually for the best new play by a woman playwright.

Reviews of the play, Goldsby reported, used such words as "disgusting" and called it an "example of Western imperialism." Or the reviewers simply fastened onto the incestuous relationships. "They focused not on the play but on what they found to be morally offensive material," Goldsby said. "The critics reviewed the work as if it were a piece of slime, of life from the tabloids. The audience, which had been growing during previews, dropped sharply when notices came out. The house went to 30 percent. Two staff members resigned because they felt the theater could not work."

"Nobody asked what the play is." Paton added: "I discovered that in doing new works you are asking questions that still trouble us. People get scared at that. Critics are scared—they want to trivialize it, dismiss it."

Goldsby said:

> When I read the reviews . . . well, we all want to write letters. But in writing letters to critics, you can't win. That is the Super No-No. Then one night I went to the theater and there were practically no people there. I decided to write a letter. But I thought about it for three days, slept on it—usually after thinking about it you decide not to write the letter, or at least not to send it. But in my twenty-five years I had not written a letter. I decided to. . . . I sent the letter to twenty-two critics of the Bay Area Critics Circle. I was outraged. I never wanted to work again. . . . When I had written the letter to the critics there was no reaction. That was a pretty good punishment.

DANCE

In the United States dance criticism is of relatively recent origin, keeping step with the rather extraordinary flowering of dance in the past four or five decades. It was not until 1927 with the appointment of John Martin by *The New York Times* that the first dance critic began writing for a major daily newspaper.

Bella Lewitzky, the choreographer who heads her own company in Los Angeles, recalls that in the 1940s and 1950s when her company went on the road, the editor of a newspaper would send a society reporter, perhaps a theater or music critic, or maybe a sportswriter. "I suppose he figured that there was movement in all of them. But practically never was anyone sent with a knowledge of the dance."

Despite the fact that Lewitzky acknowledges that there are now very knowledgeable critics across the nation, she does not have great confidence in their criticism. In the end, Lewitzky says, it is all a matter of personal opinion, and no critic or even a group of them should control the destiny of dance. "Some companies, some artists will survive, some will get lost. Dance doesn't need someone to say who shall die and who shall live. Creation is a very private affair."

Nevertheless, Lewitzky says she has benefited from the work of critics who cared deeply about the dance, such as Walter Terry, formerly of *The New York Herald Tribune;* Doris Herring, who used to write for *Dance* magazine; Paul Horst, of the *Dance Observer;* Deborah Jowitt, of *The Village Voice;* and *The New York Times*'s Anna Kisselgoff—who, like her predecessor John Martin, "see themselves as educators, put more into their critiques than their own opinions and proclivities, see dance in the context of dance history."

The determination to be independent of the critics is reflected across the country, articulated tellingly by New York's Eliot Feld. Artistic director of the Feld Ballet and an internationally known choreographer and former dancer, Feld says that when he reads the critics he frequently hears the sound of coins. Feld points out that if it costs his company $350,000 to perform in New York, the group depends on reviews to bring in audiences for its month-long New York season. And when he talks about reviews, he really means *The New York Times. The Village Voice* has some influence, as does Clive Barnes at the *New York Post,* but it is primarily and nearly overwhelmingly the *Times* that calls the tune. But this, Feld claims, has just fortified his own independence and his determination to do the work he believes in:

> I listen to no one. You must separate the artistic, personal, and economic. Your job is to lead, not to follow. Do the critics like it or not? No effect. For my own sanity, clarity of mind, and pur-

15

pose I must keep that in mind. Talent is not always enough. You need temerity, something close to obsessiveness. In dance you must go it alone. If you keep doing what you're doing you may survive. A new critic comes, another goes, critics change their minds. In some instances I know the critic will never like something I'm doing, but I go on.

Peter Martins, Danish-born dancer and choreographer who with Jerome Robbins originally took over the responsibilities of George Balanchine in running the New York City Ballet and is now its ballet master in chief, has also worked as a choreographer on Broadway. He found a startling contrast between the critics' impact on Broadway and in the ballet. Bad reviews or good, the ballet goes on, but Broadway is a different story, Martins observed. Martins made his Broadway debut as choreographer with Andrew Lloyd Webber's *Song and Dance*. It was panned by Frank Rich, but nevertheless had a respectable run (the *Times* can more easily close a straight dramatic play with bad reviews than a musical). Martins found the critique to be personal in a nearly vicious way and sensed what he perceived to be the critic's conviction that Andrew Lloyd Webber could do no good. "I believe he'd seen it in London, did not like it there and was not going to like it in New York," Martins said.

In the world of ballet, Martins claims critics don't matter much; a critically disapproved ballet will not be taken out of the repertoire and the company will do what it pleases with the highest artistic goal in mind. Conversely, a ballet raved about as a masterpiece will stay in only if those running the ballet think it is a masterpiece. In dance, he notes, "We don't let critics dictate to us."

There are well-informed dance people who would disagree with Martins even while agreeing that ballet is not as critic-dependent as theater. But they claim that ballet is not at all oblivious to critical comment. They will tell you, for instance, that Mikhail Baryshnikov, formerly artistic director of the American Ballet Theater, withdrew his *Cinderella* when it was blasted by the critics even though it was a success at the box office. Nevertheless, those who run ballet companies in New York City are at least as influenced by attitudes of the audience as by those of critics, and the ballet crowd is far more likely than the theater audience to make up its own mind.

Martins thinks critics often write for the record, for their own posterity, with the thought of how they will be judged in years to come taking priority over their own reactions. He believes they are very reluctant to take a stand lest the future hold them responsible for a wrong opinion. George Balanchine told him that John Martin used to write devastating reviews of Balanchine's ballets and purportedly never got over the fact that Balanchine became famous and his ballets became masterpieces. Balanchine said:

> I could imagine that that could be a critic's worst fear, to make a blunder like that. Look what the leading critic wrote about *Sleeping Beauty* when it was first performed in Russia. He wrote that this brought ballet a step backward and that it was unimaginable that Tchaikovsky, our great Tchaikovsky, could write a score as mediocre as *Sleeping Beauty*.

The power of critics of *The New York Times* is greater than that of any other newspaper in the city or nation. The paper's broad coverage of the arts, the shortage of competitive newspapers in New York, and widespread consumer dependence on critics are all elements of this power. But the fact is that critics on the *Times* have had extraordinary clout for decades. In those instances where a critic has left the *Times* to go elsewhere, he has usually discovered how much less power his voice then commands.

When *The New York Times* brought John Martin on to its staff in 1927, he not only helped create the power of the *Times* in the dance world but also contributed handsomely to the development of dance in the United States. Thomas Lask, who also played an important role in arts coverage over a long career with the *Times*, notes that John Martin raised the consciousness of an entire generation during the 1930s and 1940s and by his advocacy and dedication had a positive effect on audiences and dancers alike.

With power go possibilities for the abuse of power. This story about Agnes de Mille, the prominent choreographer, is an example of the latter. John Martin turned upon her professionally over a private matter, using his power in ways she claims injured her career. Through the dances of *Oklahoma!* and a string of Broadway hits, de Mille changed the look and quality of the entire American musical theater. She started her career in 1928, a year after Martin had come to the *Times*. De Mille knew him to be an exceptionally fine, discerning, and knowledgeable critic, but claims he had a weakness that could corrupt his judgment:

> He used to fall in love, now and then, with some of the dancers. When anything threatened them in any way, or worked against them, he didn't hesitate to use his great weapon of *The New York Times* personally. I think this is wicked. Well, I displeased him

17

because I wouldn't favor him in certain ways relating to certain young men that he was interested in. He simply ignored me for seven years.

But because she was on Broadway, her works were reviewed by both Brooks Atkinson and Walter Kerr, once the influential theater critics of the *Times* and *The New York Herald Tribune,* respectively, who gave her rave notices.

Ironically, the *Times* consulted Agnes de Mille on Martin's successor. Clifton Daniel, managing editor, invited her opinion and de Mille, recounting the conversation, informed Daniel that the new critic must be an American, and should be a man,

> because dancing is considered effeminate and sissy and we labor under that stigma. I think you must get a man who can write and, if possible, a virile man. Clifton Daniel looked at me with big wide eyes as though he were an innocent child and said, "I'm not aware we ever had any homosexuality in our critical forces." I said, "Mr. Daniel, we've been drinking tea up to this point and I suggest we switch to whiskey."

After a short interim appointment, Clive Barnes of London was appointed to the job. According to de Mille, Barnes came to New York with a "monstrous" prejudice against her. "I hadn't a prayer . . . he attacked and attacked." De Mille's experience with Barnes provides a telling insight into the dilemma of subjectivity, which is an essential element of criticism, especially when the opinion of the critic carries such often-decisive power. "When I'd meet Barnes he was quite affable and charming. He said, 'I have to write the truth.' I said, 'I don't see why, most people don't.' "

In fact, Barnes was writing the truth from his point of view. He was not an admirer of de Mille as a choreographer, although he admired her theatricality and believed her writings on ballet to be outstanding within the literature of dance.

"Because he was the only one," she says, "he was relentless and he was *The New York Times.* This was the only voice in America. What the *Times* said was the voice that was listened to in Los Angeles, Chicago, Dallas . . . if you couldn't get a notice in the *Times* you were stopped and that is very wrong. When you get that power with no rivals, this is what's wrong and very few in America have been trained to make up their own minds." De Mille says that she had ballets that were not mounted and ideas for ballets that were never developed because of Barnes's bad reviews. But she did have a champion—Lucia Chase, a founder and director of American Ballet Theater, who supported and encouraged her.

For Edward Villella, former principal dancer of the New York City Ballet, criticism never took on that much importance because of Balanchine:

> He always said to me he never read critics. He said "audiences are like critics—you have to educate them, you have to show them, they're like your children, like your bad children. If you have a child that is difficult, what do you do? Well, you try to look after it and hope they will pass through the phase." He felt you had to be very patient because they wouldn't be able to see it the first time. It would take them time. This put criticism in perspective for me. I was not dancing for critics, I was dancing for Balanchine. My critics were George Balanchine, Lincoln Kirstein, and Stanley Williams of the School of American Ballet and the single greatest teacher and coach in the world. These were my critics.

THEATER

Theater is probably most immediately and most crucially affected by critics, and this is so most of all on Broadway, where the odds against mounting a production that will last are particularly high. There is so much riding on each new production—so much money, so many hopes, such a chilling realization that everything better go absolutely right on the night when critical appraisal will be made. Beginnings and ends of careers are in the wings.

The theater audience is far more frequently guided by the critic, and not infrequently dominated by him, than is true for other performing arts. Theater is less protected by subscription audiences and more dependent on box-office sales, therefore less critic-proof. What happens on Broadway is read about throughout the country, just as what happens in regional theaters throughout the country is followed in New York. Increasingly, they are interdependent. But New York is supremely the place for the playwright to make his mark. A playwright who wants to make a career out of his profession and has a hit on Broadway is virtually guaranteed the economic freedom to try again.

Those involved in theater list the critical reception on opening

19

night as one of their overriding concerns. What follows is a representative sampling of the comments of those in the theater.

Discovering Why Not to Listen to the Critic

Katharine Hepburn's early experience on the critical firing line is typical of that of many performers. Her talent was discovered as she was given small roles on the stage, and she was encouraged by enthusiastic notices. Hepburn says: "I think when you start you are enchanted by anyone who says anything nice about you. . . . It's irresistible to read nice things about yourself."

As Hepburn became subject to more criticism, she ran into stormy weather. This happened with *Death Takes a Holiday* by Alberto Casella, starring a major actor of the day, Philip Merivale. In out-of-town performances prior to Broadway, first in Washington and then in Philadelphia, Hepburn got a wonderful review in one of the major newspapers in each city and an insulting review in the other. "One would say a lovely Maude Adams-like girl appeared and enchanted us and the other would say a tough-looking unattractive skeleton appeared last night with a harsh voice that sounded like icicles dropping into a slot. There were opposite reviews and then I got fired."

Katharine Hepburn's experience suggests healthy diversity of opinion within the critical community as well as a demonstration of the terrors of the "roll-of-the-dice." What if there had been but one critic? Which one? Few factors of criticism are more on the mind of performing and creative artists than that of the part that chance plays in their lives.

> Before I left the company Philip Merivale said, "You should never read reviews. You have the kind of personality that is either going to be liked or loathed and you're going to be faced with this situation." And not only don't I read the reviews. . . . I really don't want to know what one individual has to say about it . . . criticism is just one man's opinion, isn't it, and it depends on the man. And I'm so self-conscious that it would affect me. I might wait fifteen or twenty years before I would read criticisms of anything I'm in.

It was in *The Lake* that Hepburn's performance evoked Dorothy Parker's lethal one-liner heard around the world, "She ran the gamut of emotion from A to B."[6] In her biography of Katharine

Hepburn, *A Remarkable Woman,* Anne Edwards describes something of the turmoil the remark caused:

> Parker was not a theater critic, and the cruel remark was not an excerpt from a review that might have also said some flattering things to offset it. Yet this quote (because of Dorothy Parker's celebrity and its obvious humor) was printed in almost every major newspaper in the United States and England. The effect on both Hepburn's stage career and the fate of *The Lake* was devastating. Brooks Atkinson at *The New York Times* had cited her "limitations as a dramatic actress . . . and a voice that has an unpleasant timbre." Another critic called her "too young and too shy in the presence of an audience to seem as commanding a personality on the stage as on the screen." Robert Benchley at *The New Yorker* had said, "Not a great actress by any manner of means, but one with a certain distinction which, with training, might possibly take the place of great acting in an emergency."

"I didn't know what I was doing that opening night. I just walked through it in a state of absolute terror," Hepburn herself acknowledges, and continuing, says about critics:

> Oh, I think they have great power. I don't think they have as much power in the movies. Sometimes they like me and sometimes they don't like me. And I just struggle to do my best always. You know, it's not carelessness that makes me do something that they don't like. And yet I think I have the kind of personality that is irritating. I know that. I would be irritated if I looked at me. I look as if I'm so sure of everything. I'm not, my theatrical career has been straight discipline. It has terrified me until now, acting in the theater. . . . You can't do a retake, you either do it or you don't. . . . Acting in the movies I adore because it's careful and [when you finish a film] then you are away from it, you know, you don't have to be there when they throw bricks.

Timing

Public rejection of a performer's professional competence can seem a rejection of every element of his or her person. Failure is visited upon us all at one time or another, but that special kind of public celebration of it seems peculiarly reserved for the arts. This is a point made time after time by the artists. Moreover, when rejection hits—early or late, with success following failure or vice versa—it is something the artist can neither foresee nor control; it is a kind of inescapable cycle. This applies to the playwright, the choreographer, the dancer, the singer, the composer. There is a complex rhythm involved, composed of many elements, including the role of the critic as shaper of destiny.

Edward Albee, author of *Who's Afraid of Virginia Woolf?*, raised to Olympian heights by the critics, was given his critical comeuppance two years later with *Tiny Alice*. From then on he has seemed to be on a roller coaster of critical approval-disapproval. Of the mad ride, he said in a *Paris Review* interview:

> It seems inevitable that almost everyone has been encouraged until the critics feel that they have built them up beyond the point where they can control them; then it's time to knock them down again. And a rather ugly thing starts happening: the playwright finds himself knocked down for works that quite often are just as good or better than the works he's been praised for previously. And a lot of playwrights become confused by this time and they start doing imitations of what they've done before or they try to do something entirely different in which case they get accused by the same critics of not doing what they used to do so well.[7]

Other Reasons for Not Reading Reviews

Other reasons both for reading reviews and for not reading reviews are forwarded by actress Colleen Dewhurst. She claims that on stage she has found that praise a critic may have given her for a particular scene made her self-conscious about that scene with the result that it became distorted: "You are no longer in the boat . . . you are in a 'wonderful' scene." On the other hand, Dewhurst says tryouts could pay dividends in terms of helpful critical comments. Dewhurst notes that Elliot Norton, Boston's leading critic prior to his retirement, made suggestions on how a play she was in could be improved, suggestions she believed helped the work become a success by the time it got to New York:

> If the critic is a knowledgeable professional who is respected by those involved in a play, he can be of help if he feels the cast and writer are close to something—if he feels the work is a horror he must so state.

Assessing his overall rating as far as critics go, Stephen Sondheim says that he regularly gets about 50 percent terrible criticisms, about 30 percent good with reservations, usually a bit condescending he adds, and about 20 percent very good. As a means of sparing himself the distress of reading the reviews as they come in, having figured the odds on favorable-unfavorable reviews and knowing that it would be the terrible ones that stick in his mind, the good ones being what he describes as "passing pleasures," he decided to confine his reading to those he considered most influential at the box office, those in fact that could help make a show the hit he wanted it to be—*The New York Times,* the *New York Daily News,* the *New York Post, Time, Newsweek, New York* magazine, and most recently, *USA Today.*

Fate, Destiny, and Karma

For all human beings there are times when they are at their best, times when they are not. But the show will go on regardless—whether a performer is ill, in a bad mood, deprived of that energy and concentration which must underlie every good performance, or suffering from a family tragedy or a fight with a spouse. Wrong notes, missed cues, a dancer tripping—they can all happen, and their price must be measured in the critics' reaction. Accidents involving scenes, lights, or props are not subject to dispensations on opening night. The writer can see where that one line could be changed and the scene *would* work. But the critic won't see it with the change. Or perhaps the critic who likes Brahms and hates Mahler is the only one available for the all-Mahler concert. Fate, destiny, karma, and caprice are in the wings opening night.

Jerry Herman, the composer of such musicals as *Hello, Dolly!, Mame,* and *La Cage Aux Folles,* talked about the all-or-nothing aspect of opening night reviews in *Variety*:

> When I look back at what I've done each time, it makes me wonder about my sanity. To take two years of life, work daily for two years and ask people to believe in what I've done to the tune of $6,000,000 and let it all ride on one night. You have to be demented to do that . . . yet I do it each time.

Gordon Rogoff, *Village Voice* theater critic, has pointed to the special risks that actors take, especially facing the critics. He believes they are "alone at the edge of the abyss . . . the most dangerously placed artists in the most dangerous art."[8]

Martha Clarke, the innovative director whose work has given

23

performance art (works presented essentially in theater terms but depending heavily on dance and music) a new dimension, says:

> Having success is like roulette, roll-of-the-dice. You can do your best piece but it may have an unfortunate performance or do a piece not as good and it will have a brilliant performance. About half the people I know who saw *The Garden of Earthly Delights* liked that the best, and the other half liked my *Vienna: Lusthaus* best. Rich [of the *Times*] came to *Garden* on a night when a string was broken on the cello and since we had only three musicians this was important. No one [in the production itself] at the time knew what the problem was but everyone held back. Dancers are extremely sensitive to music. It was a strange and lifeless performance. Rich gave it a negative review on the radio and wrote in subsequent articles that, in effect, he didn't have time for the likes of Martha Clarke. When Rich came to *Vienna* it was a brilliant performance. Rich gave *Vienna* as brilliant a review as he ever gave.

The Playwright—the Most Fortunate, Often the Most Vulnerable

On balance, it is the playwright who probably can most quickly be raised to Olympian heights by the critic, or be hurled to Stygian depths. Certainly this is true on Broadway, where the hit-flop cycle is unyielding and where, as playwright Robert Anderson has said, you can make a killing in the theater but not a living. But when Broadway is properly working, it is doing so in the interests of the theater and the public. It is doing so when production costs and ticket prices can be kept within balance and within reason and when these economic conditions encourage producers to take risks with new works. That is not the case today save for a few notable exceptions. One example was the presentation on Broadway of August Wilson's *Fences*, which won for the author (who also wrote *Ma Rainey's Black Bottom* and most recently the Pulitzer Prize-winning play *The Piano Lesson*) a Pulitzer Prize and financial resources that will enable him to be a playwright for life should he so choose. That kind of critical and public attention with the ensuing financial rewards, which can so spectacularly launch a playwright, can most readily happen on Broadway, and represents Broadway's capacity to play an indispensable role in the nation's theater system.

For the playwright the intensity of the experience of a Broadway opening breeds an intensity of feeling. David Mamet, who won a

Pulitzer Prize for *Glengarry Glen Ross,* is one of the leading American writers for both the screen and the stage. Mamet says:

> There are several people whose work as critics is worthy of respect. And my experience with the rest of them has been that they are frauds and fools. Or frogs and fools. Want some names? Frank Rich of *The New York Times* is a perfect example. He's someone who pretends to a knowledge which he does not possess. Therefore he's a fraud and he doesn't act either in the best interest of himself and/or the constituency which he is supposed to represent. Therefore he's a fool. He doesn't act in his own best interest or the best interest of that constituency which supports him . . . the professional theater community and an informed theatergoing public. . . . His stock in trade is *ad hominem* argument and he does it consistently and recognizably and it seems to be that for which he has been hired. . . . I mean, if one wants to take a psychoanalytic view, one could say that allowances should be made . . . he is obviously very bitter and one could surmise that he was wronged in early childhood.

Of *New York* magazine critic John Simon, Mamet believes that

> he's writing about himself. Like all of us, what he sees in the world is what he sees in himself, and what he sees is an unlovely fraud—someone who is trying to put something over on us . . . and I would like to say that I hope when this book is published that these critics take my unsupported rantings in the way in which we in the theater are supposed to take theirs. . . . Good natured badinage or avuncular suggestions. The purpose of this book, frankly, is to give you, the author, a good time. It's a book you want to write. Your book isn't going to change anything. It may, on the other hand, give a good time to a bunch of other people. I didn't mean to single out your book. No book, any more than any play I write, is going to change anything.

A Career Launched by a Critic

Arthur Miller's career as one of the most important and distinguished of contemporary playwrights in the American theater was launched by a critic. But Miller also has gone through a period of devastating critical rejection:

> My career was started as a result of a one-man campaign by Brooks Atkinson of *The New York Times* which turned *All My Sons*

25

(1947) into a hit . . . the reviews of the other critics were not good enough to have launched the play . . . I was unknown when that play opened.

Miller pointed out that while the play's director, Elia Kazan, was known, he was not then the commanding figure he was to become, nor did the play have any stars who might have garnered press attention; in addition, the theme was controversial, and the play very serious. Miller explains:

Without a rave review it would have closed in short order. Atkinson picked it up and ran with it. He insisted that it was an important play, and that I was an important writer . . . we weren't sold out before Atkinson wrote his second piece which was a real exclamation point. The results were that we ran about a year and a half. I won the Critics Award,[9] the same critics, incidentally, who had been doubtful about the play.

But another incident had a marked effect on Miller's trust of critical judgments. Miller went on to more successes, winning a Pulitzer Prize for *Death of a Salesman* in 1949 and writing many other award-winning plays. Some twenty years later he was asked to write a play for the new Lincoln Center Theater. The play was *After the Fall,* suggested by his life with his second wife, Marilyn Monroe. The Lincoln Center Theater was an attempt, Miller notes, to create a noncommercial, high-level, professional theater in this country. He recalls being astonished at how almost universally the critics scoffed at the idea and became hostile to it. The hostility, he believes, washed over on to his play, which received negative notices. Two one-act plays in 1987 at the Lincoln Center Theater, even after several changes in management, fared no better than his effort almost twenty years earlier.

This experience fortified Miller's distrust of critics who permit factors other than those directly relevant to the play to get in the way of their judgment. Miller said:

Atkinson had the courage of his own convictions. I don't recall him being a man who followed any particular fashion. In other words, if something was of a different style than people were accustomed to, or an old style, or an avant-garde style, he'd try to see it in terms of its own pretensions. He did not have, I don't think, *a priori* preference of one style as opposed to another. He did not feel that something was good because it was avant-garde, or bad because it wasn't. There was an attempt to see it on its own ground, with its own limitations as it declared those limitations. There was also a common sense element in his work. He was a reporter and tried to give you an idea as objectively as he could what the thing was about so that you might draw a different conclusion than he had drawn from it. Most of the time his conclusions came at the end rather than at the beginning.

This idea that conclusions about a work should come at the end of a review has a particular relevance at the moment: the current major theater critic at the *Times* does the reverse—often writing a review that is best described as a first-paragraph killer.

Businessman and civic leader Martin E. Segal provides a final and particularly telling view of the universe of anxiety. Segal, who has served on a galaxy of arts boards and has played an important role in New York City's cultural life, was chairman of Lincoln Center. As a businessman Segal considers himself lucky he does not have to face the critic day in and day out:

My first reaction to the role of critic . . . is how precariously placed the artist is compared to the businessman. A product is developed in business by professionals, and if they are lucky all goes well. There is the test marketing but it is rarely a case of do or die; rarely a disaster nor is the imperishable stamp of disaster left. Imagine if you are an artist, trained for years, you appear in a play or whatever, then, in a way that immediately affects your career, there is the critic, but the effect of criticism is out of balance with everything that went into that career!

2 ★ The Impact on Performing Arts Companies: Theater

Theater is the litmus test of the critic's impact in the world of the performing arts. A production often takes on the coloration of success or failure within hours of a critique. Opera, music, ballet, and dance respond to critical attention too, of course, but in a less intense fashion. It is in theater where, within hours, destinies can be shaped by the nature of critical reception, albeit a vast complex of factors go into the success or failure of a work and supersede the critique itself.

As mentioned earlier, Martha Clarke's 1986 work, *Vienna: Lusthaus,* did not bear the marks of becoming one of the hits of the season—until Frank Rich gave it a rave review. Then every ticket for the presentation's limited engagement was snapped up in a day. The glowing review set in motion forces which gave her group an underpinning of financial support it had never known. As Clarke said, there was food on the table now for everyone for a longer time; "the wardrobe man will be employed because of Frank Rich." Economic uncertainty is one of the most debilitating and destructive forces attacking that artistic planning which is vital to the development of any company, and Frank Rich's review had a profound effect in releasing the company's energies and opportunities.

But consider the other side of the coin. James Duff's 1985 work, *Home Front,* looked like it might become one of the hits of the season. Duff, a playwright in his late twenties, was writing about the Vietnamese war and its implications for American values. The play would be produced by the late Richard Barr, then president of The League of American Theatres and Producers and one of Broadway's most innovative and experienced producers. Its director was to be Alan Schneider, one of the country's most prestigious directors, but, tragically, Schneider was killed in a traffic accident prior to the launching of the project. The direction was taken over by Michael Attenborough, then artistic director of London's Hampstead Club, where Barr had decided to open *Home Front*. Presented under the title *The War at Home,* the play opened to raves from London's five all-important Sunday newspaper critics. The daily press also carried mostly favorable reviews. The production played to capacity houses, and the wait on the box-office line quickly climbed to an hour and a half. In New York, *Variety*[1] trumpeted the success of the London production, saw an excellent chance for a Broadway presentation, and compared it with another American play that had recently gone from initial success in London to success on Broadway—David Mamet's *Glengarry Glen Ross.* Douglas Watt of the *New York Daily News,* visiting in London later in the summer, sent a column home urging a New York production. The play had already been done by Israel's Habimah Theatre and productions were set for Germany, Sweden, and at playwright Athol Fugard's theater in South Africa.

The Broadway production of *Home Front* went forward on mounting waves of optimism over the prospects of its becoming a hit, but the dream unraveled on 44th Street west of Broadway. James Duff recalled that moment of reading the notice by Frank Rich:

> I read the first paragraph and it was O.K. and the second paragraph and I knew . . . and I looked at them [director Attenborough and his father, the noted British film producer and director Richard Attenborough] and I said, "Well, sorry guys." That's what I said. "Sorry. It doesn't look like we'll be able to do it" . . . and everybody understood that. You know . . . *The New York Times* goes against you, and you don't run.

Douglas Watt in the *New York Daily News* and Clive Barnes in the *New York Post* registered rave reviews, as did William Henry III when *Time* magazine came out. Television reviews were generally negative save for that of Dennis Cunningham, who gave the work a favorable review on CBS.

Barr later recalled that

> The audience had screamed and stood on its feet that night. I thought the *Times* reflected absolutely nothing of what had gone on in that theater . . . and I consider it irresponsible reporting on [Rich's] part and he is simply not qualified, in my opinion, to be a critic at the absolute core of American theater where he is.

29

There was a striking irony, represented by the roll-of-the-dice, as James Duff said, that element of gambling, of chance, which professionals in the arts, particularly in the theater and particularly in New York, where one newspaper has such power, find so frustrating. Some years earlier the critic for *The New York Times* had been Clive Barnes. He covered both theater and dance for some ten years before Executive Editor Abe Rosenthal removed him from theater criticism, followed not long after by his being taken on by the *New York Post*. Barnes had written in his *Post* review, "Last night, James Duff's searingly memorable play, *Home Front*, started Broadway's New Year with a whole cannonade of bangs." Had his rave review been in the *Times*, *Home Front* might well have been a hit, with Richard Barr and cohorts presiding over the hottest ticket in town. As playwright Duff put it in an interview after the closing of his play, "If Clive Barnes were writing for *The New York Times* today instead of the *New York Post*, my career would be made in the shade." With a wry laugh the playwright went on to say that he felt his career was at a

> reflective state, I suppose . . . I'm going to write more plays . . . Frank Rich will have more opportunities to say I have not written plays, I've written television. John Simon will have more opportunities to insult me. They're not getting rid of me, in other words.
>
> [But] I will not allow my next play to be done on Broadway. I am not going to go for that ridiculous roll-of-the-dice. It's not worth it . . . the only reason I can think of now to do a play on Broadway is to make a killing, because that's what happens, you either make a killing or you get killed.

The point of this cautionary tale has little to do with whether *Home Front* was really a good play or not—there were knowledgeable and discerning people who made a convincing case for both possibilities. Rather, together with the example of *Vienna: Lusthaus*, the incident maps the territory in which the critic of *The New York Times* wields awesome power. And he throws a wide net. His review will be read across the nation, setting the prospects, or all but eliminating them, for local productions or bookings into theaters in major cities. With rave notices, reams of glowing copy will hit the papers and magazines, Hollywood will take notice. And maybe London, Paris, and Tokyo.

For the profit-making theater, a good review in *The New York Times* means there will be profits for backers, producers, theater-owners; substantial sums and sometimes a fortune for author, director, choreographer, composer; and long-term employment for succeeding companies of performers. Tax dollars generated by the show will help enrich New York City coffers and the show will draw more tourists to the city. If a nonprofit theater is involved, there will be a temporary surcease from the endless and often frustrating fund-raising. *A Chorus Line,* which Joseph Papp produced at his nonprofit theater and which then transferred to commercial auspices, endowed Papp's New York Shakespeare Festival with more than $38,000,000—the annual budget for NYSF is about $14,000,000.

In myriad and significant ways, then, a *New York Times* review is going to affect the work. But while a rave in the *Times* may speed a work into the stratosphere of success, a merely good review may do no more than stimulate audience attention for a limited time.

Take *Ma Rainey's Black Bottom* by August Wilson. It got a splendid review from Frank Rich, but the production never even gained back its investment. Similarly, an enchanting valentine of a review from Rich for Rosemary Harris in Noel Coward's *Hay Fever* and near-raves for the rest of the cast could not turn the play into a hit. Nor could a superbly mounted revival of one of the major American plays, Eugene O'Neill's *The Iceman Cometh,* starring Jason Robards, Jr., and given a superb review by Rich, hold its own on Broadway. In the case of the blockbuster musical, a *Times* review is unlikely to have much effect at all.

Unquestionably, the role of chief theater critic at *The New York Times* has been of quintessential importance in the fate of score upon score of productions, but it has worked only with the concurrence of the audience. This audience seems increasingly to consist less of theatergoers than of hit-goers, and it appears increasingly to be dedicated to the less-than-demanding attention span of television than to serious drama. In addition, the audience is so buffeted by high prices that it frequently opts for the VCR or movies. And it would appear that a substantial section of what traditionally had been part of the theatergoing audience—young professionals —has come to enjoy the "theater" of dinner in trendy restaurants at least as much as the drama of Broadway or its environs.

Even if the core of theatergoers in New York City is vastly diminished, there are still many who would go if they could afford it. The nonprofit Theatre Development Fund sponsors numerous programs aimed at stimulating the theater, including a subsidy plan for works of artistic merit on Broadway and Off-Broadway and Off-Off-Broadway, and at Times Square and the World Trade Center half-price ticket booths which have filled millions of seats.

But the generally high cost of tickets, according to some producers, gives the potential audience the "out" it needs not to see a play. Harold S. Prince, producer of a glittering string of hits, says that "any excuse an audience can have not to go to the theater they take." At this point the price is high enough so that a dissenting notice is often used as a good excuse.

Conversely, there is the hit-going psychology. Quite apart from the corporate expense account crowd (whose importance economically to Broadway is undeniable, while corporations, of course, want to impress their guests with hit shows), Bernard B. Jacobs, president of the Shubert Organization, sees in the hit-going psychology a strain that is deep in our national life: "There is a public attitude as well as the critical attitude permeating our society that you are nobody if you are not Number One." Another problem, Mr. Jacobs says,

> is that the attention span of our audiences has been affected by the thirteen-minute television segment, a fifteen-minute span with two minutes for advertising. As a result, in America particularly, we tend to limit the running time of a show. The average musical now runs from two hours, ten minutes to two hours, thirty-five minutes. The average play may run from two hours to two and a half hours at the most.

The Lively Life Outside New York

The most vibrant theaters in communities across the nation, often providing Broadway and other centers with some of our most enterprising plays, are usually not-for-profit theaters. These theaters can take on the high-risk jobs of presenting new playwrights and innovations, or mounting risky revivals that commercial theaters often cannot or will not support. Their revenue is derived from earned income, which is largely composed of ticket sales, and from government funds (federal, state, and very limited local funds), individual patrons, corporations, and foundations.

Characteristic of many of these theaters is their heavy reliance on subscriptions. This provides a pre-season guarantee of funds, an estimate of the expected audience, and, if the subscription audience is large enough, an insurance against the roller coaster of critic-dependency. The critics can hardly close a subscription-supported play. This system encourages greater independence on the part of audiences, generally helps put criticism in perspective, and provides a certain stability for the theater company. This is not to say that the critics don't matter. A critic's praise of the works of such a theater is of great importance in encouraging single-ticket purchasers, in stimulating foundation and corporate gifts, in building up the subscriber lists for the next year, and in improving the chances for a move to Broadway as well. Negative critiques do the reverse.

The highly acclaimed Seattle Repertory Theater plays to an audience composed of about 80 percent subscribers and so, according to artistic director Daniel Sullivan, a negative press is not a death blow. But Sullivan is acutely aware of the importance of critical comment to his theater, including its effect on the board, local foundations, and corporations. He does not believe, however, that the critics have an effect on funding from the National Endowment for the Arts.

Sullivan argues that, ideally, criticism at the highest level—positive or negative—is going to help theaters do their best work. Knowing the efforts that are made to stage works of high artistic merit, Sullivan wants newspaper coverage that matches such efforts in professionalism.

Gordon Davidson, artistic director of the Mark Taper Forum in Los Angeles, also relies on the insurance of a subscription list. His theater has gained a preeminent place both for the quality of its traditional productions and for its willingness to break new ground. Davidson says the critic can't close a show because of the size of his subscription audience, but a negative notice makes the difference between a show doing very well or just getting along. An enthusiastic audience can turn a play into a hit of major proportions regardless of the reviews.

In Davidson's view, the essence of the critics' impact is less in the day-to-day, play-by-play reaction than in the way they help create a climate in which the art form is either nurtured or not. There are many factors involved—for example, the way critics talk about the theater and the appetite they transmit to an audience for theater. He emphasizes that a critic can be critical of plays but the reader can still know that the critic "loves going to the theater, loves aspects of the theater, loves acting." In this regard he cites the writings of Harold Clurman, Kenneth Tynan, and Brooks Atkinson.[2] Davidson added: "And I guess every artist dreams and prays that somebody is going to talk about what the creative intention was, what the vision was, what the means of execution were and then how well it was achieved ... [but] that's what's sorely lacking, I find."

The most notable directors of performing arts institutions are men or women of artistic vision and distinction. For an artistic director, therefore, to be dictated to by what critics write could be to fatally transfer artistic responsibility. But it can happen. The pressure is sometimes there. The subject is not too openly discussed, but managers in theaters, as well as in the other performing arts, sometimes read advice from critics to include in the season more of this kind of play than that, less modern ballet and more classical, cut out Phillip Glass and stick to Mozart. Davidson says:

> They become arbiters. Dan [Sullivan][3] loves to say things like, "The Taper's mandate is to do new plays." From his mouth to God's ear. I mean where does that come from? I opened the theater. I created it. I gave it its shape in terms of new drama but it wasn't a mandate. That was my interest at the time. I also feel now that it's very important that we deal with the classic repertoire and I'm trying to mix the two. And he scolds me when I do one and not the other.

By indirection critics can tell managers what to do and what not to do, rather than analyze the success or failure of what is actually on the stage. Davidson recounts mounting a revised version of Arthur Miller's *The American Clock*. Miller did new work on the play, and Davidson aimed at a production which he felt got back to Miller's original intent. He thought it was successful and the audience response was good, but not the critical reviews. They said that the play wasn't another *Death of a Salesman* or that Neil Simon had done things better with *Brighton Beach Memoirs*. Davidson says:

> I went crazy. The play had nothing to do with *Death of a Salesman* or *Brighton*. That's not what Arthur was trying to do with this piece. He was stepping out into a new area. He was using elements of realistic drama and storytelling and mixing it with an epic scale and trying to create another form. Now you can say, Mr. Miller tried to do this and it doesn't work or I don't like it but you can't say it isn't *Death of a Salesman*. And you can imagine what it does to the writer, I mean, forgetting about my own work on it.

The impact—and importance—of the critic on the arts institution is given a unique perspective in the case of Joseph Papp's New

York Shakespeare Festival, if only because of the extraordinary scope of its activities and the nature of its director. Papp is involved with classical, experimental, avant-garde, musical, commercial, and any other kind of theater that may emerge. He is involved with minority theater, international theater, and, to some extent, with films. His Public Theater in lower Manhattan and his free Shakespeare in Central Park emanate waves of theatrical innovation and excitement or shock waves of disaster around the city and, for that matter, often around the country.

Acknowledging the crucial role of the critics—even if on occasion he has tried to bar certain of them from his theater—he knew from the first that he needed them, especially when they did not recognize his existence until he forced the issue in a most Papp-like way.

Papp started his theater on the supposition that there was a mass audience for classics and it did not have to be highly educated to enjoy Shakespeare. His first audiences numbered twenty or thirty in a hundred-seat church on New York's Lower East Side. At that time, Papp says, the major critics would never go to Off-Broadway productions, which were relatively new in 1954, let alone cover a venture such as Papp's. Finally, after his persistent efforts, *The New York Times,* alone among other newspapers, sent a critic. Papp recalls he was a third-string critic, now retired, who was a nice chap but didn't know much about Shakespeare. But he recalls they got a decent review.

People started to come. Papp was encouraged to move his theater to the better East River Park Amphitheater and decided it was time to get the chief theater critic for the *Times,* Brooks Atkinson. Papp tells how he

> went to the *Times* and sat there ten hours waiting for him to come, and they all asked me to leave and I said, "No, I'm not going to leave until I see Brooks Atkinson." He finally arrived and I sort of accosted him and he kind of jumped back a bit. I asked to speak to him . . . I said, "I'm trying to start this thing" and told him what it was all about. He said, "Pick me up at the Harvard Club next Wednesday and you take me there." I arrived in a big truck and I brought him down to the Lower East Side to see *The Taming of the Shrew* with Colleen Dewhurst.

Atkinson wrote that the play was one of the best Shakespeare productions he had seen in a long time. Among other benefits, the critique enabled Papp to approach a number of foundations to ask for support. Papp says:

> Foundations are impressed in a general way by good notices. Even today, maybe an individual notice may not be one thing or another, but if you keep getting bad notices you won't get any funding if you apply. . . . It wasn't just the review . . . Atkinson began to talk about the nature of the company and what we were trying to do, which was to reach audiences. He was very much impressed by the fact that the audience on the Lower East Side was hardly your Shakespeare audience. He was very impressed by the response and the quality of the work.

With hundreds of productions behind him now, having mounted contemporary plays and introduced new playwrights, many successes and failures too, and with works that have gone on to Broadway to become smash hits, Papp has become perhaps both more philosophical and more analytical about criticism. For one thing, Papp says he never thinks of the critics when he puts on a play; if he did he'd have no idea at all what to put on. "The only thing critics can influence is whether or not people will or will not go to see a show, and we're talking about *The New York Times,* and that's called commerce."

Turning to a 1986 production of *Hamlet,* for instance, with Kevin Kline and directed by Liviu Ciulei which got mixed notices —frequent praise for Kline, dissatisfaction with other performers, a variety of conflicting opinions on the often innovative staging— Papp claims most of the critics had no idea what the play was or that their ideas were shaped primarily by having seen certain actors play the role of Hamlet:

> How do you dare send people to the theater to evaluate a play by Shakespeare which some of them may have never read? If I did *Titus Andronicus,* I know that a lot of the critics would come who would never have read *Titus Andronicus,* let alone have seen it.

Aside from the matter of background and knowledgeability, Papp believes the critic's first requirement is to be able to write well and to have developed a point of view toward his craft. "But no matter how astute they are or how deep they may be, critics will always be in an adversarial position to people that produce the product," Papp says.

Every enterprising performing arts institution—dance, music, theater—sets for itself certain goals that are expressed through the level and thrust of its programming and that define it, no matter how modest or grandiose the institution. These goals need not be inflexible and sometimes they are disarmingly modest, no more than to present popular works that will keep the seats filled. Every arts organization, of course, must sell tickets and strive to fill its seats, but many work with a high and defined purpose, failing and succeeding, but characterizing the nature of their institutions through their goals. In theater one such goal is developing new playwrights. No place is the risk or the need for informed criticism greater. The artistic directors and managers know the importance of the critics, tend to be protective of their playwrights, glory in their successes, and share in their despair when the work does not succeed. As arts institutions, their future is intimately involved with that of the playwright.

Matching Papp's passion for William Shakespeare is his passion for a formidable array of new playwrights who have had either their first works or early works done at the Festival's Public Theater. Papp's interest in providing the opportunity for new theater voices to be heard importantly defines his theater. His sense of commitment to the playwrights can be prodigious and he can relate to them in an extraordinary way, albeit sometimes in hostility which on occasion has explosively destroyed a relationship. But perhaps his fiercest battles in the theater have been on their behalf.

For an arts institution such as Papp's where the development of playwrights is a high priority, rather special measures may be taken to support the playwright in the face of criticism. And damage can occur not alone from negative criticism, although that is the major problem. Sometimes a new playwright gets knocked down early, Papp says, or a playwright who isn't ready to be praised is vaulted to too great a height. But being brutally knocked down is the great danger that Papp sees, with the consequence that some people stop writing for long periods—as did David Rabe until a star-studded Mike Nichols production of *Hurly Burly* seemed to offer reassurance. The same happened to Dennis Reardon, author of *Leaf People* and *Happiness Cage*. A very talented writer, Papp says, Reardon was nearly destroyed, stopped writing plays for ten or twelve years, and is just trying to make a comeback. After the last reviews he couldn't get up the next morning, couldn't function. Papp says, "I've had people who are suicidal about these things." He went on to say:

Every time we used to open a play by a writer who was doing his first play I would have four or five writers meet the evening of

37

the reviews and we'd sit around and if the reviews were negative he'd have people around him. The impact of devastating reviews can be mortal . . . and the other effect which is even worse than the attack on the writers is that the public loses as a result. . . . The public is deprived of certain writers and the theater then is poorer for that fact.

A Diversity of Development

There are, of course, numerous theaters in New York City as well as across the country devoted to developing playwrights, such as San Francisco's Magic Theatre, the Actors Theatre of Louisville, the American Repertory Theatre in Cambridge, and in New York, the Ensemble Studio Theatre, Circle Repertory Company, the Manhattan Theatre Club, and, among a handful of others, Playwrights Horizons.

In these and other theaters, playwrights are able to enter into that sustaining relationship with the theater which makes life tolerable in a profession so fragile, so fraught with uncertainty and often loneliness that it would be nearly intolerable without such a bond. The relationship is perhaps typical of that found in all the best developmental theaters, with the artistic director playing the pivotal role of guardian, friend, champion, and critic. Something of this commitment to the development of the new playwright informs the attitudes that Andre Bishop, artistic director of Playwrights Horizons, takes toward the realm of criticism. (Among the playwrights involved with Playwrights Horizons are Wendy Wasserstein, Albert Inaurato, Ted Talley, Christopher Durang, A. R. Gurney, Jr., and James Lapine.)

Knowing the pervasive and often decisive effect of criticism on theater companies, and knowing too that presenting new playwrights carries particular risks, Bishop is troubled by the fact that of the relatively few critics now writing, some are out of touch with new writing and the avant-garde. He finds Frank Rich hospitable to new writers, and talks admiringly of *The New Yorker*'s Edith Oliver, some writers from *The Village Voice*, Robert Brustein at *The New Republic*, John Simon of *New York* magazine (but "he can be very cruel"), and a few others. Bishop thinks too much criticism is simply reportage and too many critics are unsuited to review a younger generation of writers.

His own experience parallels Papp's in his description of living through the despair of the authors upon which his company depends in so large part when they have been attacked by critics. In addition there is the personal aspect for Bishop: "Am I supposed to say, 'I am so stupid; I've picked such a ridiculous work, such an error that I should be killed for it'?"

But mainly Bishop himself suffers for the gifted playwright who is confronted in print with the critics' judgment that he lacks talent for his chosen profession. He said:

> Take the writer who said Wendy Wasserstein should not write for the theater. [Ms. Wasserstein is considered one of the most talented of the Playwrights Horizons writers, author of the Pulitzer-Prize-winning *The Heidi Chronicles,* the earlier *Isn't It Romantic,* and numerous other works.] He wrote she should write short stories because everyone comes on stage and they sit down on a couch and they talk. So he concluded that her talent was not drama. We redid the play, but not enormously, and the critic wrote it was the best play of the season! It was a different production but the same lines. No one minds a bad review—one that is intelligently thought out; you're sorry but you go on. What artists are afraid of is insane attacks—these are fragile careers.

Bishop concluded that there is not much talk publicly about critics in the theater. "We are all so scared; we don't want to alienate them. It's our lives; we need them."

The Long Critical Reach

The reach of the New York critic is a long one, but there are numbers of competent critics across the country who have played a vital role over the past thirty years or so in the emergence of what in effect is a national theater—first-rate theaters in scores of cities whose high professionalism, vitality, and originality have supplied much of what is best in the New York theater for their communities.

Take Chicago. Such nationally known organizations as the Steppenwolf Theatre Company, the Goodman Theatre, and the Wisdom Bridge Theatre have drawn critics from New York to Chicago. The New York press, which for most theaters around the country means *The New York Times, Newsweek,* and *Time,* can raise attendance, create interest in other cities, and generally stimulate the work of a theater in a city like Chicago.

The reverse is also true. Robert Falls, one-time artistic director

39

of the Wisdom Bridge Theatre (presently director of the Goodman Theatre) recalls a play highly successful in Chicago, John Olive's *Standing on My Knees,* which fared well at the hands of New York critics with the exception of *The New York Times.* Falls explains:

> It was devastating. . . . It took me months to recover . . . [from] a state of depression from that review. Try as an artist may, it has a great deal of effect . . . we are very vulnerable. Also, if I'm going to be aghast or hurt, or in disagreement of the bad reviews, how can I possibly bask in the glory of the good reviews. Isn't it a rather interesting double standard? It has created a personal dilemma for me my whole professional life.

In addition to self-esteem, there was the depressingly practical result that commercial producers had been interested in the work, but after *The New York Times* review none of them would come forward.

Falls believes Frank Rich is read by the opinion makers but he himself also reads *The Village Voice*—is particularly an admirer of Michael Feingold; John Simon, not because he necessarily agrees with him but because he finds him entertaining; Jack Kroll (*Newsweek*) and William Henry III (*Time*). Falls regards Richard Christiansen, entertainment editor and theater critic for the *Chicago Tribune,* as the city's equivalent to Frank Rich in influence, with drama/dance critic Glenna Syse of the *Sun-Times* following importantly. Lenny Kleinfeld, critic for *The Reader,* is also influential, as is columnist Irv Kupcinet of the *Sun-Times.*

With two major newspapers as well as noteworthy criticism in the so-called alternative press, Chicago's arts coverage is lively, and almost unique in that a certain collegiality characterizes many of the relationships among the people running the theaters and the critics. This feeling surfaces throughout many conversations. Larry Sloan, associate director of the Goodman Theatre, noted that both Richard Christiansen and Glenna Syse have seen the entire theater movement in Chicago burgeon from a few theaters to the present panoply of extraordinary activity:

> They are like the aunt and uncle, have worked to nurture, to enlarge, to make it known, taken their role beyond, "This play is worth seeing." They are friends of many. They go out of their way to make themselves available . . . lunch, will say, "yes," will come to reading of plays, meet for breakfast, really keep abreast

of developments. . . . Lenny Kleinfeld of *The Reader* is the third important critic.

Sloan says that around Chicago reviews can make or break productions, especially in the case of smaller theaters because they have such small ad budgets. The Goodman has some 20,000 subscribers; they constitute about 60 percent of the total audience for a play.

Recognizing the importance of the New York press in Chicago and in most cities around the country, Sloan points out that this influence also reinforces the love-hate relationship the rest of the country feels toward New York: "Wow! Look at what they're saying about us in the Big Apple. I guess we really are pretty good/Who the hell needs their approval, anyway!" And he adds that good New York notices are great for local fund-raising and public relations. Jeff Perry of the Steppenwolf Theatre Company, which garnered some extraordinary notices in plays brought to New York, says the New York notices cut two ways, not only bringing new local attention to Steppenwolf, but raising expectations all around in ways which are more demanding of them. In the end, though, what is important is that "the New York notices jacked up attendance at Steppenwolf 50 or 60 percent."

And a favorable critique from Europe of a local production playing abroad can be advantageous, particularly if local pride has impelled the hometown newspaper to send over its own critic. Word from American critics writing back home can do wonders. The Wisdom Bridge Theatre took its production of Jack Henry Abbott's *In the Belly of the Beast* to Glasgow and London. Robert Falls explains:

> We were the first Chicago company to be seen in Great Britain. We invited Christiansen and Syse to Europe. Both reported back almost daily on European response to this event. Very beneficial to our fund-raising, to our image.

From time to time Chicago may experience an excess of enthusiasm among its critics emanating from the town's collegial spirit, but there is an underlying discernment among them. The arts institutions are essentially well served by the critics, according to the testimony of most of the heads of Chicago theaters.

A problem that makes itself manifest in too many communities is that of critics who simply are not qualified to evaluate performances—through a lack of training, experience, or temperament. Perhaps this is because editors do not take the arts seriously enough to offer critics the opportunities to do the better job required—in terms of salary, space available in the paper, or opportunity to grow in the job by permitting them a reasonable degree of specialization. Regardless of the reason, a heavy penalty is levied on the arts.

Atlanta is a city with an arts life full of vitality, including a symphony orchestra, a ballet, the Alliance Theatre, the Academy Theatre, and the Theatrical Outfit among others. Not only do most artistic directors in town fully acknowledge the importance of the *Atlanta Constitution* and its associated evening and Sunday newspapers, but they are generally appreciative for a supportive attitude on the part of the critics. Nonetheless, there is a widespread belief that neither arts coverage nor arts criticism has kept up in sophistication with the growth of professional arts activities in town. There are encouraging signs, though, particularly in the search by the editors, conducted on a national level, to hire an outstanding music critic.

But one director of an Atlanta theater vehemently claims that his work is being judged by people who don't know theater. He recognizes their goodwill and sincere efforts but argues that they don't write well, don't bring insight, depth, and knowledge to their writings, and don't write from a consistent viewpoint. New works, or avant-garde works, seem in particular peril from the inadequacies of local criticism. He claims: "I've become very resentful of criticism; I want criticism by qualified people." Rarely, he says, has there been a critic whom he could learn from artistically. Too often, he adds, the critics seem to see their job as getting people to the theaters, claiming a play has to be outrageously bad to be commented on negatively.

At the same time, this director says some artists don't want better critics or more rigorous criticism, are afraid of being exposed, and are willing to settle for mediocrity. "There is a lot of hypocrisy around," he says.

The Alternative Newspaper: An Often Invaluable Voice

As is the case in several communities, alternative newspapers—not the most prestigious or widely read ones—may have the most capable critics. For a time, Tom Boeker, one-time theater editor and critic for Atlanta's *Creative Loafing*, brought some of those qualities that were found lacking elsewhere. According to one person involved in the Atlanta theater, Boeker brought to his writing a deep level of understanding: "He is very opinionated, many times I don't agree, but I can learn from him." Another theater director writes him off as a misplaced hippie, but admits that Boeker's approval matters.

Another theater director puts it this way:

> The background and training of many of those involved in the theater is much ahead of the background of those who criticize and evaluate it. I resent the hell out of it. . . . Criticism plays a very strong part at the box office. . . . What I would like to see is a strong handful of critics who have either academic training or hands-on experience that I feel I have and some of my colleagues have. I don't mind a slam if it comes from a point of view.

How Avant the Avant-Garde

A limited number of institutions in the performing arts are dedicated to avant-garde works. While the avant-garde is in need of particularly discerning critics, both to forward what is meritorious and to identify what is meretricious, it is too likely to be all but ignored by too many major critics because it is outside the interest of mainstream audiences. Initially, perhaps, avant-garde works can prosper with very little criticism, and since much avant-garde activity emerges in the laboratories of small and obscure theaters, that is often the case.

Once the so-called avant-garde begins attracting major audiences it turns into something else, because it is a species of theater that requires dedicated and daring audiences as well as dedicated and daring artists. The need for discerning criticism thus asserts its importance.

The Next Wave Festival, mounted annually by the Brooklyn Academy of Music (BAM), has made the Academy, if not the bellwether for the avant-garde, a place not that far from the cutting edge of much in music, dance, and theater, from Pina Bausch to Robert Wilson to Steve Reich. Before the New Wave there were scores of performing arts organizations experimenting in myriad ways, including the pioneering and politically conscious Julian Beck and Judith Malina and their semiclad or nonclad performers of the Living Theater. Harvey Lichtenstein, president and chief executive officer of BAM, says that BAM is not on the leading edge of the avant-garde, for essentially he believes BAM is too big for that and cites instead The Kitchen and P.S. 122. But by nearly any standard, it is an enterprising and sometimes courageous operation, which has built an audience that appears not only willing but enchanted to be entertained, amazed, mystified, and sometimes stunningly bored.

The New York Times is the most important by far of the newspapers that write critiques of BAM, which generally showcases works that have short runs; therefore weeklies and national magazines don't have much effect, although Lichtenstein makes special mention of *The Village Voice* (a weekly) even if it often writes after the fact for BAM presentations.

The avant-garde, when reviewed, attracts all kinds of biased reactions, favorable and not, Lichtenstein says:

> If the *Times* sends its music critic [John] Rockwell to a piece by Glass or Reich, you know he is open to it; you know Henahan will pan a work. Henahan was assigned to do something here this year, it was a negative response from word go. We thought we might protest, but we decided not to because it would not have made any difference. So when you've got someone like Donal Henahan you've got a real problem.

In this category he also named Andrew Porter of *The New Yorker* and John Russell, art critic for *The New York Times*.

Lichtenstein says that what a critic needs who is dealing with new works, possibly innovative works, is an open attitude, informed by enough background and training so the work is not placed completely out of context. He says:

> Looking at new work is nothing more than a state of mind . . . nothing more than a willingness and a readiness to be open, to be aggravated, to be prepared to see a lot of material which isn't very good and to still keep your equilibrium and your equanimity.

Among the Few Surveys

Very few directors of arts institutions fail to make their own mental surveys of just where the various critics stand relative to the work of their companies, but very few institutions have made formal surveys of the direct effect of criticism on their presentations.

The John F. Kennedy Center for the Performing Arts in Washington, D.C., however, did make a survey of how ticket sales are affected by reviews. David Richards of *The Washington Post* quite unsurprisingly emerged as the most influential theater critic in town. Included in the survey findings was information on average daily ticket sales of theater events, which after positive critiques were found to be three to four times larger than average ticket sales before the review, save in the case of those productions with a big star or large advance sales.

Roger L. Stevens, chairman of the board of the Kennedy Center, sees problems in criticism as a key difficulty facing the arts today because of the critics' power to make or break careers, because of their power to decide on whether or not new forms are to be developed, and, in essence, because of the power involved in what is often their uncertain evaluating abilities. Stevens is in a good position to understand this power. A real-estate tycoon who made a fortune, starting in the 1950s Stevens put large sums into the Broadway theater and was a prolific, innovative, and venturesome producer as well as a champion of new playwrights, numbers of whom went on to become among the important theater voices of these times.

Stevens believes that today critics are writing more for posterity than for the public. Nor has he the same confidence in the nature of critical evaluation that he once had and which helped him to proceed with a certain confidence in estimating the odds for success or failure of each of the 120 plays he has produced, mostly on Broadway. And he had always been willing to take considerable chances with works he simply believed in. Hits were fine, but not necessarily what he was after. He felt confident that 25 percent of the plays he produced would be big hits, 25 percent would be a *succès d'estime,* for another 25 percent the perception of the critics would be crazy, and in the case of the final 25 percent Stevens said it was he who would be crazy.

Finally, Stevens is convinced that the arts will never be better than the criticism that surrounds them.

From Stevens's vantage point, and looking at his record, which reveals that he has produced some two hundred works at nearly every point in the spectrum of theater, his words command attention. The weight given to the impact of critics by managers and artistic directors around the country, as sampled here, seems incontrovertible, even if the extent of critical influence may be arguable. What does not seem to be arguable, though, is the importance of raising critical standards, and the need for the media to give coverage of the arts a priority commensurate with their importance.

3 ★ The Impact on Performing Arts Companies: Music and Dance

Music, dance, and opera companies are less immediately affected by criticism than theater, often because they have more insurance in the form of larger subscription audiences. But the insurance for the companies can cost them artistically, holding them in a vise of conventionality their subscribers may demand, thus limiting artistic freedom. On the other hand, with a "guaranteed" audience there is equal potential for greater artistic freedom.

Criticism in music particularly tends to be limited to performance—the orchestra, soloists, conductor. How many times can you critique the music and story of *Carmen?* Another factor is the loyalty of opera, music, and dance audiences. If Pavarotti is singing, if Baryshnikov is dancing, if Bernstein is conducting, who cares what the critics say? Both Bruce Crawford and Beverly Sills, until recently heading, respectively, the Metropolitan Opera Company and the New York City Opera, neighbors at Lincoln Center, know that unless the elephant gets drunk in *Aida,* the faithful will usually come regardless of what the critics say.

None of this is to suggest that criticism is unimportant or uneventful in the life of dance, music, or opera. The evidence is otherwise.

OPERA

Bruce Crawford says that about 50 percent of the Metropolitan Opera audience comes from subscription lists, with an average overall attendance of about 85 percent; a very good review might raise attendance to 90 percent. Assuming ten performances of a single opera during the season, nine of them on subscription, and a potential box-office total of $1.5 million, depending on the mix of Saturday and other days, and with advance box-office sales, Crawford estimates $100,000 to $200,000 worth of tickets are likely to be affected by reviews. And even then, he says, the reviews would have to be extremely good or bad to have an effect, and on a very popular opera they will have almost none. For certain works, early Mozart or certain twentieth-century works, for example, the review could be absolutely stunning and won't do much good, Crawford claims. But if in *Falstaff* a singer gets a good review, it has an immediate impact on the box office. On the other hand, if a new production gets a poor review because of the production itself—decor or decoration—the review may or may not have an effect. Crawford claims that the Metropolitan is still a singers' house in the minds of the audience and the production is not the prime motivation for their attendance. If Luciano Pavarotti is singing, or Placido Domingo or Joan Sutherland, all seats are filled, as they are if *Boheme* or *Traviata* is being staged, and the critics won't keep audiences away regardless of the reviews.

The Metropolitan Opera has received particularly negative attention from *The New York Times* critic Donal Henahan. Crawford takes a somewhat fatalistic view about such negative criticism:

> Sometimes I feel we'll get criticized whichever way we jump. If it's innovative, new and different, we'll be criticized for the fact that it isn't serious and important and it's trivial. If we do a more traditional production, we'll be labeled conservative!
>
> Basically, what we are trying to do is to create productions that are as dramatically important as we can make them with sets and costumes that will have a life span of some considerable time, because they are expensive for this theater, and we have those factors to take in mind.
>
> We also have to use directors that will be good for the kind of artists that we have. There are some artists that are very effective dramatically and there are some great singers who aren't. We have all those factors to consider, so we can't spend much time on how the critics will react. Jean-Pierre Ponnelle[1] never gets good reviews here. [Franco] Zeffirelli doesn't either. Both work for us a lot, and both consistently get bad reviews here. They are two of the most effective directors and designers. The conductors and singers love working with them; our technical staff loves working with them. It comes together—it works. Everything they do lasts for years. We think they are the best. Why don't critics appreciate this? Certain major critics . . . believe Zeffirelli

47

overproduces, goes more for grand stage effects and spectacle than he does for true direction and motivation of the principal artists. He relies on spectacle drama . . . they're never going to let up on him until he does something completely different. Ponnelle is accused of commercialism because he tends to work in a similar fashion, and he repeats his work sometimes from theater to theater, and tends to repeat colors and tones and yet the art world is filled with painters that did not have a great variety of style.

A leading New York agent in the music business would take issue with Crawford's fatalistic view on criticism and warns that it is never wise to ignore criticism. He advocates a meeting between the critics and Crawford. Others would endorse Crawford's stand.

When to Pay Attention to the Critics

Beverly Sills has contemplated critics and criticism thoughtfully, sometimes benignly and sometimes sulphurically, during two careers—as one of the leading opera singers in the world and as an opera manager and administrator of the New York City Opera. It is about this latter career Sills speaks here.

In contemplating criticism, she says, she has found particularly disturbing the near-impossibility of a single person mastering the scope of knowledge and expertise which she believes is a requirement for an opera critic—mastering, in short, the worlds of music, dance, and theater with fluency in at least three languages. An unreal demand, she acknowledges, but she wants to know why, if she requires her opera singers to be gifted in their art form, she can't expect critics to be gifted in theirs.

Does Sills pay attention to what the critics say? Acknowledging that in her early days of managing the New York City Opera the company was bankrupt artistically as well as financially, she believes the criticism was well founded. Even if they were not able to make positive estimates of the performances, Sills found most critics essentially supportive. After reading a negative review in which she sees merit, she will deal with it by discussing it with members of the company—artists or technicians—and "improve things where they need to be improved . . . but I pay no attention to snideness. It's a sign of incompetence, lack of knowledge, insecurity and ineptness. . . . *Opera News* is really critical of this company, unfairly so, snidely so, sarcastically so, which really diminishes *Opera News,* not us, because everybody says, well, of course it's a Metropolitan house magazine [*Opera News* is published by the Metropolitan Opera Guild]."

Sills finds the whole situation exacerbated out of town, with even fewer informed critics and sometimes infuriatingly ignorant questions thrown at her in interviews. Sills continued:

> We here in New York are quite lucky to have a large number of critics. In smaller towns the problem is that with young peoples' careers in the palm of your hand, you can have a critic with no background. In Los Angeles we always are beaten up by Martin Bernheimer. But I could count critics I admire on my one hand and he's one. Henahan is wonderful, Rockwell good and lively. Bernheimer is a brilliant critic. But he wrote that a singer in the company looked like someone in drag . . . she wept. I called him and I said, "Tell me she sang badly, tell me she acted badly, tell me you thought her costume was bad, but don't be brutal." He agreed. I usually don't call anyone at a newspaper, but I feel privileged to scream at Martin because he screams at me because we are family!

"I love them all" was the reply of Ardis Krainik, the formidable general manager of the Chicago Lyric Opera, who kept candor and diplomacy in a careful balance when an interviewer asked her what she thought about the critics. Known as a tough and effective administrator, Krainik said she decided you get nowhere by opposing the critics; rather, she says they are part of the team, not the enemy, and you go to lunch with them, have a talk with them, keep them informed. This attitude reflects the collegiality of arts institutions and critics that appears to mark many of their relationships in Chicago. When there are suggestions she likes from the critics, she takes them gladly, she says. John Von Rhein, music critic for the *Chicago Tribune,* printed a list in a newspaper of some of the world's major opera singers who had not appeared recently in Chicago but who he thought should. Krainik agreed and kept Von Rhein up-to-date as she engaged them at various times. "It wasn't necessarily that I learned something from him but that I had the same point of view and I let him know it," Krainik said. She does, she says, want critics to reflect audience reaction: "The public has a voice and an intelligence. If the public just loves something, I think the critics should just say so."

Of course, with a subscription audience occupying between 80 to 85 percent of the seats, Krainik notes that critics do not exert much impact: "But a sockeroo review will help at the box office . . . and the Board sees what is said, so for fund-raising the reviews are very important."

On the Pacific Coast in Seattle the collegiality of Chicago is not cultivated. Seattle has a very lively performing arts community, including the Seattle Repertory Theater, the Seattle Symphony Orchestra, the Pacific Northwest Ballet, and the Seattle Opera Company, but the conviction within the arts community is that the media neither understand the arts community nor recognize its importance. In fact, for these reasons Seattle is rather more typical than Chicago of a great many communities across the country.

Speight Jenkins, general director of the Seattle Opera, widely considered one of the most successful in the country, and himself the former music critic for the *New York Post,* has articulated some of the concerns of the performing arts groups in Seattle and in so doing has taken on the media rather directly.

The genesis of Jenkins's rebellion was the sense of frustration regarding critics shared by many performing arts groups. They find that they are not taken quite seriously by the press or the electronic media. They claim that the resources devoted to coverage of the arts is inadequate, the budgets for salaries and travel relatively low, the level of expertise not matching those found in other pages of the newspaper, and the place of the arts in the paper not commensurate with their importance to the community. As a generality, virtually all arts institutions want more space, more attention, and more approval than any newspaper could reasonably give: the probability of the arts ever being satisfied with coverage is low. Nor do they always take into account the practical problems of the newspapers themselves, including putting out a newspaper that attracts the interest of its readers and the strictures imposed by the economics of publishing.

Despite Jenkins's reservations, he lauds much of the criticism, noting the opera has had splendid reviews, and he admires Melinda Bargreen, who, as music critic for *The Seattle Times,* is the most important critic in town. He also spoke approvingly of Richard Campbell, music and dance critic for the *Seattle Post-Intelligencer.*

The Seattle Opera is only a few years old, during which time it has placed emphasis on its singers and on its production values, resulting in some elaborate presentations. It is also venturesome in its choices—not usually the road to the heart of regular operagoers. Among the operas Jenkins has mounted are *The Ballad of*

Baby Doe by Douglas Moore, *L'Elisir d'Amore* by Donizetti, and *Jenufa* by Leos Janacek, as well as *La Boheme*, which "sold out 100 percent because *Boheme* is *Boheme*." The recognition by the critics of the good work being done has been important to Jenkins even if it has not mitigated his great distress at the failure of the press to give the arts the kind of attention he believes they merit.

Jenkins's distress was intensified by the circumstances under which *Jenufa* was produced. Because of the demanding nature of the work, it was necessary to have two casts, but, until he fought for his position, *The Seattle Times* was going to cover only one of them. Jenkins says:

> The idea that I would give people here a brand new second cast, and that in a town of so little opera [five operas are presented for five performances each] the critics wouldn't come to review the opera was just incredible to me. I made my stand; I stood on my head and I got them to come
>
> Both papers will give an article on the Friday before an opera, and that's very nice, but they won't do Sunday articles prior to our opening. You talk to the critics and they say they have nothing to do with it.

Jenkins went to various editors, some of the visits arranged through his board to whom he had gone with the problem:

> I had long sessions with the editors. Basically there is not much musical background, nor much interest in opera among their readers, I was told. I said to Donn Fry [arts and entertainment editor, *The Seattle Times*], "I don't give a damn whether they're interested in opera or not, opera is an important thing for the community of Seattle. A newspaper does not just publish what it is interested in." When I went to the *Times* in anger I told them about the new *Baby Doe* . . . the most elaborate production Seattle ever saw, not even an apology. The star of *Baby Doe* was Michael Devlin. He has sung at the Met, at Covent Garden. The story should have been in because he lives in Seattle.

But the struggle between arts organizations and the media is unequal. Newspapers *do* have the last word. All the more reason for arts managers to demand better critics.

DANCE

The dance is nearly a new arrival among the performing arts—at least in terms of the tremendous surge of companies, the huge audiences, and the general level of interest that have surfaced since the 1950s. Many, but certainly not all, of the most sophisticated dance critics are in New York. In many communities across the country the dance critic is often not a dance expert but is doubling from reviewing one of the other performing arts. In too many national publications the resources to cover dance do not seem to be commensurate with the proliferation of performances.

Kent Stowell, artistic director of the Pacific Northwest Ballet in Seattle, would like to broaden the national coverage of dance. It is Stowell's belief that the dance world in New York does not want to give up any of its turf and is reluctant to say that anything important is happening beyond that turf. Much of the writing about dance around the country is superficial, according to Stowell. He would also like to see a dance magazine on the West Coast.

Stowell believes the dance critic is faced with very special problems and is too often denied the means of overcoming them. While plays can be read or scores seen or listened to, there is very little documentation on the dance. In addition, dance critics are exposed to few major dance companies: only a handful come through many cities and critics don't have the opportunity to travel to centers where they can watch a variety of ballet and other dance. So the main reference point for too many dance critics is the company they are reviewing at the moment and that just is not enough, Stowell maintains. Seattle newspapers themselves, he believes, do not see the importance of dance criticism, and he is aware that word from outside the community by a major publication is still more important than what is being written locally.

In Atlanta, Kenneth Hertz, executive director of the Atlanta Ballet, reflects on the tentativeness of commitment to the arts he sees in the city's now-combined newspapers, *The Journal* and *The Constitution*. He finds it frightening to read the Sunday section with so much space devoted to "films and celebrity interviews" and so little to dance, since he knows the importance of arts coverage to the ballet. Favorable critiques, Hertz reports, can cause a surge of 15 to 20 percent in ticket sales along with mounting pride at the ballet company itself. He also finds that if the critique is bad but the word-of-mouth is good, the criticism won't count at the box office.

In the matter of the unequal space devoted to "films and celebrity interviews," Hertz touches on a dilemma wrestled with across the country: how do newspapers both fulfill their responsibilities to their readers' interests—which they will justifiably claim lie more in films and celebrity interviews—and at the same time cover with distinction a city's cultural life?

Hertz knows that among the results of a bad review may be telephone calls from members of his board of directors. Virtually all nonprofit theaters, symphony orchestras, opera, dance, and theater companies are governed by boards who serve without compensation and are usually drawn from the community. Their primary responsibilities include overseeing fiscal management of the organization, raising the money beyond ticket sales required for the operation of the companies—which can range from thousands to millions of dollars—and hiring and if necessary firing the artistic director who runs the company. Artistic freedom is of the essence for artistic directors, but the funds that the board is supposed to raise for the survival of the organization are equally vital in this equation. Complaints from board members about bad notices therefore can have disquieting implications.

Because many board members of arts organizations are recruited mainly for their abilities to raise or donate funds, they are not necessarily sophisticated in the art forms over which they preside. Indeed, their function is very decidedly not to determine arts policy; that is the realm of the artistic director. At best, boards should be sensitive and knowledgeable in the arts, albeit many artistic directors would just as soon have their boards' knowledge confined to money matters. But the fact is that budgetary decisions carry implications for artistic matters. It is a very tricky minuet.

The prestige that might accrue from membership on a board can be important to some board members. Good notices, therefore, can be meaningful, even if meaningful for the wrong reasons.

Tom Armstrong, former director of the Whitney Museum of American Art, held a job that in certain respects was analogous to the directorship of a performing arts organization. He recalls that after the opening of one of the museum's biennial exhibitions of works of new American artists a highly negative critique of one of the paintings (along with the suggestion that perhaps the director was not the right man for the job) appeared in *The New York Times*. A trustee called and wanted the painting removed. It was not, and Armstrong dealt with the matter by convincing the trustee that controversy was not only acceptable at the Whitney but respectable.

When William Schuman was president of Lincoln Center for the Performing Arts, he found that the only problem he had with boards was over reviews. "I'd have to explain to them that you couldn't run your program on the basis of whether you please critics or displease them," Schuman said. Boards of directors, he believes, must learn to deal with the whole range of criticism, so he fought the disposition of some managers to send only the good reviews to board members.

Schuman also has advice for artistic directors and the artists themselves on the use of quotes from favorable reviews in advertisements and publicity releases:

> I guess I would say that if they are willing to live by the sword, they have to be willing to die by the sword. By that I mean, they all just jump on the first pleasant adjective they can find in a review and they just build it up. They build up the power of the critics by relying on what they say to sell their product. So, as long as they do that, they have no cause to complain, because they want the support of the very source they denigrate. They don't denigrate that source when it's in their favor.

The Critic and Fund Raising

Critics' reviews can affect all funding sources—government (federal, state, and local), foundations, corporations, and individuals. Officials at funding agencies want to see seats filled at organizations they support to justify their expenditures of public funds. Arts institutions receiving government support often feel pressure to show mounting attendance rates in order to prove that the enterprise is not hopelessly elitist. That sometimes puts an unbearable pressure on the demands of artistic achievement over popular appeal. Good or bad reviews can be a factor in the decision-making process. The National Endowment for the Arts, most agree, relies heavily on the visits its panel members make to arts organizations in deciding on funding it may provide. Robert Marx, former director of the theater program at the New York State Council on the Arts, recalls that the council was so determined to rely on its own system of evaluation that reviews were not allowed on the table; in fact, if an applicant submitted a portfolio of reviews they were not looked at. Mary Hayes, executive director of the Council under its dynamic chairman, Kitty Carlisle Hart, did say that a good review "*does* affect us [in] that it expands the number of Council people who will see a given work and more people become interested in it [which] is helpful for that company."

Many foundations request arts organizations that apply for grants to send press critiques of works they have done. Indeed, favorable reviews are sent even when not requested. While the largest foundations funding the arts usually have staff members who are sophisticated and knowledgeable in the arts, this is not invariably true, and smaller foundations often have no arts specialists on their staffs. Professional criticism therefore can be an important factor in foundation giving. Furthermore, virtually all foundation staffs are under the control of a director who is responsible to a board of trustees. The arts are rarely a subject of board expertise and good reviews of works supported by a foundation cause trustees to think well of the staff and give them a feeling of pride in their decisions, a pride reflected in community responses. Too many bad reviews, on the other hand, can make trustees very uncomfortable indeed, and they are not likely to be secretive about the matter with the staff director, however subtly they may raise the point. The correlation between favorable reviews and funding is evident in the testimony of the directors of arts institutions around the country.

The situation is understandably exacerbated in the case of corporate foundations. Corporations rarely mistake their purpose in life—to make money. Corporate giving is in one way or another part of public relations programs whose purpose is goodwill and profitability for the corporation. Some corporations are extraordinarily generous and discerning in giving to the arts and a few have skilled and well-informed staff members supervising their giving. Good reviews, particularly if they mention specific sponsorship, are music in the boardroom. Reviews of controversial works, however worthy, or failures, however honorable, are likely to sound discordant notes in that same room.

Critics of the support system also find that private or corporate foundations, and government, are sometimes overly indulgent of that which is frivolous, or artistically phony but parading in kingly robes. Howard Kissel, the highly discerning and sometimes acerbic drama critic of the *New York Daily News,* made the point in his only partially capricious review of Martha Clarke's *Miracolo d'Amore:*

> One of the great innovations of our time is theater specifically created for critics, dilettantes, and dispensers of grants. [The press has presently turned its attention to Martha Clarke.] Her works ... address important themes, but since the texts are either nonexistent or incomprehensible, there are many blanks to be filled in, which allows critics, dilettantes, and dispensers of grants to display their own erudition and brilliance. Clarke's

work may be puzzling to the average theatergoer. This proves she must be ahead of her time, and thus a logical recipient of grants from those whose support of the arts is based on the surfer's eagerness to catch The Next Wave.

But the record proves that, at the same time, foundations, corporations, and government have been the indispensable support, across the country, of the major and minor companies providing works of the greatest quality and frequently of the most exhilarating and important innovation. Without the support of these funding sources the arts in this country would be a spindly plant, barely existing as they do now, nor would they be able to serve the increasing audiences that attend arts events.

MUSIC

Gerard Schwarz, the conductor of the Seattle Symphony Orchestra, among other assignments, protested against a critic who he was convinced simply did not know what he was talking about in telling Schwarz's audience, his players, his board of directors, and other funding sources of his deficiencies.

Schwarz recalls being taken to task by the critic for conducting a Mahler symphony in 84 minutes' running time when Bernstein took 93 and Klemperer[2] 102. Aside from the dubious racecourse sensibility being brought to bear on the work itself, Schwarz was troubled over what he saw as a pervasive evil in music reviewing: "I look at something like that and I realize that the man probably hadn't heard Klemperer do it and probably hadn't heard Bernstein either, but he has records, which he listens to, which is the great tragedy of music criticism." Schwarz claims too many critics learn from records, records being a very different performing medium from a concert: a recording is a rendition of but one performance. Schwarz notes that

> when we make records we are concerned about music and mistakes; there is none of the spontaneity and excitement that you get from concerts. The mistakes are not that important in an otherwise fine work, but the critics trained on records won't know this. They come to the concert hall and all too often they want to hear the performance that they heard on the record, and they are so used to a certain way of hearing it . . . [that they] have difficulty hearing it any other way.

Schwarz had one final word: Mahler himself said that the symphony in question should take 80 minutes!

Schwarz was dealing with a particular kind of conflict, but there are others. One involved Zubin Mehta, one-time conductor of the Los Angeles Philharmonic, and Martin Bernheimer. Heavily involved was Ernest Fleischmann, general director of the orchestra, because attacks against a regular conductor and musical director of a symphony orchestra become in effect an attack on the institution, or at least involve its management as well as its board, and ultimately its funding sources and the audience.

Bernheimer saw the orchestra growing under Mehta, being televised, and making recordings. In Mehta he noted a compelling, charismatic, and commercially salable public figure who made music seem glorious and important in ways that it hadn't always seemed before in Los Angeles.

Bernheimer said, "At the same time I had to say, 'Hey! Much of what Mehta does is superficial, exaggerated, insensitive.' He does Mahler and Strauss well, and Mahler and Strauss insensitively." Bernheimer questioned Mehta's many absences from the orchestra, claiming that the orchestra was coasting on a name, not a presence, and that standards fluctuated enormously when he was not there. Bernheimer wanted to know who was running the show. While he applauded the fact that something was happening, he regretted its uneven quality.

Bernheimer's criticisms were unyielding over the years but he points out that while he was yelping and howling about things that were wrong with Zubin Mehta, the orchestra was flourishing and Mehta enjoyed an unparalleled popularity for fourteen years. "The emperor has no clothes," Bernheimer claimed, "all that glitters is not gold." Bernheimer saw an enormous hype machine grinding out what he viewed as often false information about quality, and he believed it was his job to remind his readers of what *wasn't* happening. Bernheimer recalls:

> And they didn't like it. I mean until I had come here there was a great deal of knee-jerk approval of major musical activity in this city and they were kind of surprised and shocked when this funny young man from New York came and said, "Hey! It's not so terrific all the time." I offended a lot of people and I made it difficult for the fund-raisers. I also sold newspapers. I became controversial. Editors do like that.

Finally Mehta left Los Angeles for New York's Philharmonic,[3] driven out, many said, by Bernheimer.

Donal Henahan wrote of a recent season of the New York Philharmonic: "Mr. Mehta's own contribution to the season fluctuated widely in quality, as usual." In an interview Henahan expanded on the matter:

Mehta is a very talented musician and in some ways an extremely sensitive one and he's not a hack. He's a first-class musician. What he's not able to do so far, and he's quite well into his regime here, is to consistently make that orchestra play better than it knows how—to get it to that next level. Other conductors, maybe not thought of as highly as Mehta, are able to do this.

Mehta declined to be interviewed for this work, his office reporting that he does not discuss his critics.

"In a way this is the best of all possible worlds," Bernheimer says. "Mehta did what he had to do. I did what I had to do. And we coexisted, if not amicably, at least professionally."

It is Bernheimer's contention that he did not drive Mehta out: "He left because he had a better offer in New York." And that better offer, it is estimated, brought Mehta a rise in income from a six-figure salary to over $1 million. Bernheimer is similarly accused of causing the demise of the Los Angeles Ballet, a company he did not admire:

They finally went under after ten years of an unhappy existence. And it was very easy at postmortem time to blame the demise of the company on me or on the *Los Angeles Times*. And I don't lose sleep over this. My response really has to be—prove it to me that I did it—not that they did it to themselves.

Two items on Bernheimer's office walls are instructive. One is a photograph of two camels copulating in a tent. A third camel is taking a peek. The caption says, "You always have to have a critic." There is also a wooden plaque with a quotation from Voltaire: " 'But for what end was the world created then?' said Candide. 'To make people mad.' "

PART II

The World of the Critic

★ IF IT IS evident that the critic has a considerable impact and influence on the arts—including performers, performances, entrepreneurs, and audiences—then it becomes of transcendent importance to know who the critic is. What is the critic's education, training, experience, philosophy? How well qualified is the critic to be the critic? From what backgrounds are critics chosen? What are their aims? How do they view their jobs and their responsibilities? How does the critic cope with conflicts of interest and a variety of pressures and temptations?

To evaluate the work of critics and the role of criticism it is necessary to explore the entire frame of reference in which criticism is set, including, in particular, the publisher and editor who ultimately define the realm of criticism. How are newspaper and periodical critics chosen, and once in the job, what are the parameters of their independence and the scope of their opportunities? Can they travel throughout the worlds of the arts to enhance their capabilities? What are their salaries, their standing within the media world (print or electronic) in which they operate?

Together, these are the major factors in the galaxy of issues that determine the quality and nature of criticism. They will be considered in this section.

4 ★ Profile of the Critic: The Accidental Route

"There is no way of becoming a dramatic critic," [1] wrote George Bernard Shaw, who became one of the world's great dramatic critics. Shaw explained:

> It happens by accident . . . when the accident happens, it happens to a journalist. . . if the dramatic critic dies, or goes on another paper, or drops journalism, you have your chance of succeeding him, if you have shown the requisite capacity. That is the regular way. . . . Remember, to be a critic, you must be not only a bit of an expert in your subject, but you must also have literary skill, and trained critical skill too—the power of analysis, comparison . . . I have had to go through years of work as a reviewer of books, a critic of pictures, a writer on political and social questions, and a musical critic, in order to qualify myself for the post I now hold on the staff of *The World*. You must not think that because you only heard of me for the first time the other day or thereabouts that I got such reputation as I have cheaply. I came to London in 1876, and have been fighting for existence ever since. . . . In London all beginners are forty. [2]

Things haven't changed that much in the last century. Critics are still, all too often, critics by accident. Preparation for becoming a critic is very much undefined; Shaw's precepts far from invariably followed. There is relatively little information on the texture, quality, and circumstances of being a critic. There have been few surveys of critics of the performing arts; a modest one was made for this book. [3] It was carried out by telephone in 27 cities involving 130 dance, classical music, and theater critics and 76 media executives. While necessarily selective in scope, the survey provides insights into a number of elements of the critic's realm.

General Characteristics

Nearly two-thirds of the newspaper critics are male, the over-whelming majority are white, and their median age is around forty. Most critics have completed their B.A. and over half have taken some graduate courses; more than one-third have advanced degrees. Most theater critics majored in English and the liberal arts. Only about a quarter of the music critics majored in music or studied music at all. In the ten cities the author visited (all had major performing arts companies), few critics were hired originally for the critic's job, nor did many have arts-related experience before being given assignments as critics. Only a few major newspapers made determined efforts to discover well-qualified critics. Salaries across the country for newspaper critics range between $600 and $750 a week, higher in the largest cities, and highest in New York City. News magazines generally pay more and, comparatively speaking, the salaries for critics on television are astronomical.

A large majority of critics in all disciplines said they had role models, albeit no overwhelming favorites emerged. For theater, most often mentioned were George Bernard Shaw; Walter Kerr, formerly theater critic of *The New York Herald Tribune* and subsequently *The New York Times;* John Simon, *New York* magazine; Frank Rich, *The New York Times;* and Robert Brustein, *The New Republic.* In dance, Arlene Croce of *The New Yorker* was named most frequently, followed by Deborah Jowitt of *The Village Voice*, Tobi Tobias of *New York* magazine, Marcia B. Siegel of the *Hudson Review.* Music critics cited as role models were Andrew Porter, *The New Yorker;* the late Virgil Thomson, formerly of *The New York Herald Tribune;* Martin Bernheimer, the *Los Angeles Times;* Harold Schonberg, formerly of *The New York Times.*

It is evident that Shaw was right: there is no single road to take in becoming a critic. Samuel Lipman provides one example. A pianist, music critic, and publisher of *The New Criterion,* he was giving a concert at the Aspen Music Festival one evening. In the course of a pre-concert dinner with Lionel and Diana Trilling, whom he had never met, Mrs. Trilling told Lipman that she thought he spoke very well and that he should write. "I will arrange it," she added. Within three weeks she had invited Lipman to her home in New York to meet Norman Podhoretz, editor of *Commentary.* Not long after, Lipman was writing music criticism for the magazine.

William Henry III, theater critic for *Time* magazine, started his working life with a summer job at *The Washington Post,* writing features and theater reviews; the next summer, he was an arts writer on *The Boston Globe.* That position extended into freelance assignments covering television, smaller theaters, various arts events, and some city rooms. In less than a year, he became a staff arts writer covering movies and other entertainments. Henry said:

> I was pretty close to incompetent, and I became the paper's dance critic. I had taken some dance courses because I was an actor, but my knowledge was very limited. I didn't even know the technical terms. People praised the freshness and originality of the prose, which was a polite way of saying, "He doesn't know what he's talking about, but he's imaginative and making up for it." I did that for a year.

A personality clash with an editor precipitated a change in assignments, and Henry turned to political reporting. But three years later he accepted the post of television critic for *The Boston Globe* and went on to win a Pulitzer Prize. He subsequently accepted an offer from the *New York Daily News,* as critic-at-large, then moved on to *Time,* first in the "Nation" section, then in other sections until becoming the replacement for Ted Kalem, theater critic. Henry thinks that the final audition for the job may have been a cover story on Shirley MacLaine focusing on her Broadway show. Henry's story is characteristic of the random way in which critics become critics much of the time.

A lifetime theatergoer since age seven, David Richards, appointed critic for *The New York Times* Arts and Leisure section in 1990, had been theater critic for *The Washington Post.* He has two master's degrees, one in speech and drama, one in French. Having decided he wanted to work on newspapers or in the theater itself, he started his writing career on the *Washington Star* on its Sunday Magazine and within a year was asked to be the theater critic before joining *The Washington Post* as its critic. As part of what he sees as his training, he lived in France, where he did much theatergoing, acted in Vermont, and spent time with a touring theater truck-and-bus company because he believes that a knowledge of the mechanics and dynamics of theater, knowing how to put a work together for the stage, is important for a critic. "One of the greatest mistakes in theater criticism is misattribution," Richards says, referring to the placement of praise or blame for various elements of a work given to the actors or the director or the playwright without the critic understanding enough about theater to know where the often-subtle lines of distinction are among the responsibilities of actor, director, and playwright.

Fundamental to Richards's view of criticism, after education and training, is a profound commitment to theater:

> A lot of criticism is casual, offhand. For me it is vital—right there after water and bread. I think that lends a certain convictive passion ... I have enormous affection for theater ... I'd fight for it with my dying breath. But if this wonderful instrument has been misused, bastardized, that brings out my ire.

Fundamental to the calling of most gifted critics is a passion for the art they are involved with so that they are able to pass on it unflinchingly when it falls below their standards or to celebrate it with exuberance when they see it triumphant. Witness dance critic Arlene Croce.

In high school and college, Croce wrote as a critic on film, her great interest at the time, largely inspired by the writings of James Agee. She turned her interest into a profession when, having moved to New York from North Carolina, she successfully submitted samples of her film criticism to various publications:

> But my interest dried up the minute I saw ballet, and I became a ballet nut, and it seemed like the most wonderful thing I ever saw ... when I saw the first night of Balanchine's *Agon,* and *Apollo* on the same night, that was it for me. Rilke says in a poem about Apollo, "You must change your life." Those pieces had a moral impact on me, because that's exactly how I felt ... stop all this that you are doing now ... it wasn't just stop movie criticism, that just faded away ... I wanted to watch these dancers, I wanted to know everything I could about Balanchine and ballet. Now I know why I've come to New York—here are my waters.

Once Croce knew she wanted to write on the dance, it was not so easy to actually do so. In 1965 she started *The Ballet Review.* She says, "I never really got paid until I went to *The New Yorker.* I hadn't even gotten press tickets—most of my salary went to ballet tickets."

Deborah Jowitt, the critic for New York's *Village Voice,* got into criticism through a series of "fortuitous accidents." A dancer and choreographer, Jowitt was asked by a friend to talk about dance on a program on radio; that was her first effort at criticism and led to a new career.

But not every critic is a critic by accident. Harold Schonberg, music critic for *The New York Times* from 1960 to 1980, is among the exceptions. Schonberg started studying the piano at age three, "and from the age of twelve I wanted to be a critic because my one talent was not playing the piano, it was not composing, but it sure was listening. I could hear a piece twice and commit it to memory." His first job was on a now-defunct musical magazine. "I didn't get paid a cent but I got tickets and a by-line. And that's important because of its exposure."

Another exception is Matt Wolf, a young critic, graduate of Yale University, whose career choices had veered between academia and writing. He had started writing theater criticism for his school paper and went on to write criticism for the *Yale Daily News*. After completing college, and with an accelerating interest in theater, Wolf determined he would give himself "a graduate education" by steeping himself in theater in London. Although he planned to take a job in a book shop or in publishing or wherever he could find one while getting his "graduate education," he found an opening at the Associated Press doing feature stories, interviews, and general cultural stories. He later began writing for the international edition of *The Wall Street Journal*, for the *Chicago Tribune*, for *The New York Times*, and for British publications. Wolf believes he could never have started in New York, where he was brought up, with its paucity of outlets, so different from London, where he finds such great theater vitality and so much writing about theater.

What combination of education, formal or informal, and experience prepares a critic to be a critic? The need for practical experience in the theater itself is held by some as essential, by others as not.

Frank Rich believes that actual involvement in theater is not important for a critic: "The two most important factors, I found, are having seen an enormous amount of theater (and read an enormous number of plays) and reading a lot about theater." Rich went to Harvard because it offered the broad liberal arts education he sought: "I wanted to study all sorts of things and in fact majored in a hybrid honors course called History and Literature . . . I feel there's no such thing as a critic who knows only theater . . . and they had this wonderful theater, the Loeb."

Rich went on to say, "There's no substitute for seeing theater, and it's not something that can be picked up late in life. In a sense I created a Theatre Development Fund[4] for myself by becoming a ticket-taker." This was at the National Theater in Washington, then becoming an important Broadway tryout house, which gave

Rich the opportunity of standing in the back of the theater, missing maybe seven minutes of a play in counting the tickets, but seeing free plays as often as he wished when he was thirteen. Rich explains:

> What I learned was that shows would come in and they'd be good, bad, or indifferent, but theater professionals in those days, in the out-of-town tryouts, would work on them day and night. They would put in new scenes, fire actors, throw out the whole second act. . . . Being there every night I'd see Neil Simon and Mike Nichols put in something new in *The Odd Couple* during its tryout every night. Or, I'd see, I believe it was Peter Brook work on a production of *The Physicists*.[5]
>
> . . . You would see new plays in progress as they were being refined, fixed, destroyed, improved, whatever. I saw all permutations of it. I had that experience with a new play every three weeks . . . I often feel that I learned more about the theater from that experience than anything else I've ever done connected with the theater.

Jack Viertel, one-time arts editor and theater critic for the *Los Angeles Herald Examiner* and presently an executive with New York's Jujamcyn Theaters, also went to Harvard and also had some involvement with its Loeb Drama Center. After college he went to London with his friend Frank Rich, where they "did nothing" but go to the movies and to the theater. That experience, Viertel claims, was probably his most important training for a job he never sought—theater critic for the *L.A. Reader*. He and his wife had settled in Los Angeles, where he was barely making a living, he says, as a screenwriter. A friend told the *Reader*'s editor that Viertel had "never written a review but knew an awful lot about the theater" and he got the job. After two and a half years, Viertal was asked to become theater critic of the *Los Angeles Herald Examiner*. Viertel says:

> Every other kind of writing that I had ever done . . . I always had the sense that I really didn't know what the hell I was doing. With this I knew what I was doing. You might agree or disagree with my opinion or my abilities but at least I understood what I thought I was doing. At that point I said, "Well, I guess I'm a theater critic."

Eventually, the job as critic became less than fulfilling for, as in other cities where there is one dominant newspaper such as the *Los*

Angeles Times, it is the critic of that newspaper who is most seriously read and listened to.

Dan Sullivan is the theater critic for the *Los Angeles Times*. His circuitous road to becoming a theater critic took him through an early stint as a music critic for the *Minneapolis Star and Tribune*, which let him go to Tanglewood to study music for six weeks and later to the University of Southern California as part of a two-year sabbatical, with the second year as what he describes as a kind of apprenticeship in *The New York Times* music department:

> I rewarded the *Minneapolis Tribune* by never returning . . . this is another reason why papers are sometimes leery about letting their people have sabbaticals. This was a wonderful paper that believed in letting their young people have as free a hand as they could.

A highly instructive incident in his music training, he recalls, was attending classes in criticism with a guest teacher, Virgil Thomson. "If you are reviewing a violin recital," Thomson said, "go to it with a violinist and ask him questions about the violin if you don't know." Sullivan recalls saying to Thomson that he thought such an action might be dangerous, concerned that his editor might see him, acknowledging in a sense that he didn't know what he was doing. "Tell him Virgil Thomson said it was all right," the master replied.

Sullivan's study of music fortified his conviction about the importance of intensive study as well as practical experience to prepare himself as theater critic. In college, Sullivan had studied English and literature. He had the opportunity to study theater firsthand when he won a Professional Journalism Fellowship from the National Endowment for the Humanities. He went to Stanford —hung lights, painted sets, studied acting. He says:

> Only an actor knows how to take a line and make it a living statement. "Where's all the furniture, honey?" (from *Waiting for Lefty* by Clifford Odets). Is it a joke, accusation, what? At least it gives you humility. Damn hard to make a play live on the stage. If I had the money I'd give it to the twelve youngest, best critics in the U.S. to get this knowledge of the theater.

The frequently expressed opinion around newspaper city rooms is that you bring into the job of critic a man who is first of all a highly professional journalist—and he'll take it from there. This theory was tested, with mixed results, in the case of Richard Eder, formerly chief drama critic for *The New York Times* and now the book critic for the *Los Angeles Times*. Eder went to Harvard, majored in history, wrote for the *Harvard Advocate* (the college literary magazine). He went on to become a copy boy at *The New York Times,* subsequently achieving his ambition of becoming a foreign correspondent. Working abroad, he found theater of particular interest because in some authoritarian countries theater had become an alternate voice. At the end of his tour as a foreign correspondent, he was in England and began writing feature articles on the arts. When he talked to the editors at the *Times* about his return to New York, the suggestion was made that he write on culture, and he became the *Times*'s second film critic under Vincent Canby and did occasional theater criticism. When Clive Barnes left the job of theater critic, Eder succeeded him.

He found Broadway at a low ebb of energy. He notes that "after Clive Barnes . . . my somewhat sharper, more strident, less modulated voice came as a shock." The question he himself had asked— could a foreign correspondent be a critic?—was soon answered in the negative by those in the theater world. And there were lessons in the internal politics of the job. He became aware of pressure from Broadway producers and playwrights to replace him. The message he got from *Times* Executive Editor A. M. Rosenthal was that he was too judgmental, too cutting, and didn't have enough humor. According to Eder, both Rosenthal and Deputy Managing Editor Arthur Gelb (the *Times*'s most influential editor in terms of arts coverage) conveyed a message that he should relax and ease up a bit.

Within two years, Eder left to work for the *Times* in Paris, a departure neither voluntary nor amicable. Looking back, Eder says:

> I think the reason [Rosenthal] replaced me was that Broadway pressure was there and I think he internalized it to some degree. It wasn't him taking orders from Broadway, but I was an uncomfortable critic for him to have. He made suggestions about being more humane and less judgmental. The classic thing was his telling me that as a foreign correspondent I always seemed to have such sympathy for the people I wrote about and yet when I met a play I didn't like, I was very cutting. I replied that clearly a work of art, or a work of entertainment, is not a person, any more than a corporation is a person. His point was, "Why can't you be nice to plays as you are to people?" . . . [He] said over and

over again, "We're not going to tell you to like something if you don't like it, but it's the way you write about it, it's the way you treat it."

Does this mean that Eder's problems were mainly political or a function of his own training? Probably something of both, according to his own testimony:

Clearly my weakness was a lack of expertise, an inability to make comparisons because of my limited experience, but what I used was my whole experience, a relationship of culture to life . . . it didn't do me much good on Broadway . . . I wrote as if there were no unspoken rules. But there were Broadway's unspoken rules and there were *The New York Times*'s unspoken rules.

These unspoken rules which Eder believed applied to him were to emphasize the positive; to be especially careful with a "big" show; and if a play or musical had to be condemned, to show sadness and regret, to write sympathetically. He notes: "What I was trying to do was to be a critic of theater at *The New York Times* without any hidden messages . . . I think I did a great deal of good because the critic now has a slightly stronger hand."

Better training and more profound experience in theater would probably have given Eder not only the frame of reference indispensable to the critic but also the authority to stand up against the onslaught of theater people when they feel abused and against the public when it is outraged over what it considers unjust criticism. In addition, such training and experience will give a critic the authority to stand up to his editor, when necessary, if he is to remain reasonably independent. Or it will, at least, give him a fighting chance to do so.

If publishers and editors exercise arbitrary authority over a critic's work, they are more likely to do so prior to hiring him; they will engage someone they are confident will meet the paper's standards or views.

Everyone believes himself to be an expert on theater, but few editors claim to be so knowledgeable about music and dance. The music critic may thus have fewer people looking over his shoulder. To be a music critic, according to most experts, requires considerable study, including reading scores and playing at least one instrument. But the route Joseph Duncan McLellan took to become music critic for *The Washington Post* provides a classic example of how impossible it is to lay down rules for the education and training of even a music critic.

McLellan started at the *Post* as a copy editor in the book review section, where one of his jobs was editing new record reviews. He occasionally substituted for the chief music critic and was asked to do part-time concert reviews. After becoming a general assignment reporter he decided on an intensive plan of study that would eventually qualify him for the job of music critic if it should become available.

McLellan found a paucity of formal courses for music critics, so he invented a course of study of his own. His background at that point consisted of a master's degree in French and work as a journalist on *The Boston Pilot,* a Catholic newspaper. McLellan's own curriculum included learning how to read a score, how to play the classical guitar ("you can explore musical theory thoroughly and economically with a classical guitar"). He read music histories, biographies, and books of structural analysis, took an intensive course on Bach, among others. He explains:

> You check your ear against other critics. I'd listen to records . . . then check what others thought about it even if no two people hear exactly the same concert.
>
> My editor noted that I'd come back from my lunch hour with a musical score or a recording under my arm. He asked me to do a review, then another, and I was asked to do more.

He got the job.

Although a certain passion and excitement are perhaps the key to outstanding criticism, they do not come with training any more than does a critical sense or any other kind of talent. Yet only education and/or experience appear to provide the vast majority of those critics interviewed with the background from which these other qualities can be effectively released.

The Formal Study of Criticism

A survey of critics across the nation reveals that very few have depended on formal classes in criticism for learning their trade. Yet some excellent teachers of criticism are at work in quite a number of universities and conservatories.

David Littlejohn, professor of journalism at the University of California at Berkeley, who is himself an opera critic appearing weekly on television in San Francisco, teaches two programs that originated with grants from the Rockefeller Foundation. Littlejohn has mixed feelings about what should be the criteria for critics. He has found that sometimes those with the best academic training are not good, in fact, that there can be something deadening about such training. He teaches two seminars for undergraduates but does not expect more than one out of ten to respond thoughtfully to an artistic experience. He puts before them films, some live theater, some live music (Elton John or Mozart), and accompanies his students to all the events he asks them to attend during a fifteen-week course.

Heavy emphasis in Littlejohn's course is placed on good writing, which, to the extent possible, will enable the critic to re-create for his readers the experience he undergoes. He advises students to read scripts, reminding them that they are judging a play as well as a production. He warns his students to watch out for pedantry and to avoid showing off in an effort to be witty or clever, and to avoid pouring out an opinion without reason. On the question of bias, Littlejohn tells his students that the best way to deal with it is to write so clearly that it will be communicated in a way that will let the reader decide.

Littlejohn tells his students that he reads Arlene Croce's dance criticism in *The New Yorker* and sees on the page the dancers and their movements. "By far the most important theme I teach," Littlejohn says, "is that in the end your opinion is dispensable, your theories are dispensable, your academic training is dispensable . . . the verbal re-creation of your experience, what went on on the stage . . . that is indispensable."

The Critic in the Classroom

There are probably over 250 college courses in criticism given across the country,[6] and, according to listings in the National Directory for the Performing Arts/Educational,[7] the vast majority are in theater criticism, with less than a handful in music and dance. Some associations of dance, music, and theater critics show an interest in educational programs for their members, with the Dance Critics Association stepping out well in front with a varied and stimulating program at its annual meeting exploring the world of dance criticism as well as providing a workshop, led by senior critics, on writing about dance.

The American Dance Festival at Duke University has seminars for critics. The Music Critics Association has conducted institutes, workshops, and other educational programs, but often without continuity because of a lack of funds. The Peabody Conservatory of Music of the Johns Hopkins University offers a master's degree in music history and criticism, the first institution, according to its description of the course, "to establish a degree program in which music critics must first satisfy the performance requirements for graduation from a conservatory of music and then add on a broad range of knowledge and skills, combining studies in music and musicology, with those in journalism, aesthetics, philosophy, history, sociology and creative writing."

One of the most ambitious of all critics' workshops is for theater. It is the National Critics Institute of the Eugene O'Neill Memorial Theatre Center, founded in 1968 and held each summer for six weeks in Waterford, Connecticut. The center is a force of considerable importance in the American theater, its National Playwrights Conference each year selecting from the thousands of scripts offered by new playwrights a few that are given staged readings by professional actors, often supervised by leading directors from around the country. The Critics Institute's director is Ernest Schier, former theater critic for *The Philadelphia Inquirer,* who selects each of the institute's fifteen fellows from the ranks of young, working critics and students interested in becoming critics. The institute, Schier says, is one of a kind, dealing with day-to-day questions a critic will face.

The emphasis at the institute is on writing under deadline a critique of one of the plays being given during the session, and then having the faculty—drawn from established critics—do their own critique in class of what has been written. More emphasis is placed on what elements must be included in a critique than on the philosophy and underpinning of criticism, which gives the program an imbalance. Guest speakers drawn from a variety of publications or television are also involved, but many of the rather extraordinary resources of the O'Neill Center—visiting playwrights, directors, actors, dramaturges, and theater celebrities who wander into the critics' sessions from time to time—are not regularly a part of the program. This appears to be a missed opportunity, one which has on occasion distressed some of the students, however good the rest of the program may be.

Nevertheless, the student critics do have the opportunity, when their schedules permit, to watch the birth of a new playwright's work, to see it develop, and to gain insights into the discrete and overlapping roles of author, director, and actor and to plumb something of the mysteries of how the play itself changes as others get involved. The Institute has well over 150 graduates, a substantial number of whom work as critics, on staff or freelance, at publications around the country.

Center for Arts Criticism

In the course of discussions and interviews with critics around the country, it becomes clear that there is a need for more accessible training centers and for workshops on a continuing basis for active critics. Beyond this, there is also need for a systematic effort to address problems relating to the practice of criticism as well as to encourage more favorable conditions for critics who work on newspapers. One organization addressing itself to some of these questions has been set up in St. Paul.

Minneapolis and St. Paul are home to a remarkably varied number of arts institutions, endowing the Twin Cities with a rich life of the arts. They have the Minneapolis Opera, the Minnesota Orchestra, the St. Paul Chamber Orchestra, the Guthrie Theatre (one of six Equity theaters among some thirty or thirty-five other theaters). Minneapolis is also the home of the imaginative Theatre de la Jeune Lune. The Walker Art Center presents high-quality and highly innovative performing arts works in addition to being among the nation's distinguished art galleries. There are also some dance groups as well as other music organizations.

The Twin Cities area is a perfectly logical place, therefore, for the establishment of a unique organization, the Center for Arts Criticism. The center's purpose is "to improve the quality and quantity of criticism of all art forms and media. The center seeks to accomplish these goals through direct programming, grant awards, and administrative services. The center is predicated on the conviction that its constituency is the substantial community of critics, artists, and audiences who want sustained and serious consideration of the arts rather than superficial promotion of the arts." It was established in 1985 with support from the Jerome Foundation, the Northwest Area Foundation, and the Minnesota Humanities Commission.

Providing grants to Minnesota critics for projects and activities directly related to their growth as practicing freelance or staff critics is one of the center's priorities. Examples include a grant for a critic to attend the Aldeburgh Festival (travel grants are among the center's most important activities), another to advance a critic's capabilities in the field of photography, and still another for the completion of a critical analysis of the life and work of French avant-garde filmmaker Dimitri Kirsanoff. Lectures by established critics from outside the state, workshops on criticism, and a variety of publication and other grants are included in the center's program.

Patrice Clark Koelsch, the center's director, has a Ph.D. in medieval philosophy from Ohio State, taught philosophy and ethics in Illinois, and did postgraduate work in feminist literary criticism. A native New Yorker, Koelsch moved to the Twin Cities and started working for the Minnesota Humanities Commission as a program officer, which led to her present position.

Koelsch is particularly interested in such questions as the need for more newspaper space for criticism, for improving the quality of criticism, and for finding ways to encourage more substantive criticism. But in this regard the center seems unduly accepting of what newspapers themselves see as "practical" and "appropriate" in the amount of substantive, interpretive criticism they carry. Too many newspapers are all too "practical" about their allocations of space, time, and money for criticism and coverage of the arts. There is ample evidence that if the arts were to gain a higher level of importance in the eyes of publishers and editors—commensurate with the place they hold in the lives of an increasing number of communities—money, time, and space could be found to upgrade arts coverage "appropriate" to its importance. Without playing a more vibrant role of advocacy, the center appears to be losing an opportunity. Nevertheless, the center stands as an important experiment that, with some modifications and additions, might well be worth replicating elsewhere; moreover, it is presently reviewing its entire program with the possibility of taking a more activist role.

That Critical Dollar

The best critics, whoever they are and however they got to their posts, are not going to be around long if the monetary rewards are not adequate. On the way up, many critics are willing to make concessions, and will even do so as their careers progress. Most do not aspire to star status such as that accorded to top sportswriters, but all seek payment commensurate with their experience and capabilities.

A features editor of a prominent newspaper in the West said

that he made a determined effort to get critics' salaries to the top of the pay scale, a fact that he acknowledged would greatly upset other writers in the section, if they knew. Critics on this newspaper, and most others, are categorized as reporters for salary purposes and salaries are in large part governed by how many years a writer has been at the job. Accordingly, editors interested in raising the quality of criticism must overcome institutionalized barriers before a beginning critic can be properly compensated for the special experience he may bring. Only critics brought in with experience from another newspaper can be brought in at top pay scale.

Save for the larger metropolises, according to my own informal survey, there are no "official" figures to be drawn upon. The American Newspaper Guild, which is the major force in setting pay scales on newspapers across the country, has no category for critics. Critics' salaries across the country range between $600 and $750 a week. In Chicago, the *Sun-Times* critics' pay equals that of the highest paid reporters, starting at $800. The senior theater critic is said to get much more. David Richards, when he was interviewed and was theater critic for *The Washington Post,* probably among the better-paid critics, said he did not consider criticism a viable way of making a living. He augmented his salary by writing feature articles.

The New York Times is in a class by itself among newspapers when it comes to salaries. Frank Rich, according to an estimate, earns something in the nature of $85,000 to $90,000 annually; the chief music critic earns close to that, and the dance critic probably a little less. At *Time* magazine, with stock options, profit sharing, and occasional $1,000 fees for special assignments, the total compensation for the theater critic is likely to be in the $90,000 to $95,000 range. Moreover, until recent austerity budgeting, travel and entertainment allowances could amount to $50,000 or so in addition. In New York, television critics are likely to make $100,000 and more.

Freelance critics are used by some newspapers, even some of the larger ones, including *The Washington Post.* Washington has become a city flooded with musical events. The single music critic of *The Washington Post* must therefore rely on freelancers to provide adequate coverage. The *Los Angeles Times* also uses freelance critics, but many newspapers will not, sometimes claiming that the American Newspaper Guild looks askance at the practice. The guild claims it frequently approves the use of freelancers; thus, it is possible to conclude that the newspapers are using guild disapproval as a convenient excuse to avoid spending extra money to improve arts criticism. In any event, freelancers generally fare badly when it comes to compensation. Thirty-five dollars, maybe forty-five, per critique plus free tickets to the event seems to be par for the course. The rate can go up to $150, but that is rare. John Koch of *The Boston Globe* uses many freelance writers with fees up to $100—high by comparison with others "but still insulting," he says.

Chief sportswriters make more money than chief critics by a wide enough margin to drive a Maserati through—cause for commentary throughout an arts community that sees inadequate coverage as detrimental, yet is repeatedly told by editors that there is no money to increase or upgrade arts coverage.

Who Plays First Violin, Anyway?

Kenneth D. Towers, managing editor of the Chicago *Sun-Times*, faces the salary question of arts critics and sportswriters unequivocally. Towers admires his feature editor, Scott Powers, who oversees arts coverage, but in making decisions on space and other questions, Towers says he keeps his eye carefully on the readership as he knows it. Towers says:

> Sports gets far more space than the arts because of much wider interest. We can say with great certainty that there are far more people who know the make-up of the Cubs or the White Sox baseball teams than there are who know who plays first violin with the Chicago Symphony Orchestra. . . there are more sports fans than there are fans of the symphony orchestra. So we make that judgment without any equivocation. . . . We know we are pretty damn good [the arts in Chicago] so we can safely assume there's an interest. Not in our lifetime will it catch up with baseball or football, but baseball is an art form!

Richard Schaap, who appears as a sports commentator on ABC's television program "World News Tonight," is an author of the record-breaking sports book *Instant Replay,* former city editor of *The New York Herald Tribune,* and editor-in-chief of *Sport* magazine. He once served as a theater critic and considered doing so full time. He believes that criticism requires more taste and knowledge than sportswriting:

> If a pitcher pitches a no-hitter a moron knows that that is something unusual, but an unknowledgeable person may hear the

greatest performance ever of a Beethoven symphony and not know it. Most sports is so measurable and statistical . . . sportswriters are qualified only in the sense that a huge percentage of American males consider themselves by the age of ten to be experts at sports.

Schaap estimates that there are a few sportswriters in New York and Los Angeles whose salary is in the low six-figures. On television there are probably seven or eight sportscasters in the million-dollar salary league, with Brent Musburger, formerly of CBS, heading the list with a $1.8 million annual salary. Leaving aside those legendary sportswriters who are gifted writers and are endowed with original and insightful views into the world of sports or their own specialty within that world, Schaap was asked why, if critics require a greater training than sportswriters, there should be such vast discrepancies in salaries. His answer was:

Probably because sportswriters are the stars of the paper. In almost every city the leading sportswriter is a local celebrity while the arts critic normally is not. He's a celebrity because more people read the sports pages than the cultural pages. When Nixon was President I was speaking to Herb Klein, White House Director of Communications, and Klein said that the first thing Nixon read each morning was the sports pages. Sports is the great American pastime. You can watch sports twenty-four hours a day on television. You cannot watch cultural events. I wish you could.

Freelance literary criticism is no better paid than arts criticism, according to a National Book Critics Circle Survey by Carlo Romano of *The Philadelphia Inquirer.* Reporting on the survey in *The Village Voice,* Nicholas von Hoffman wrote: "For a professional writer, the call from an editor with a book review assignment is as welcome as a summons to spend the next two weeks on jury duty. In actuality, jury duty is preferable because you don't work and the pay is better." According to the survey, fees ranged from zero at the *Charlotte Observer* in North Carolina (which has subsequently been "shamed into changing its policy," according to von Hoffman) to $100 for shorties, and up to $500 for a full-scale review at *The New York Times.* Von Hoffman adds:

That's not great money, but the *Los Angeles Times* is the only other paper that equals it. . . . *The New York Review* and *Grand*

Street, which is partly subsidized, are the only papers around that pay their reviewers decently.

Among performing arts critics, salary does not appear to be their most pressing concern, although it is amply evident that there is a need for higher salaries commensurate with training and expertise. The need for money and opportunity to travel, for a more enlightened system of choosing critics and advancing them, and for adding opportunities for first-rate training, both at the outset and along the way all are among the priorities. Clearly, all of these are dependent on securing greater recognition for the arts in the media.

Sustaining the Enthusiasm, the Boredom or Outrage

If you can't take your one thousandth Beethoven's Fifth, you'd better get out of the business. That is the advice of one music critic. And what's more, he advises, be ready to find something new, surprising, or exhilarating in it, understanding all the time that the "dud" concerts will probably outnumber the triumphs. Dance and theater require the same intrepidity, the same sense of hope, and the same capability to sustain boredom or even outrage at the pretentious.

Richard Gilman wrote in the sixties:

> . . . it would not be endurable to be a drama critic in these days if it were not for the exceptions, the accidents, sudden, unaccountable, miraculous in their power to renew hope and restore perspective.
>
> . . . There seems to be a fixed number of them every season, no more than four or five, as though hope were meant to exist within a narrow, unchanging strip of territory, a running track around the central reservoir of theatrical staleness, lies and corrupt gestures. These accidents, these triumphs within a climate of defeat, are what make us able to go on.[8]

But Gilman did not go on, dropping his job as drama critic, first of *Commonweal* and subsequently of *Newsweek* and *The New Republic.*

Gilman is sure that if he had answered the question of what he wanted to be when he grew up with, "A drama critic," his parents might have decided he needed therapy—and he would concur with that decision.

Rotating the Job?

In the best of times the stress of constant attendance night after night at concerts or dance and theater events can be numbing. The idea of some respite, of rotating the job, for instance, to provide some time for that refreshment of spirit, of eye and ear, of heart and mind, that will permit a rekindling of enthusiasm, a renewal of a perspective that may have gone askew, is virtually unattainable from the point of view of most editors. Who do you get in temporarily? Who will willingly go off when the critic returns? What do you do with the critic who is on "leave"? The very idea of rotation or even a sabbatical seems to send newspaper assignment desks, editors, and financial officers into a panic, and perhaps with reason.

5 ★ Publishers and Editors

Major factors governing critics and criticism are the character, the nature, and the complexity of the newspaper industry. Survival for the industry depends on advertising, and advertising depends on raising circulation. The arts are not considered important in increasing circulation and consequently do not command major attention on most newspapers. This combination of circumstances does not provide the most hospitable environment for encouraging the best criticism.

While many newspapers are profitable, many of the larger urban newspapers that are the most important for arts coverage are struggling for survival. Some, of course, turn a fine profit, often increased by other holdings, but the largest profit margins (20 percent) are realized by small newspapers. These are not beset by the far higher wage scales and rising costs of the larger newspapers in metropolitan areas, or by the fact that many of their readers have emigrated to the suburbs, or by the formidable competition for readership and the advertising dollar from television and the proliferation of an astonishing range of specialized publications.

Newspapers have responded to these trends with a variety of special sections (home, science, technology, sports, arts)—often to the advantage of arts coverage. According to *Editor and Publisher,* while the number of weekday newspapers in the United States shrank from 1,763 in 1960 to 1,676 in 1985, Sunday newspapers increased from 563 to 798 in the same period.[1] Figures for circulation are distressing: despite a rise in population in the United States between 1960 and 1986 of over 62 million,[2] newspaper circulation rose by less than four million.

Business Realities and the Critic

Little wonder that the controller and the editor are vying—or worse still, cooperating—in ways they never did before. Concerns over these problems surfaced at a meeting of the American Society of Newspaper Editors.[3] *The New York Times* reported that the annual convention of the Society has become less a forum for devising ways to maintain the independence of editors and more a gathering devoted to the virtues of cooperation between the news and business sides of the newspapers. "For instance," the *Times* reported, "one segment of this year's program was titled 'Business Realities: Their Impact on the Newsroom.' The reality was that editors were now part of a management team whose purpose is both profit and a quality newspaper." Perhaps the editorial side has come too far from the not so distant days when editors looked tolerantly at the denizens of the business departments as people perhaps indispensable to the enterprise but hardly colleagues in their own magic circle.

Financial conditions exacerbate the struggle the performing arts have to wage for space in newspapers. Motion pictures draw in advertising in spades, theater does not; rock concerts do, classical performances do not. Advertising in print media generally accounts for 50 percent to 60 percent of the total space of the publication.[4] For the performing arts pages, advertising accounts for 20 percent to 30 percent.[5]

According to the Newspaper Advertising Bureau, local advertising expenditures on the performing arts, compared with television and radio, are negligible. In 1984, live theater advertising brought in $61 million, compared with $550 million for film advertising. For opera, ballet, and concerts the 1984 total was $44 million (an increase of 150 percent over 1975). Television, radio, and record stores spent a total of $546 million in advertising (an increase of 474 percent above 1975). Revenues for ads for sporting/boating, for example, brought in a total of $290 million in local advertising; eating and drinking places, $201.4 million. According to these figures, it would appear that newspaper executives would be most responsive to general merchandise and apparel advertisers who spend nearly $5 billion annually.[6] This is not to say that editors allocate news and feature stories according to advertising, but it is an added pressure, another complexity in the equation.

With each department in the editorial section of a newspaper vying for a larger slice of the budget, the decision over whether or not to hire a dance critic and a music critic runs into many competing demands. Editors and publishers make decisions about where to put their resources with meticulous care—should it be in the sports pages, or to maintain a foreign correspondent in Rome or Hong Kong or Caracas, or for a new financial writer or political pundit? The arts pages are rarely the winners.

This is so despite the fact that the arts have become an increasingly important factor in the life and economy of scores of American cities. According to the National Endowment for the Arts, arts organizations of professional orientation and standards eligible for support have grown markedly since the Endowment was established in 1965 (see the figures on p. xv). Private support for the arts and humanities (not including educational institutions) rose from $223 million to $4.6 billion between 1967 and 1984.[7] A great many of the most important and vital works on Broadway now have their genesis in regional theaters; composers and choreographers are developing their talents and works in cities across the country.

In some communities, newspapers, impelled by local pride as well as by the practicalities of news coverage, have been quick to respond to the increased activity in the arts and have been willing to gamble that their readership is going to be receptive to expanded coverage of the arts. This recognition by the local press is frequently given impetus with a successful Broadway production of a hometown playwright or coverage of a regional arts group by *The New York Times* or a national news magazine. But local coverage of community initiatives still varies markedly, and with certain admirable exceptions, the problems of providing professional criticism on an acceptably high level are evident across the country. All too frequently critics who could be brought up to a higher level of excellence are denied opportunities for travel or study by budgetary decisions, even when funds are not in such short supply.

There is no question, then, that financial restrictions put pressure on the shaping of editorial choices. Many publishers and editors believe that the arts are simply not that important and do not command the attention of most or even many of their readers, but instead interest mainly a small elite. Indeed, these attitudes reflect the perceptions of the general public. The arts are growing but still fighting to find acceptance and sustenance in mainstream America. However, for whatever rationales of financial survival or raising circulation the publishers put forward, there is one major inconsistency: most publishers and editors of good newspapers aim at editorial excellence, but that is hard to achieve if arts coverage is not on a level with the best coverage in other parts of the newspaper.

How It Works from the Inside

Martin Bernheimer put the matter succinctly when queried as to why he thought criticism was not of a consistently higher standard across the country. "That's easy," Bernheimer said. "The fault lies primarily with the newspapers. American journalism—I'm talking about the editors and publishers—places a very low value on critical writing. Therefore they don't pay enough to attract the best minds. There is a general feeling out there still that anyone can be a critic and what a fun, easy job it is. You just go to concerts and performances and then sit down and write about whether you had a good time or not. The *Los Angeles Times* has a pay scale of $75 for buying a review from a nonstaff person. But if you're buying a breathless interview done over the telephone with an artist written by the same person to whom you pay the $75 for a review and covering the same amount of space in the paper, we pay $200 to $300. And we pay well. Some papers," Bernheimer continued, "don't have to pay critics at all. They just give the critic the free tickets to the concert and publish his stuff in the paper and that's ample recompense they think."

The problem of getting federal money for the arts, Bernheimer noted, is difficult because the arts are considered frills and not important, and that same attitude is often reflected by the people who run the newspapers.

"We don't put money into music education in this country either," Bernheimer continued. "It's a disgrace what we do with music in the public school system. And if the kids are not going to get it at home and they're not going to get it at school why should they support it when they become taxpayers? Americans don't value the arts."

Search for a Critic

An important responsibility of an arts editor or a features editor is to hire the paper's critics, but frequently there is a failure to appreciate the complexities of the job or to recognize the discrete areas of training and experience required to competently critique the different performing arts.

Accordingly, there are still too few newspapers that are willing to take the time and effort, with the accompanying costs, to make an effective search beyond the confines of their own newsrooms for the best critic or, if a member of the staff does turn up who might qualify, to show the willingness to invest in his training.

One exception was in Atlanta, where the *Journal and Constitution*'s managing editor, Edward Sears, and the assistant managing editor, David Osier, who is responsible for the arts pages and has an M.A. in journalism followed by training as a reporter, undertook an operation to challenge some of the traditional thinking among news executives about arts coverage. They conducted a national search for a new music critic, having decided that neither their own staff nor local possibilities would provide the kind of critic they wanted. In looking for the new music critic, Osier noted that he himself did not have the requisite expertise to make the selection, and instead looked to experts for advice. Applications came "from everywhere, from all around the country." The choice was Derrick Henry, second-string music critic for *The Boston Globe,* with advanced degrees in musicology from Yale and a number of published works on music to his credit.

Osier does not think that the general level of criticism is on the rise, noting his discouragement with what he saw when he was reading clips from nationwide newspapers during his search. "Things haven't changed much . . . and not many places (except New York) turn out good critics. As for the smaller newspapers, those with a circulation under 60,000, forget it, they can't afford it."

Despite Sears's determination to bring in fine critics, he is not sanguine about receiving the kudos of the arts world. "In the back of my mind I have the feeling that these people want not good critics but good notices. I always hear that when we get calls. They want drumbeat, but I say to them the best drumbeat is best critic."

Sears reported that "in the sixties, Robert Shaw [former musical director and conductor, Atlanta Symphony Orchestra], a difficult person to deal with, argued that the paper did not have a good music critic. The answer came from Jack Tarvey, a master of the one-liner, through the publisher's office: 'And you're damned lucky we don't have one.' "

Winston-Salem, North Carolina, population over 130,000, is a community rather remarkably alive with arts activity. It is the home of the North Carolina School of the Arts, a constituent institution of the University of North Carolina, with departments in theater, dance, and music. The school mounts an enterprising program of public performances at its newly renovated 1,380-seat Stevens Center, named for Roger Stevens,[8] in downtown Winston-Salem, as well as at several smaller houses on the campus. In addition, the Stevens Center hosts a varied bill of touring attractions. The city is also home to the Winston-Salem Symphony, a number of theaters, and several outstanding museums, including the Southeastern Center for Contemporary Art, the Museum of Early Southern Decorative Art, and Reynolda House, with one of the most distinguished collections of American paintings in the country.

The arts in Winston-Salem are given a boost by RJR Nabisco Industries and the Hanes Company, which provide support, with members of the Reynolds and Hanes families personally involved.

Managing Editor Joe Goodman of the combined *Winston-Salem Journal and The Sentinel* determines the character of all coverage in the paper. At the time of my visit, there was a single critic to cover all the arts and a single assistant for theater, a manifestly impossible task if high-caliber criticism in all the arts is a criterion. Was this decision dictated by editorial considerations, economic ones, or was it a matter of value judgments? And how in general are such decisions made?

Goodman believes middle America is not really convinced of the importance of the arts, and consequently the resources of the newspaper—its money, its space, the time it has available—should be allocated accordingly. The paper has done readership surveys which it considers "90 percent definitive" that found that the arts clientele—audiences, participants, and patrons—is rather small relative to Winston-Salem's population; this finding must be balanced against the interest, for instance, in stock-car races. He further noted that the paper's readers range from the deepest rural dwellers to the most cosmopolitan, from corporate executives to pulpwood cutters; most do not consider the arts a high priority. These sentiments are echoed by editors and publishers across the country.

The one additional critic Goodman would like to employ would be an architectural critic to respond to the increasingly aesthetically destructive glass-box-tower syndrome infecting Winston-Salem's skyline.

In response to a question as to whether it would not be possible to add freelance critics to reduce the load on Jim Schertzer, who covered all the performing arts and film with only one assistant who also covered cultural news, Goodman said there really were no freelance critics of sufficient competence around. This is a frequently made claim and perhaps is correct in some cases, but not in Winston-Salem's or a great many other communities with many arts resources. As a matter of fact, one would have to look no farther than the *Spectator,* a free weekly guide to what's going on in the triad of Winston-Salem, Greensboro, and High Point. There Stephen Amidon, a critic in his mid-twenties who is paid approximately $25 per review, got high marks for the insights and depth of understanding he brings to his job as theater critic.

Amidon is a promising critic. A graduate of Winston-Salem's Wake Forest University, he was a philosophy major taking many courses in theater, literature, and history. Along with several other students, he started an independent theater group that went to the Edinburgh Festival to present a play he had written. Similarly, alternative publications across the country have some potentially excellent critics who need to be encouraged to enhance their own possibilities as well as the profession itself. Major newspapers all too frequently fail to use or develop this local talent even where the needs on their own papers are evident.

Whether or not the *Winston-Salem Journal and The Sentinel* could afford to augment its critical force is debatable, but one former high official of the newspaper thoroughly familiar with the paper's operations and privy to its finances does not doubt for a second that funds for improving arts coverage would be available if the interest were there. It is a matter of perception as well as budgets.

The problem of maintaining enough qualified critics to match the art form is omnipresent. In Minneapolis, the *Minneapolis Star and Tribune* has two theater critics—unusual for a newspaper in a city the size of Minneapolis—but one is also responsible for dance. There is also a music critic. Roger Parkinson, publisher of the *Star and Tribune,* has great pride in his newspaper's arts coverage and points to the prominent role that John W. Cowles, former publisher, and the Cowles family played in establishing the internationally celebrated Guthrie Theatre in Minneapolis.

A place where they are likely to hear complaints about the extent of coverage, Managing Editor Joel Kramer adds, is in the area of serious music, where they have one critic. They also have a writer on popular music. What they want to do, he says, is to view the whole field as one and think of arts and entertainment together, appealing to the complete range of entertainment tastes, including television, film, and popular music. Reflecting a nearly universal dilemma in newsrooms across the country, Kramer says that if there is an area of tension, it would probably be in this competition for space, recognizing though that the artistic community in Minneapolis is unusually flourishing in what might be called the more highbrow areas. Equally, he points out, the majority of the audience is not as excited about the performing arts as the people who participate in them.

But the dance community in Minneapolis does not accept as adequate the coverage the *Star and Tribune* gives to dance. A professional dance critic is a necessity, members of the dance community contend, not alone for the extended coverage and added visibility they believe would come to the dance but also out of a conviction that the dance merits coverage as professional as that given theater or music. One knowledgeable member of the dance community reported that funding sources asked for copies of newspaper reviews to accompany requests for financial support and were sent reviews written by critics without the degree of sophistication that would validate a critique. This situation underlines the consequences of inadequate criticism in the press. Granted that the critic's responsibility has nothing to do with fund-raising, anything less than professional criticism on a high level can nonetheless have various adverse effects.

In Seattle, Virgil Fassio, the thoughtful publisher of the *Seattle Post-Intelligencer,* which sponsors the Seattle Chamber Music Festival and has been a longtime sponsor of the Seattle Opera Guild benefit, presides over a newspaper viewed by much of the Seattle arts community as being insufficiently aware of the importance of the arts to its readership. He acknowledges that some might be aghast at the amount of coverage the paper gives rock music at the expense of some more esoteric performances and concedes that Seattle is "hot" for a trained critic who will write exclusively on the dance. The present arrangement consists of a combined classical music–dance critic, but Fassio maintains it would not be practical to have a critic for each of the performing arts. (He adds that the newspaper is precluded by union rules from using freelancers to cover specific events, but the national office of the American Newspaper Guild claims that it often makes allowances to do so.)

Hometown Pride

What influences publishers and editors to increase coverage of the arts is often unpredictable. In Chicago, national and international recognition of the city's performing arts raised the consciousness of the local media remarkably, resulting in significant added coverage.

On one wall of the office of Ken Towers, managing editor of

the *Chicago Sun-Times,* is a Norman Rockwell poster showing a youngster—perhaps a Little League player, in baseball regalia, the shirt emblazoned with *Chicago.* An equally prominent poster of the Chicago Lyric Opera or the Goodman Theatre or the Steppenwolf Theatre or the Chicago Symphony Orchestra hasn't made it to Mr. Towers's wall, but there is a new appreciation of the arts in Chicago, in his thinking and in the paper—and it is related, too, to a new confidence by Chicago in itself and perhaps a slight redressing of balance in the love-hate relationship that Chicago, in common with most arts centers around the country, has with New York.

"There's no longer any second-city syndrome; any inferiority complex that Chicagoans might have about the arts vis-à-vis New York, San Francisco, or world capitals," Towers said. He attributes this change to the emergence of Chicago arts companies on the national and world stages, noting the successes of the Chicago Symphony, the Lyric Opera, and numbers of neighborhood theaters in addition to the well-established ones. Towers notes that the Chicago Symphony plays to worldwide acclaim and that the *Sun-Times* sent its critic to Europe with the orchestra and covered the tour as a news story. Towers also notes that David Mamet had some of his plays first performed in Chicago and that the actor John Malkovich got his start there.

"We are doing more in covering the arts because we are more sure of ourselves," Towers says. "We know we are pretty damn good so we can safely assume there's an interest."

The arts community quite understandably wants to exert pressure on the local newspaper to give more attention to the arts, even to be on occasion their advocate, claiming with a good deal of justice that they are a major treasure of the community. This is so throughout the country. But editors have limits on what they either can or should do, when to boost something or when, in the interests of professional journalism, to resist. Linda Picone, the assistant managing editor of the *Minneapolis Star and Tribune,* is in overall charge of arts coverage. Her response to any kind of boosterism is unequivocal:

> I personally would suffer if the Guthrie Theatre were not to be here, but it's not my job, or the job of the people who work for me, to keep the Guthrie here. It is their job to report accurately on what the theater is doing. On the one hand, many people want the newspaper to be a citizen of this community and to support the things that make this community great and help push them—and it isn't only with the arts—and on the other

hand they want you to be independent and a voice that won't be stilled, or won't simply take on the common wisdom. You can't do both of those things all the time. So, we try to do the latter, as do most newspapers.

Number Two — Tough Even if You Try Harder

Publishers and editors of newspapers in cities in which they are number two or three in a market dominated by a single paper often have particularly intransigent problems in covering the arts, even when they are enthusiastic in their determination to give excellent coverage. Los Angeles offers a particularly instructive example. The *Los Angeles Times* dominates the newspaper market (circulation 1,116,334) and has by far the greatest impact on the arts. The owner's family is interested and involved in the arts and the parent Times Mirror Company even contributed some $5 million to the Olympic Arts Festival held in conjunction with the Olympic Games of 1985. The *Herald Examiner* has a circulation of 235,252 and the *Daily News* a circulation of 170,809.[9] But those figures do not tell the whole story. A look at the attitudes and problems of these newspapers is important as well.

Jane Amari is feature editor of the *Los Angeles Daily News* and in charge of arts coverage. She is a veteran journalist who came to this job after working on some twelve newspapers with a wide variety of assignments. She sees the arts in Los Angeles as an important story to cover, but has the usual problems in providing the kind of coverage she would like. In her case, they are compounded by being in third place.

In discussing the special problems encountered by being Number Three—behind the *Times* and the *Herald Examiner*—Amari said,

> The *Times* has a great deal of money, an enormous staff, and my problem, say with music, is that Richard Ginell, the music critic, covers classical music and opera and he tells me when the jazz is worth covering and then we scratch around trying to find other people to do it. The *Times* has seven people to cover rock music alone; their calendar section on Sunday frequently is more than one hundred pages, while the best I've ever done is sixty to sixty-four pages.

Underlining her point with a wan smile, Amari noted that the Dorothy Chandler Pavilion (of the Music Center of Los Angeles) does not take out ads in the *Daily News:* "So if I spend an entire page covering a music event at the Pavilion we are not going to get any ads from it. And a small percentage of our readers, maybe 5 percent, will actually go to the musical event—the opera, say—but it is important that we not ignore it."

Even if Amari says she is willing to fight for space for the arts among the competing editors of other departments, sometimes taking the heat from editors for the amount of space she extracts for the arts, she acknowledges the preeminent importance of viewing newspapers as a business. Amari sees the necessity, therefore, of targeting coverage to readers/consumers between eighteen and forty-five if the paper is to attract advertisers. (Sears retail clothing advertisers, for example, would like to know that the paper has a substantial readership of people under thirty, the ones buying back-to-school clothes for their children.) Yet newspapers must serve readers of all ages. And there's the heart of her complex problem.

Amari recounted the philosophy of an editor she once worked with who decided whether or not something was worth a story or good coverage by this criterion: if you put it on the side of your delivery truck would you sell more papers? Amari thinks the problems of covering the arts in newspapers around the country are wound up in a perception that the arts are something "very tony, you know, something very highbrow and not for the vast majority of people; the vast majority of people have entertainment, the upper crust has the arts." But underlying the limited readership for the arts, Amari says, is a problem that in part is the newspaper's: "We don't explain why these things matter."

A striking advantage for any newspaper is to be able to put arts coverage under either a features editor or an arts editor who by training and experience, both in the arts and in journalism, is able to exercise the kind of direction which can enhance all of the paper's arts coverage. Such an editor can go about the job of hiring a critic discerningly, and once the critic is in place, will be on a firm footing to involve himself as the need arises, without stepping over the line which might deprive the critic of the requisite freedom of opinion. Finding the best critics and arts writers is a crucially important and complex process. It is too often slighted at newspapers under the pressures of time and financial limitations, and without the guidance and knowledge of a competent arts editor.

Charles Champlin, arts editor of the *Los Angeles Times,* has selected all the critics there: two full-time theater critics, two full-time music critics (classical), a dance critic, and a number of part-time critics and/or freelancers. He is former film critic for the paper and sometime book reviewer. An English major at Harvard, Champlin went on to become a trainee at *Life* magazine, remaining with the Luce organization seventeen years, writing on national affairs for both *Life* and *Time* magazines, stationed in New York, Denver, and Chicago, and from 1962 to 1965 serving as arts correspondent of *Time* in London. Subsequently, Champlin joined the *Los Angeles Times.*

In hiring the critics, Champlin has had the resources to conduct searches on a national scale, to offer the requisite salaries, and to attract the people he wanted. He also has had the enthusiastic backing of Jean Sharley Taylor, the associate editor in charge of arts coverage.

Writing skills are what Champlin demands most in a critic, followed by knowledgeability and passion. He insists that critics think about criticism as an end in itself, not as a stepping-stone. The critics he most admires understand criticism as an art form. "Look at Tynan or Kerr or Atkinson," Champlin says. "I think standards come of experience—how it is done, what was done. You can't be blissful in your ignorance."

Guidance for the Critic?

The line between interference or even censorship and helpful editorial guidance for the critic as the occasion arises is a thin and treacherous one in an area where independence and integrity are prized. For new critics, professional guidance, or hints along the way, can constitute invaluable training—or, if the guidance is uninspired, a stunting experience.

At *The New York Times,* according to William Honan, now chief cultural correspondent, the disposition is to listen to outside criticism of their critics, but to stand by them. Honan believes the relationship between critic and editor must be confidential and not an interfering one, but he acknowledges that while he was culture editor he might have suggested an idea to a critic, might have pointed out where there could have been more exposition for a public that is intelligent but not composed of specialists, or might have warned against a critic speculating on motives, for example, "This play could only have been produced with movie sales in mind." Unless the evidence is overwhelming, Honan thinks it important to avoid any kind of *ad hominem* attacks. And on a subject of pervasive interest—how to deal with the power of the *Times* critic—Honan says he handled it by selecting the best critic for the job. These issues, and the general area of standards in criticism, are likely to be a basis for discussion at weekly *Times* luncheons of editors and critics.

Jean Sharley Taylor says that the *Los Angeles Times* pays serious attention to informed criticism of the critics, watching for critics who may be going amiss. "If we come to the position where we think that a critic is inept, then it is our business to find another. But while we have him under our roof, we put our name behind him . . . defend him just as we would any reporter." Taylor made the point, however, that judging the work of a reporter was simpler than judging that of a critic, since criticism, being so largely a matter of opinion, is a shadowy area.

Ernest Fleischmann, general director of the Los Angeles Philharmonic, claims there are no more than two or three qualified critics in all of Los Angeles. "I don't know how many critics outside New York City or how many in New York City have been exposed on an ongoing basis to all kinds of international levels of performances, to new works, etc.," Fleischmann says. "Certainly in Los Angeles, it's embarrassing to read the totally superficial and unenlightened clichés that parade in the name of criticism."

Fleischmann raises crucial questions. The arts at a high level of professionalism require a lifetime of training, discipline, and commitment by performers and creators. Fleischmann demands that this be reciprocated by those who judge them and often influence their careers. A central problem for editors in the arts is to match the highest level of performing and creative artists with the highest level of professional criticism. And this must be done under difficult economic conditions and within traditions which all too often see those who cover the arts as second-rate citizens in the world of journalism. But without dealing with this problem effectively, standards of journalism are corrupted, the readers victimized by second-rate reviewers, and the arts demeaned.

What the Arts Should Expect from the Print Media

Building readership and attracting advertising in order to ensure profits, and assuring profits in order to ensure survival, must be priorities for publishers. An editor without an appreciation of this —even if he has an uncompromising obligation to be editorially independent of the concerns of the advertising department—would be headed for oblivion. But journalism with integrity requires striking a balance between fiscal requirements and editorial responsibility.

The point is eloquently made with reference to the arts by Managing Editor Joel Kramer of the *Minneapolis Star and Tribune*. Despite the fact that Minneapolis is an artistically strong city, Kramer holds that the average reader is more likely to see a Rambo movie than to hear the Minnesota Orchestra:

> That's the constant balance that we are trying to strike between reflecting our artistic community and reflecting our audience's interest. . . . We are a mass medium. The fact that even in a community like this where they have the concentration of painters, sculptors, dancers, and actors there is still a greater number of people interested in television and movies. That's true of any place in the United States. It's true of any newspaper's audience except possibly *The New York Times*. But I think that while a newspaper to a significant degree has to reflect its audience's interest, it also has to lead the audience and represent what might be described as the higher values in life.
>
> Like most newspapers, we provide more coverage of government than our readers probably want because of our belief in the role of a free press in informing people in a democracy. So the newspaper is partly going to reflect what its audience wants and partly some higher values about what really should matter to people. I would put the arts in the same area as government in that respect, in that you give them more coverage than you would get by purely relying on public opinion polls because they are important. They somehow represent what is the best of life in the community.

6 ★ The Critic's Career: The Hazards and the Perils

One fall day William K. Gale, president of the American Theater Critics Association, arrived in New York from Providence, Rhode Island, where he is arts writer for the *Journal* and *The Bulletin,* to attend a meeting. Gale, a robust man in his late forties, strikes one as the very essence of a congenial companion at a bar at dusk. But when the meeting ended, he did not head for a friendly waterhole. He set out on a more esoteric mission—to buy his first ballet shoes.

Not aiming to displace Baryshnikov, Gale, as he explains it, was preparing to do the best job he could as dance critic, an assignment recently added to his job as drama critic. He had started taking ballet lessons and classes in modern dance in addition to reading intensively about dance, as he had done about drama in preparation for his assignment as theater critic after long experience as a newspaper features writer and a reporter. While he is sure that reading a description of an arabesque or a *port de bras*[1] is essential, he is convinced there is no way to learn the technical side of dance without trying the dance itself. But by defining his own standards, Gale is among a praiseworthy few. Had he opted not to study the dance, let alone take to the *barre,* it is likely that the job nevertheless would have been his. This way, he will be way ahead of most critics who are asked to play multiple roles.

Gale's assignment as a critic of both theater and dance is a significant hazard for a conscientious critic: how can a critic be a jack-of-all-arts when the complexities of mastering the knowledge of even one can be a life's work? Yet in nearly all cities outside major centers, critics on newspapers are given multiple assignments, required to cover more than one of the performing arts— theater, film, music, dance, and opera—and perhaps all five.

It is certainly not impossible to cover more than one of the arts, and there are interrelating elements that can be used to give criticism in any of them greater depth. The time, effort, and experience required to master knowledge, insights, and experience—the essentials for first-rate criticism in *any one* of the performing arts— however, diminish the possibilities of becoming a first-rate critic in more than one. Looking at most of those critics who have been accepted as outstanding and qualified, they have written about dance *or* music *or* theater, albeit there are striking exceptions. (George Bernard Shaw is one, his renown as a music critic equaling his renown as a theater critic, but he finished with the former position before setting out on the latter.)

The Variety of Hazards

Being given multiple assignments is but one of the hazards critics face. Another is conflict of interest, which comes in many guises and is as familiar on the news or the sports or financial or book pages as on the arts pages. In the arts, conflicts may arise out of the critics' wish to find additional income, perhaps by writing symphony program notes for an orchestra and then reviewing that orchestra. Conflicts may surface for the writer assigned to critique an artist whom he has interviewed prior to writing the critique or in balancing personal relationships within the arts world with the need to retain critical integrity. There is the hazard of personal biases, which everyone has. The question is how to deal with the variety of hazards that confront the journalist as critic.

Lack of opportunity to travel, for example, can be a hazard to writing first-rate criticism through preventing exposure to a spectrum of music, dance, opera, and theater. For this, travel is a requisite. The lack of opportunity for training is also a hazard. Very few critics are likely to be asked by their editors to put on dancing shoes, to learn to play a musical instrument, to serve a stint at a theater, or even to take a few graduate courses. If they have not already prepared themselves for the job of critic, there is virtually no pressure to embark on an even modestly rigorous training or educational program. In fact, even those eager to seek formal training or practical training usually will find it hard to get the cooperation of their editors for the time or expense involved.

Being a critic demands a certain valor that often goes unrewarded, and frequently carries with it the certain knowledge that the odds are against your doing the best possible job—and the knowledge that there are not enough people who care. This is also a hazard, intangible but real.

The Hazard of Multiplicity

The hazard of multiplicity of coverage obtains across the country. Unfortunately, it is a hazard to the performing and creative artist and the audience as well. All are ill-served if the critic is writing in areas in which he is not qualified.

But the problem is often difficult to overcome. In many communities there is not a sufficient amount of performing arts activity to justify a critic in theater *and* dance *and* music. The economics of the newspaper industry impose often justifiable limitations. But with sufficient understanding of the role of the arts and attention to high journalistic standards, publishers and editors can take measures to ameliorate some of the problems.

Press coverage of the bountiful arts activity in Winston-Salem, for instance, with its art museums, symphony orchestra, theaters, Stevens Center, and the North Carolina School of the Arts, is chiefly in the hands of Winston-Salem's jointly published morning and evening newspapers, the *Winston-Salem Journal and The Sentinel,* and in no small part dependent on them. Also important to the arts is the *Spectator,* a free alternative publication serving Winston-Salem, Greensboro, and High Point.

At the *Winston-Salem Journal and The Sentinel,* Jim Schertzer was listed as film, theater, and music critic until his switch to a Florida newspaper. No one was listed under dance, but Schertzer covered that as well. And for good measure he was listed under amusements—thereby reporting on arts news as well as reviewing performances.

With the best of intentions and the most admirable industry, as well as with a serious commitment to the arts, all of which Schertzer possesses, no single critic can do a good job in all these areas (even with the help of an assistant for theater, which Schertzer had). Yet the situation is common among newspapers across the country, making it instructive to look at arts coverage in Winston-Salem.

Schertzer's preparation as critic is similar to that of many critics, having come to the job largely by chance. He started on the *Winston-Salem Journal* with a part-time assignment writing obituaries, subsequently moving on to other assignments, including occasional film criticism on the way to his present position. His assistant, Roseanne Howard, covered all cultural news, and considers herself a jack-of-all-trades: "I don't think I want exclusively to be a critic, but if I were just dance or just drama I could go into depth; as it is, I just skim the surface."

The *Spectator* has a special interest in the arts and publishes a calendar of events. Rick Mashburn, the *Spectator*'s associate editor, notes its strong commitment to finding the best reviewers available on a freelance basis, a task he says is difficult but not impossible (the rate of pay is $25 to $40 a review). There are freelance critics for theater, classical music, rock—and he was considering adding someone for jazz, for film, and for the visual arts. Of all the newspapers, the *Spectator* seems to cover most adequately Larry Leon Hamlin's North Carolina Black Repertory, a theater deserving of more attention than it gets. The *Winston-Salem Chronicle*, a black newspaper, does not carry reviews, despite Hamlin's efforts to persuade it to add a critic. Reviews are important to Hamlin, he says, not alone to attract audiences, but in seeking corporate and financial support.

Joe Goodman, managing editor of the *Journal and The Sentinel,* is generally satisfied with arts coverage, although ideally he says he could take on two or three more critics. He acknowledges receiving many complaints over the years from the arts community about the paucity and quality of the coverage, but he believed that Schertzer never stopped learning and studying about the arts and had become well accepted. (This was not borne out by talks throughout the arts community, which frequently faulted Schertzer for not being able to cover adequately the spectrum of the arts offered in Winston-Salem.)

Mike Steele is multi-critic for the *Minneapolis Star and Tribune*. Steele was hired as a general assignment and cultural news writer, and with what he describes as the cultural explosion in Minneapolis, his job turned into full-time cultural reporting. When the theater critic left to go to London, Steele also got that job; in addition, he covered the visual arts. Steele reports:

> Then dance began to develop and I took that on, dropping visual arts. . . . I had not been involved in dance, other than going to performances, and as a consequence I came to it through modern dance rather than through ballet. I was conversant with the formal questions the modern dancers were dealing with, if not technique. I have done an enormous amount of work . . . taking some dance classes, reading, seeing videotapes. . . . In an ideal world you have full-time specialists, but not in the real world. I advise youngsters coming out of school to be cross-cultural and to hone their journalistic skills. No critic outside of New York is just a critic. . . . We all do interviews, news.

CONFLICT OF INTEREST— THE UBIQUITOUS HAZARD

Critic, Interviewer, Reporter—Time Bomb

On most newspapers throughout the country critics are required to double as art news reporters and interviewers. (Or is it that reporters and interviewers double as critics?) The arrangement can breed conflict of interest, for the purposes of each are quite separate. It may not be wise to combine the stance of supposedly informed and disinterested opinion involved in writing criticism with reportage on possibly highly charged news. Such a combination can work to the disadvantage of the writer, the reader, and the artist. The decision to combine the two jobs grows largely out of both budgetary decisions and editorial predilections.

The conflict of interest asserts itself when an interviewer, a role which can foster a certain personal involvement, subsequently fills the role of critic, which must have no personal involvement. It can be difficult to write a critique of an artist with whom one has spent an hour or two the day before. The interviewer has become somewhat familiar with the artist's hopes, fears, and aspirations, and has had either a positive or negative reaction to them. These reactions may be reflected in a later review.

"Traditionally, newspaper editors do not allow themselves to regard these conflicts as a problem," Hilton Kramer, former art critic for *The New York Times* and presently the editor of *The New Criterion,* says, "because it would cost them too much money" to hire separate persons to do the two jobs. Kramer believes most professional journalists understand the conflict in soliciting answers to questions about an artist's career on Tuesday and slamming the same figure in a critique on Wednesday, or in sitting down to dinner one evening with a director and the next day saying the work he directed is terrible. Kramer says, "One would have to be lobotomized not to recognize that it's a problem."

Helen C. Smith, theater and dance critic for *The Atlanta Journal and Constitution,* acknowledges that combining interviewing and criticism can become very tricky, the interviewees (frequently members of the local companies) becoming a little bit like family, with the critic moving into the interviewees' camp rather than remaining on the outside. She explains: "You have been told their intent, their goals, and then they don't materialize." And the critic must say so, often acutely aware of the hurt that that can cause.

Edward Sears, managing editor of the *Atlanta Journal and Constitution,* finds the notion that critics should not also do interviews preposterous. He sees interviewing not only as part of the job but as of signal importance in the critic's understanding of the artist he will review. Sears believes that professional responsibilities must transcend any pulls of a personal nature, and that the writer must be tough enough to stand the heat. Using a sports analogy, he says, "You write about a six-foot monster and you've written he's not doing his job in the backfield and then you have to face the six-foot monster in the locker room. You have to have guts."

When the News Can Get the Reporter in Trouble

The hazards for the critic as reporter are of a different nature from that of critic as interviewer—and can be explosive. Most critics, save those on some of the largest newspapers, are expected to do a certain amount of reporting on news in their area of interest and expertise. Editors often quite rightly regard them as the best informed to do the job. To be sure, most critic-reporters encounter neither clash nor conflict. Plans for a new season at the symphony or the appointment of a new director for the dance company would appear to entail simply giving the facts in a news story. On the other hand, depending on the programs selected for the new season or controversies relating to the new appointment, the "simple" news story can become a land mine for the reporter, plummeting him into an involvement that at a later time can call into question his critical stance.

Crises rock the arts world as they do the worlds of government, finance, sports, and all others. Similarly, opposing camps often take extreme positions and feelings run high. The reporter, rightly or wrongly, is often seen as taking sides, and if he is a critic as well, his voice may be suspect from that moment on. When, for example, a question of artistic leadership or financial management dictates artistic policy, then the matter may be considered the province of the critic, as long as it is handled only in a column of critical commentary. It is the "objective" day-to-day news coverage of such crises that can threaten critical credibility. A few examples may be instructive.

The signs were all good when Michael Smuin was brought in some years ago as co-director of the San Francisco Ballet. The company was ensconced in a spectacular new building, it seemed financially stable, its works were playing to big audiences, and it was enjoying life as a major San Francisco arts institution. Smuin was approved by the board of directors on the recommendation of Lew Christensen, a noted American dancer, choreographer, and protégé of Balanchine, who would for some time be co-director with Smuin before being succeeded by him. After a relatively brief tenure the board, with the concurrence of Christensen, decided not to renew Smuin's contract. The feeling was that he was not providing the kind of artistic leadership needed for the San Francisco Ballet.

The decision to let Smuin go divided the company itself, fragmented the San Francisco ballet community, and was vigorously opposed by some members of the Ballet Association, an influential group of friends of the San Francisco Ballet involved in a variety of activities in support of the ballet and with certain responsibilities relating to the board. According to the Associated Press, they gathered enough proxy votes to force a vote to recall the board's officers over the matter. Support for Smuin was telegraphed from across the country. Smuin was reinstated for a year.

Smuin's firing would have attracted press attention in any event, but it burst forth as a news story of considerable interest with the involvement of important figures and hints of Byzantine power plays. The story heated up with the refusal of the board of directors and the lawyers of the ballet company to permit its director to speak to the press. Under such circumstances the impulse to retreat into silence is nearly always a mistake, compounding whatever difficulties are at hand, and the company quickly was perceived as being involved in some kind of cover-up. The Associated Press had taken up the story and had put it on its national wire. Editors at the *San Francisco Chronicle* and at the *Examiner* now gave their dance critics, whom they had turned to for news coverage of the story, the role of investigative reporters. The land mines were in place.

Richard LeBlond, director of the San Francisco Ballet, felt particularly on the spot, prevented as he was from dealing with the press while witnessing a mounting flurry of rumor, innuendo, and speculation that could only discredit the company. Even so, for LeBlond to deal with critics rather than with reporters in a matter of this nature would have been to involve himself with the very people on whom he depended for a disinterested evaluation of the artistic achievement of the company. He would have had to do so in a highly charged controversy, involving not only artistic policy but personalities, overall direction of the company, and the whole panoply of charges and countercharges that was threatening to pull the company asunder. As the controversy went on, it became nearly impossible for the critics either not to take sides or not to be blamed because they appeared to take sides by whoever interpreted their stories as unsympathetic. As a consequence of being involved in the news stories and the passions involved on all sides, unfortunate repercussions surfaced later when the critics returned to writing critiques. Negative reviews were considered a result of animosities created during the struggle, positive ones as vindication. Critical judgment had become inextricably involved with news judgment, or was so perceived.

Allan Ulrich, the thoughtful dance critic of the *San Francisco Examiner,* was one of the critics who became involved in the controversy through the columns of his newspaper. Ulrich says that he maintained his reputation for fair-mindedness until he had to do the investigative work as to why Smuin left, information the newspaper wanted to uncover in the face of official silence on the part of the company. Ulrich said that in earlier days Smuin had invited him to his house and to rehearsals, and that they were on good terms, although he did not generally socialize with artists in the dance world. But with the stories he wrote in the newspaper over the controversy, Smuin stopped talking to him and threatened him with physical violence:

> He claimed he was going to rearrange my face and I only hoped he would do it better than he arranged his ballets. Michael was under the impression that I had something personal against him, which I didn't at all, I just didn't like what was happening to the company under him.

Music and dance critic Robert Commanday at the *San Francisco Chronicle* worked for a newspaper that insisted he cover the story with a colleague to avoid getting into the center of the fray, although it was Commanday who had the most intimate knowledge of all those involved: he transmitted his knowledge to his colleague and most of the stories carried a double by-line:

> My position was that the board behaved unfairly, ungraciously, and, in a certain sense, dishonestly in the ways they went about it. Without questioning for a moment their right to let Smuin go, or perhaps even the desirability of it, that wasn't the question. The question is that they did it very, very badly.
>
> That hurt the company . . . that hurt the image of dance, and it hurt the confidence of the public in the San Francisco Ballet.

101

To me those are questions of principle, of honor, of fairness, of justice, of things that are at the very bottom of the whole structure.

There are, to be sure, various ways of dealing with the problem. John Finnegan, vice president/editor of the *St. Paul Pioneer Press and Dispatch,* said that if he saw a situation beginning to develop in which the critic could not, or did not, retain a reasonable detachment when covering a story, he would favor getting someone from the news side to do the reporting, despite the fact that the critic is the one best informed: "I'd use the critic as source in an investigative piece, but not to do the news reporting."

The fact is that the price for using the critic to cover cultural news in any controversial stories is simply too great. To risk a loss of confidence in him by the arts institutions, the artists, and the readers for taking sides or for the appearance or suspicion that he is taking sides is to undermine the standing of the critic and the newspaper. The bottom line is the economic condition of the newspaper *and* how serious the newspaper and the critic are about criticism.

Critical Objectivity in Program Notes

Competent music critics are very often proficient players of one or more instruments and veterans of a thousand and one nights in the concert hall. Who better, then, to write program notes for the symphony or opera? Furthermore, it is a good way for critics to supplement their income. But can a critic be retained by a symphony orchestra to do program notes, accept the check involved in the transaction, and then go on to perhaps write harshly about the program—and be asked next week to do the notes again? Some critics can, but since the appearance of conflict of interest can be quite as damaging as a conflict itself, the practice can raise problems for the integrity of the critic.

Martin Bernheimer said:

Once in a great while there is a subtle form—you can't call it bribery—but we are invited to write program notes, and from time to time we are invited to write articles for program magazines and one can argue that by accepting money for professional services from the organization that you write about you put yourself in double jeopardy. If a magazine that is not related to the Philharmonic publishes the program magazine and invited me to do a program note, I might accept it. If the Philharmonic were paying for it I would not. . . . It is very tricky. And then you start wondering, do you write annotations for record liners? Because we review records too. If all critics were to say, "No, we don't write annotations," then, of course, there wouldn't be many good annotations. . . . I make it a point . . . not to review [a] recording [where I've written the notes], maybe not even to review for a while any other recordings on that label. . . . Readers sense . . . the appearance of something inappropriate and that is discomforting. I personally avoid almost all those temptations.

Andrew Porter, one of the nation's most widely read and nationally respected music critics, occasionally writes program notes for the Metropolitan Opera, which is, of course, a major part of his beat as critic for *The New Yorker.* He has written in praise of the Met's productions but hardly seems "in their pocket," as evidenced by just one of his critiques of one of their operas:

> The Met's revival of "Aida" . . . was almost without merit: a brainless and boring presentation of the opera, undercast, and enacted without drama in ugly and ineffective scenery. . . . Luciano Pavarotti, doing his first Radames here, looked like a great gilded tent with a whiskered head on top, and sang without light and shade.[2]

Porter wrote the libretto for John Eaton's *The Tempest,* which was presented by the Santa Fe Opera Company. He did not review that opera but did review the rest of the Santa Fe season, and so had accepted recompense from an organization whose works he was reviewing.

This is not to say his critique would be any less honest. It is to say that the appearance of conflict itself is a hazard. Porter did not wish to be interviewed, but another prestigious music critic, commenting off-the-record, said:

> Porter's an opera buff, translator, wants to be stage director, and has worked with scores of opera companies. So if you apply the rule [against any involvement with an organization whose work you will criticize], he'd never be able to criticize anything. . . . A rock [critic] named Dave Marsh . . . wrote a very good and popular biography of Bruce Springsteen. Dave Marsh is a close friend of Springsteen's. Virgil Thomson was critic and also lobbied organizations to get his work performed. Harold Schonberg [formerly chief music critic at *The New York Times*] made the rule

that no composer-critics could be employed at the *Times* and fired Eric Salzman because he was a composer.

Composer Ellen Taaffe Zwilich contends that rules adopted by some publications barring composers from criticism would have eliminated one of the best critics in this country in our time, Virgil Thomson. She explains:

> I don't think people are that easily bought, and Thomson proved himself to be able to review composers whose aims were entirely different from his. The *Times* believes that it's conflict of interest. Berlioz wrote marvelous criticism. The composer brings something to the job of criticism that is worth the trade-off.

Virgil Thomson himself said the major responsibility in any kind of coverage is to the event you're covering:

> The reputable and readable reviewers of music, practically all of them, are responsible to the profession of music. Of course, it's a writing job and you're responsible to your editor and publisher . . . and you're responsible to your reader, who is entitled to talk back by writing you letters. . . . You've got to know what you're talking about. . . . The people who know about music . . . are the musicians—the composers and the performers of music. They're not the appreciators or the people who are just advertising gramophone records. And this applies to any domain of coverage.

Identifying the unique qualities a composer can bring to criticism, Thomson made the comparison of a carpenter looking at a chair to someone who isn't a carpenter looking at a chair. The carpenter would know how the chair was built. Anybody else would merely know what it looks like.

The Hazards of Too Friendly Persuasion

Friendships should not cross the footlights, some critics warn. Their concern is that subtle pressures may become a hazard to critical writing. Others believe there is little such risk, and examples are available on both sides. One of the renowned critics of this generation, Harold Clurman, was involved personally and professionally as a prominent director and a founder of the Group Theatre with scores of persons in the theater, and doubtless drew many of his extraordinary insights from his contacts with them. But the course can be a slippery one.

Mel Gussow, a longtime theater critic for *The New York Times,* has many friends among theater people and is confident that the pitfalls of friendship can be avoided:

> I think critics face this question all the time, because everyone has friends in the profession that you're in. I've personally never found a conflict at all, and I suppose were I to review, and I will, a play by Athol Fugard, or Tom Stoppard, or with Dustin Hoffman, or anyone that I've written about at length, it wouldn't stop me in the slightest from saying that the work didn't measure up to what it should have been if there is a problem with it. There are exceptions. I suppose . . . [if] a truly good friend who is an actor or a playwright . . . [gave] a bad performance or wrote a bad play . . . [one might] defer from reviewing it.

Noting his longtime friendship with Athol Fugard, Gussow pointed out that the very fact of knowing him as well as he does has deepened his knowledge of Fugard's plays and has, in effect, made him a better reviewer of them. Gussow noted that the one-time chief theater critic for *The New York Times,* Brooks Atkinson, had a reputation of going out of his way to avoid friends in the theater, adding, "It did not prevent him from receiving a signal honor from the theater community—having a Broadway theater named after him."

Further dissecting the intricacies of personal relationships for a critic, Gussow noted that he unequivocally declines to go to opening-night parties in New York, explaining: "The accidental encounter of someone whom I might be writing about, I would avoid at all cost." Gussow also distinguishes between interviews before and after a work that he is going to review opens. He does not consider it proper to interview a writer before reviewing a play. *Washington Post* dance critic Alan Kriegsman recognizes that social contacts present a problem and that there is a price to pay, but that by carefully selecting those with whom you do associate, the price is not too high. Kriegsman says:

> I wouldn't have a close relationship with someone whom I couldn't easily write negatively about without any sense of restraint. There are certain very possible fallouts in closer relationships with artists where it is possible to get to know how their minds work, how their feelings work to a degree and depth that I don't think you could obtain in any other way. So you pay a price, so to speak, endangering your objectivity, but at least in my case I'd

like to think that I've kept those relationships to situations in which the price is going to be negligible.

Andre Bishop, artistic director of Playwrights Horizons, acknowledges the anguish of nervously steeling himself for the bonhomie of greeting the critics at a post-opening reception—sometimes of a play he knows will draw critical fire. But he nevertheless sees good reason for contacts with critics:

> I don't think there's anything wrong with critics knowing you. It can get tense if there's an intense friendship, but I think if a critic knows about your institution—its aims and goals—that isn't bad, because you are going to be judged in context . . . not only on a play-by-play basis. I think a mistake I've made at Playwrights Horizons . . . has been in not calling them all up, saying, "Look, I'd love to have lunch with you, I'm not trying to do anything, I would just love to talk to you about it . . . the theater, my theater, so the next time you come you'll have a larger sense of what I do."

Paula Crouch, who assists theater critic Helen Smith of *The Atlanta Journal and Constitution,* says she talks three or four times a week with the public relations people at Atlanta's prominent Alliance Theatre, where she once took acting courses. She says that it is "really hard to keep your distance. [They] call with such longing, can you do a story, everyone knows you . . . but I feel I could not be as good a critic without the storehouse of information I get from interviews."

Much depends on the size of the community a critic is writing for, on the nature of its arts life, and on the mores of the community. In Winston-Salem, Roseanne Howard, who does theater criticism for the *Winston-Salem Journal and The Sentinel* explains:

> You're doing something others won't do. You can't be in this city and be too hard. . . . I have to ask how honest can you be; I don't enjoy doing someone in. I have attacks of paranoia . . . such and such a person not speaking to me . . . it's a little town . . . I have to socialize with people I write about. How much of an inhibiting force is that? Depends how you feel about yourself. Sometimes I feel strongly and say what I want. Other times I think I should have softened up. Sometimes, I wish I had anonymity.

Someone who didn't find it hard to keep his distance was Richard Eder, whose frequently sharp reviews of works on Broadway brought him into a wide range of disputes. Looking back, Eder says:

> I never, with one exception, mingled socially with anyone on Broadway, but Schoenfeld [Gerald Schoenfeld, chairman of the Shubert Organization] said we must get together. We had a very constrained lunch in which I think he was trying to get a message across to me . . . he was trying "between you and me Dick" and I was being exceedingly distant. Broadway's expectation is that a show that is put on by good people—a Mike Nichols show or [the late] Bob Fosse show—even if the verdict is not favorable, if it has something going for it, it's not going to get slammed and if it is slammed it will be slammed in terms that still allow a certain amount of cheerfulness to emerge.

Schoenfeld does not see it that way. He would encourage such communication. Speaking generally, not referring to the Eder meeting, Schoenfeld expresses himself unequivocally on his right to speak out, on the importance of critics, being informed about the theater. He sees theater professionals playing an important role:

> I do not believe that I am in any way circumscribed or restricted from telling a critic that I disagree with the critic's opinion, and explaining why, not as an attack but as a discussion. I don't believe that I should be inhibited about that. I do not believe that I will get a psychological reaction from a critic that will hurt me the next time out. I think that critics have integrity.

Similarly Schoenfeld sees it as his prerogative to go to an editor or publisher or others when a critic in the print media or television launches personal attacks or "transcends the role of fair comment or taste. . . . It could be rejected out of hand but I do not feel I must necessarily be passive in that regard."

Schoenfeld believes that there should be more ways in which critics can be more fully informed on the business and the life of the theater; he suggests, for example, exchanges between critics and theater professionals in such forums as the Drama Desk or perhaps in sessions sponsored by the League of American Theatres and Producers:

> I believe that a critic is part of the fraternity for which he is writing. I believe that a critic should know intimately what goes into the making of a show; why what's up on that stage is there;

what went into getting it there; the role of the director in relationship to the performer; the role of the other people [involved in the production]. In other words, every aspect of the show. I believe, also, that a critic should know the business of the discipline that the critic is involved with.

Similarly, Schoenfeld believes that the public should know about the critics who are serving as their guides:

I have always espoused a philosophy that I would like to put forward in an article in *Playbill* . . . Know Thy Critic. I would give each critic a biography: age, marital status, children, religion, education, etc. . . . what shows they liked which did not do well and the converse; were their criticisms reflective of the public's response . . . you'd be surprised at how many instances the criticism is not reflected by the public response.

Boosterism and Chauvinism

Local pride, chauvinism, boosterism, or just plain community spirit can be an energizing force for arts coverage, stimulating the print and electronic media to put more resources into arts coverage where local groups are emerging and upgrading coverage of arts news as well as criticism. There can also be a hazard if boosterism flavors criticism.

Chicago's arts institutions are among the finest in the country, the Lyric Opera among the nation's leading houses, some of the city's theaters running in the forefront of innovation for theaters around the country. The city has a healthily developed sense of chauvinism.

An official of one of the leading theaters in Chicago claims he can track one of the city's most important critics in his fluctuations of approval and disapproval, depending partly on the extent to which local actors, designers, and directors are used rather than those imported from New York or elsewhere. When more local talent is used, the work is given the benefit of the doubt more frequently than at other times.

Chicago's pride and sense of community seem to exert a force of common purpose enveloping the critics and those in the arts. Critic Richard Christiansen of the *Chicago Tribune* noted,

One tries to be supportive without being totally oblivious to the flaws that one sees. . . . I know most of the theater and dance people and I am on pretty good terms with them. No tight alliances. I don't believe in the [Brooks] Atkinson School of having nothing to do with them. They are interesting and bright.

Christiansen also sees in them an important source of news on what is going on in theater and dance.

The Publisher Involved, or Too Involved?

Newspaper publishers are by definition in the top echelons of community leadership, sometimes adding to their power with direct involvement in community affairs. A publisher's participation on a board of an arts organization is welcomed as a special prize, an opportunity to have its case heard at the top.

Publisher John Henry of the *St. Paul Pioneer Press and Dispatch* is a member of the board of the nationally recognized St. Paul Chamber Orchestra, a situation that could potentially be a conflict of interest. Henry claims such is not the case. An amateur jazz musician himself, he enjoys music and is simply interested in getting to know more about the orchestra. Henry says he doesn't allow his involvement to color the editorial treatment of the orchestra in the paper. He sees his involvement as fitting recognition of greatly increased community interest in the arts and of his paper's responsiveness to such interest. But he does not consider himself close enough to the actual arts coverage to "tell you what we really do . . . ask the editor."

The Hazards of Non-Travel

Fashion writers get to New York or Paris, spring and fall, because editors want their fashion coverage to be first-rate; sportswriters get all around the country for fall or spring training and to major sports events because editors quite correctly assume that if they didn't, a good many of their readers would rebel; but critics very rarely get to major capitals or other U.S. arts centers because editors quite correctly assume that relatively few of their readers seem to notice, let alone care, and all too few readers and editors are aware that the failure deprives them of first-rate arts coverage. Even if publications don't have their own fashion people in Paris, or can't scrape up the money for national coverage, the wire services, stringers, or others are close at hand to fill any voids, just as they are for coverage of international political, economic, or other events. But in the arts, the means to fill such voids hardly exist. What isn't covered by the paper's own critics usually isn't covered at all.

Adequate coverage of the arts is but one element in making the case for travel allowances for the critic. To be an effective critic is to hold an unending dialogue with the widest range of dance, music, and theater—with innovative works, noteworthy revivals, and works of outstanding artistic merit. Regardless of where home base is, it won't have all of this. If the music critic from New York cannot get to Berlin as occasion demands, or the theater critic from Seattle cannot go to see the work of new playwrights at the Actors Theatre of Louisville or at the Eugene O'Neill Theatre Center in Waterford, Connecticut, or if dance critics from around the country can't get to see the American Dance Festival at Duke University, then their horizons will be limited and they will be deprived of the opportunity to see immensely important presentations that can give them the capacity to measure what they see in their localities against a canvas of broader initiatives and thereby maintain standards that validate criticism.

Without exposure—to the best, the worst, and everything in between—the critic will be wandering in a cultural landscape without true bearings. Furthermore, the arts are highly interrelated, and the critic who does not have access to innovative and original productions at a high artistic level throughout the country will be at a serious disadvantage in his own growth as a critic and in what he can bring to his community. It is unrealistic to expect newspapers to give their critics unrestricted travel expense accounts; it is, however, equally shortsighted to deny critics that essential growth and stimulation provided by observing the best.

Melinda Bargreen, music critic for *The Seattle Times,* is in a community with important musical activity (led by the Seattle Opera and the Seattle Symphony) and her critiques are of considerable importance to the city's musical life. Her travel opportunities are erratic. She can get to San Francisco if she makes a strong enough case because many music-lovers from Seattle go there, especially when the opera season is scheduled to start with Luciano Pavarotti. When he canceled, the newspaper canceled her trip as well: "If you don't have a media hero to link your trip to, the trip is less likely to succeed."

Similarly, Bargreen said:

I requested a trip to St. Louis to go to the Opera Theater. It is important because it is a rather new maverick in a world dominated by great opera companies. . . . My request for that trip was not approved—not a media event.

A curious complication has arisen in extending travel possibilities for critics. Increasingly newspapers have adhered to stricter codes of ethics that prohibit their writers from accepting any free trips (in some cases even from accepting free tickets, but this is the exception). While the rule is commendable, its corollary—that the newspaper itself will pay for a trip of importance—all too frequently does not obtain.

Michael Walsh, music critic for *Time* magazine, said,

> I think most American critics are now pretty vigilant about being independent of the organizations they cover and most American newspapers, certainly since Watergate, have cut down on the so-called junketing which they allowed their critics to do. . . . This has had a negative effect in that these cheap papers will say, our critic is not allowed to take the trip to Germany at the expense of the German government to learn more about Beethoven. So then the critic says, will you send me, and [the paper says] it's not in our budget. Well, the papers have absolutely no hesitation about sending their reporters to cover their home sports teams, home and away. In baseball, one hundred and sixty-two games. Home and away they're staffed, covered, including the playoffs and even if their team is not in the playoffs you can bet that every newspaper in the United States is sending their writers to the Super Bowl. And I mean every newspaper above a circulation of six.

The New York Times is relatively lavish with travel allowances for its critics, but even so, the record could be improved. Robert Brustein, drama critic for *The New Republic* and artistic director of the American Repertory Theatre, said in an interview[3] calling for the creation of itinerant critics, that if he had the time he could go around the country writing every week about interesting and exciting productions. He wondered why *The Village Voice* and *The New York Times* did not have such a policy. He noted that *The New York Times* theater critic went to see Yuri Lyubimov's *Crime and Punishment* at Arena Stage in Washington the night a Broadway play opened—perhaps the first time in history a Broadway play was not covered by the first-string critic. At least, Brustein noted, that signified some added interest in theater nationally. But, he added, there still isn't half enough reporting outside New York City.

Roseanne Howard reports that she sees as much theater as she can outside Winston-Salem, but the opportunities for travel are limited and it must be done on her own time and at her own expense, as is the case with so many critics. Some critics traveling on their own will be paid per article for those they do while traveling, and some, such as Howard, take what is allowed as a tax write-off for their trips.

Hazards of the Job—Bribery

Is bribery a factor of consequence in the world of criticism? It does not seem to be in its frequency or overall impact, although nobody knows how many bottles of Dom Perignon arrive at a critic's home at Christmas. In the past twenty years or so newspaper managements generally have become far more sensitive to the problem of bribery or anything that could possibly be interpreted as such and that might conceivably result in more favorable treatment in its columns for the giver.

Martin Bernheimer says:

> Payoffs? I wish there were. That case of champagne or the beautiful dancing girls? No. All my life I've heard wonderful stories about critics being bribed and I keep looking forward to the moment when I can either accept or turn one down. Sol Hurok, the impresario, used to send us caviar at Christmas time which I was happy to return to him because I don't like caviar.

SCURRILOUS CRITIQUES AND THE LEGAL HAZARDS

Vitriol, abuse, and insult have all been part of the critic's armory through the ages. At some time or other, after the five hundredth "Moonlight Sonata" or the fiftieth Hamlet, perhaps performed under water for art's sake, probably every critic has felt like at least risking a libel lawsuit, if not murder. But restraint and decorum and perhaps the suggestion of an editor most frequently have won out over the most extreme critical denunciations. Nevertheless, insulting and inflammatory statements are printed and actors, singers, playwrights, directors, dancers, and other anguished souls, following disastrous reviews, have vowed revenge in the courts. By the time they get to their lawyers, however, if they ever do, they are likely to become convinced that the chances of a stunning victory in court are far less than the chances of only a stunning bill for legal fees. A libel suit over criticism is highly unlikely to be successful because criticism is opinion and the First Amendment affords protection for the maker of opinions.

In *Cherry v. Des Moines Leader et al.* (Supreme Court of Iowa, May 28, 1901) precedent was set upholding the rights of the defendant (the newspaper) against the performers who claimed that the critique was "severe and satirical . . . holding the performers up to ridicule." The decision gave little encouragement for legal redress from even the unkindest cuts if they are enshrined in a critique.

The suit arose over a critique of a performance by the Cherry Sisters. The reviewer wrote:

> Effie is an old jade of 50 summers, Jessie is a frisky filly of 40, and Addie, the flower of the family, a capering monstrosity of 35. Their long skinny arms, equipped with talons at the extremities, swing mechanically, and anon waived frantically at the suffering audience. The mouths of their rancid features opened like caverns, and sounds like the wailings of damned souls issued therefrom. They pranced around the stage with a motion that suggested a cross between the danse du ventre [bellydance] and fox trot—strange creatures with painted faces and hideous mien. Effie is spavined, Addie is stringhalt [a nerve disorder in horses affecting their motion] and Jessie . . . has legs with calves as classic in their outline as the curves of a broom handle.

Instructive legal tenets affecting all critics were more recently exposed in a New York case involving a Chinese restaurant owner and France's Gault-Millau guidebook.[4] The guidebook found the preparation and serving of some items at the restaurant below standard. In *Mr. Chow v. Ste. Jour Azur* a libel suit was brought against the publication and Chow was awarded $20,000. The lower-court opinion was challenged on appeal by the publication, which claimed that the court confused fact with opinion. On appeal, New York's Second Circuit Court agreed and reversed the lower court's decision. In doing so, according to Michael N. Pollet and Henry R. Kaufman in the *New York Law Journal* of April 8, 1985,

> . . . the Second Circuit broadly observed that restaurant reviews —and presumably all other kinds of reviews and criticism—are "the well-recognized home of opinion and comment. . . . [R]eviews, although they may be unkind, are not normally a breeding ground for successful libel actions. . . ." The Court noted, "one would

expect the review writer to attempt to use metaphors, exaggeration and hyperbole" in a perfectly proper and permissible "attempt to inject style into the review." Such stylish statements, the Court concluded, "are entitled to the same constitutional protection as straightforward expression of opinion would receive." . . . Finally, the Second Circuit observed, opinionated statements in reviews are not "objectively capable of being proved true or false." They are "clearly matter[s] of personal taste." Indeed, the Court noted, even if the reviewer's personal tastes are "bizarre and his opinions unreasonable," that "does not destroy their entitlement to constitutional protection." Even the minor misstatement of fact would not be grounds for action, according to the opinion. ". . . [A]s a practical matter, the damaging but protected effect of unfavorable opinions in reviews would almost always overwhelm the inconsequential effects of an incidental misstatement of fact."

Being a critic in London may offer more legal hazards than here, as indicated in a front-page headline of London's *Daily Mail* for December 19, 1985: "The Bottom Line is £10,000." The lead article reported that actress Charlotte Cornwell had sued the *Sunday People,* a newspaper, because one of its critics claimed that she was ugly, couldn't sing, and had "bums too big." Ms. Cornwell was also awarded £30,000 in costs and expressed the hope that her victory would perhaps help define the line between what is fair critical comment and mere personal abuse.

An editorial in *The Guardian* on the Cornwell affair, discreetly commenting on "amply padded celebrities," was more direct in its defense of "rambunctious, rude and even scurrilous" criticism as a price for free expression and claimed the case could have unfortunate implications, although noting that one High Court judgment is not a formal precedent:

> . . . the case could be an example which will subtly inhibit the scribblers in the [orchestra]. . . . Occasional rambunctious, rude and even scurrilous criticism has been one of the glories of the free press down the centuries, not least in politics but also Kenneth Tynan and Bernard Levin, for example—in arts and literary reviewing. There are a lot of singers who can't sing, actors who can't speak and comedians who can't tell jokes who will sit more easily on their fat, untalented bottoms this week as a result of Ms. Cornwell's victory.[5]

After reading an unfavorable review by Kenneth Tynan in the *Evening Standard* of his performance in *The Wandering Jew,* Donald Wolfit issued a writ for libel against the paper and Tynan. Kathleen Tynan says in her biography of her husband:

> Much to [Tynan's] anger the paper did not spring to his defense, and battle was never engaged [the *Standard* eventually paid Wolfit's costs]. Ken had made another rabid enemy in the profession. At London parties actors would either keep frigidly out of Ken's way or hang on to his every word.[6]

The Criticism of Cruelty

There is a hazard connected with "rambunctious, rude, and even scurrilous" criticism that won't land a critic in jail but that can possibly invalidate any higher purpose criticism might serve. This is the temptation to make of dissent and negativism in reviews an end in itself regardless of the injustice to performer or creative artist. Sloppy, misguided, or fatigued artistry may possibly be revitalized by negative criticism, by being hauled up in dishonor before the public. But at other times negative criticism may have cut down a promising artist at a crucial moment of his development or cast into oblivion a production, dance program, or composition which with time could find its place in the world of the arts.

The point is how negative criticism is used, and when it crosses the line into cruelty. Of course, what may appear to a performer or writer or composer as cruelty may be accurately justified by a critic as honest analysis. The uses of excess can be fatally tempting.

No one has bothered, insofar as I know, to collect words of praise by critics, but Diana Rigg compiled a book of what she describes as "the worst ever theatrical reviews," and Nicolas Slonimsky did the same for music in a work on "critical assaults on composers since Beethoven's time." For good measure there is *Rotten Reviews: A Literary Companion* by Bill Henderson. All these books have been issued in multiple editions.[7]

Patrick Stoner, a young radio and television critic (WHYY, Philadelphia), attending the National Critic's Institute at the Eugene O'Neill Theatre Center, was quick to see—if not to personally subscribe to the notion—how seductive negative criticism can be. Stoner says it is easier to write a negative review than a positive one, easier to be wittily sarcastic than analytical: "We are all good at that—I can do that with every show I've ever seen. I don't." But he adds: "If you're starting out, bomb the first ten shows, lavish disdain on every aspect, nail them to the wall in the most venomous language you can find. People will respond." He has caught the essence of the matter: it is as true in the theater or the concert hall as it is in the boardroom or at a faculty meeting that, psychologically, attack has a nearly unerring attraction and endows the critic or the board member with an authority that seems to emanate from the hypercritical posture itself.

John Simon, theater critic for *New York* magazine, lost his first job as critic for heaping praise on a play. He was a student at Harvard University, writing for the *Harvard Advocate,* and the editorial board thought he must be crazy for his enthusiasm. The play was *A Streetcar Named Desire* by Tennessee Williams. Since that time few if any have considered him crazy; few if any have accused him of overly praiseful ways. On the contrary, he is known for the vitriol of his critiques, for the ruthlessness of his attacks, for the cruelty of his assaults on the person of performers, and for his denigration of the playwright. While known for his offenses, he is also known as the champion of a number of new playwrights and as one of the most formidably erudite and perceptive of critics writing today. Simon says:

> A good critic is always his—and I mean hers as well—own toughest critic. If he is satisfied with his work, then the work is finished. He doesn't care how many readers have orgasms over it, or how many of them have apoplexy over it . . . people may read them [the reviews] or not read them, get enthusiastic about them or get furious about them, that's all secondary or tertiary. He doesn't care if the Broadway producers think that he is a great help to Broadway or a great hindrance to Broadway. He doesn't care whether he is invited to give the big lecture at the university. . . . He doesn't care whether he gets invited to many cocktail parties.

Impelling Simon in his rigorous, controversial, and often stunningly abrasive stance is, he says, a passion and commitment to the best in theater:

> I think art is a very serious undertaking. It is as serious to me as medicine, or architecture, or engineering, and bad art to me is ultimately as nefarious as bad bridge building. If a bridge collapses and thousands of people fall into the river that's a terrible thing, but if a country's art, in this case theater but it might be

anything else, is terrible and people grow up fed on that junk, that intellectual junk food, that's equally terrible and perhaps more terrible in the long run because more people suffer from it. It's self-perpetuating. The bad bridge builder may be finished for life, but the bad playwright goes right on, if he's encouraged, to write more bad plays which are more big successes, and I think people have to be protected from themselves.

But that protection may not be forthcoming, for Simon thinks most critics aren't up to the job and he has doubts about the discernment of the public as well.

Asked how he justified his personal attacks on the looks of performers, and why talent wouldn't supersede any such considerations, Simon says that to him the pursuit of beauty is a prime, if not the prime, concern in life and that his attacks on the looks of actors or actresses are made if such looks are grossly inadequate to the dramatic, aesthetic purpose. Simon pursues the ideal of beauty on the stage in every element of a presentation, including the beauty of the person:

Our ancestors, the Greeks, knew this very well, and we should have stayed with them in this respect. [In the theater] we should be able to see beautiful human beings perform. I realize that it's customary to say that acting talent is more important. It is, but I think ideally the great actor is someone who, whether he or she is beautiful or not, can simulate physical beauty by his inspiration, by his genius, if not by his actual looks, but in some cases by actually being good looking. I think that that kind of genuine physical beauty that the Greek sculpture has preserved for us is something that we have a right to look for in the theater. If we don't get it, I think we are being cheated out of something that we need to sustain us in life.

It is Simon's contention that a critic has to use "strong literary effects" to put the point across. He says:

For that you have to use very strong literary effects. When I say literary I mean that I like my criticism [to exist] not only for the moment, I would like it to be read a hundred years from now, which means it has to be exciting writing. It has to be forceful, it has to hurt people if you will. I think hurting someone's feelings today is less important than saying something in such a way that it will stick.

History hardly bears this out: the critics we read today from the past are not necessarily read for the extremity of their opinions but rather for the insights into the age they were writing about. The criticism of cruelty has little to do with this.

A Hazardous Tilt

If none of us should lean in the direction of our weaknesses, critics should never lean in the direction of their biases. Nor, for that matter, in the opposite direction in order to overcome their effect. In order to be fair to his readers and to the creative and performing artists he may be evaluating, a critic can hardly do other than to acknowledge his biases and find ways of dealing with them. This means, of course, first of all understanding what those biases are. If a critic just can't stand a playwright because he is convinced, after paying proper attention to his work, that the playwright is incompetent, it is his responsibility to so state his evaluation.

Arlene Croce believes herself fortunate in not having to write about anything that she does not have a response to.

> It is not possible to respond to all kinds of dance with the same enthusiasm. I love ballet and I am more responsive to dance that is set to music than to dance that is not, but that doesn't mean that I don't have any feelings at all, that I can't enjoy the work of people who don't conform to those particular aesthetic principles. You do the best you can with all kinds of things [but] I think we are pretty much grounded in our tastes.

Composer William Schuman puts the matter with chilling but compelling logic:

> There are two words that are all-important and that are never mentioned, and those two words are aesthetic predilection. The aesthetic predilection of an individual critic is what guides his writing . . . and is imposed upon the community which he serves for the entire length of his tenure, which can be the bulk of a lifetime of a listener.

To Schuman, the greatest defect in our system is that it lets one person become the leading critic in a single city for a period of twenty-five to forty years, and in that time to have a chance to espouse causes of interest to him and to ignore those that aren't, even if they might have an important claim on the attention of the music world. He went on to cite Harold Schonberg, whose enthusiasms included the piano and the composer Dvorak. Schuman says Schonberg did an enormous amount to bring about a resurgence in the music of Dvorak. Modern American music was not one of his enthusiasms, Schuman observes, noting that had he been enthusiastic about it, he could have been a great plus in its behalf. Contrasting Schonberg to Alfred Frankenstein, for many years the music and art critic for the *San Francisco Chronicle,* Schuman notes that even with a less powerful forum Frankenstein was a tremendous force for the American music of his day. "Now does this mean that I am making judgments about Frankenstein's view or Schonberg's view? No, what I'm talking about is . . . aesthetic predilection," Schuman says.

In saying this, Schuman is touching on something every creative and performing artist is aware of: if an important critic in the community has an aesthetic predilection against the type of work a performer does, his career can be put in jeopardy every time out. Recognizing the power of such opinions, right or wrong, Schuman comments that critics are not chosen for their humility. "And I think that's right. I don't think you can be humble and be a critic."

Joe Adcock, theater critic for the *Seattle Post-Intelligencer,* puts his cards admirably on the table, at least when it comes to Gilbert and Sullivan. In a review of *Patience* he wrote: "My own patience wears very thin where Gilbert and Sullivan are concerned. A hundred years ago, all this artifice at the service of ridiculing artificiality must have seemed scintillatingly topical. But now it just seems quaint." He goes on to sidestep any harsh judgments, and while he may never encourage a new generation to sample the works of Gilbert and Sullivan—that may be too bad, but his prerogative— aficionados are unlikely to be put off by him, knowing where he stands.

Composer John Cage is a man particularly well situated to talk about bias, having been well exposed to it. According to Roy Close, music critic for the *St. Paul Pioneer Press and Dispatch,* Cage's dictum on learning to appreciate what at first may be unappealing is: if you don't like something for two minutes, listen for four minutes; if not for four minutes, for eight. And that is the way Close says he tries to deal with his biases.

On the Infrequency of Awards

Critics of the performing arts don't have to duck to avoid awards, for their world is hardly awash with them. Even those awards directed to writers or journalists are usually presented to others than critics. But a Pulitzer Prize does occasionally go to a critic in the performing arts. Such an event creates the most gratifying ripples of excitement, a new sense of recognition at the critic's home base and throughout the community, national attention in the press, a monetary award, and a boost to the idea that the importance of the critic may be as great as that of all those other journalists who win prizes quite regularly. Similarly those giving the George Polk Awards in journalism occasionally cast their prestigious eye on a critic, as do those deciding on who gets the Capezio Dance Award.

But in the theater, and presented with continuity and discernment—as well as the biggest cash award of all—there is the annual George Jean Nathan Award for Dramatic Criticism. Nathan, a towering figure in American theatrical criticism, wrote for many publications from the period prior to World War I to 1965. He prepared a weekly review for national syndication, was at various times co-editor with H. L. Mencken of both *The Smart Set* and *The American Mercury,* and wrote dozens of books. Through his scorching disdain of much of what he found in the theater and his championing of new talent—perhaps most notably Eugene O'Neill —he profoundly changed the outlook and destiny of the American theater.

The award, which can be given for reviews in newspapers, periodicals, books, or on TV or radio, was set up in Nathan's will, in words insightful of his own view of criticism: to "encourage and assist in developing the art of drama criticism and the stimulation of intelligent playgoing." Nathan specified that the annual net income of half of his estate constitute the award, and that now amounts to $5,000. He further specified that the selection for the award be made by a committee of three consisting of the heads of the English departments of Cornell, Princeton, and Yale universities. The custom has been to rotate among the three universities the judge for press, books, and periodicals, and for the head of each department to choose from its faculty a reader to make recommendations, usually based on submissions of critical writings.

Lawrence Danson, professor of English at Princeton University, was appointed to review submissions from the press for the 1986–87 Nathan Award, among other years. Talking about the criteria for the awards, Danson singled out the critic who walks the line between advocacy and stringency; who actively seeks out what is good and is willing to go off the beaten path to find it. Danson believes that the better critic places a work within the broader world of literature and identifies its affinities with the other arts. "I look for good writing, liveliness of style, a sense of engagement, personality, vivacity that attracts our attention." Starting with Harold Clurman in the 1958–59 season, the award has been given to many of the distinguished critics of these times.

A Concluding Note

Clearly, there are various hazards that can undermine criticism to one degree or another, but rather than anguish over their existence, the thing to do is to recognize and face them. Publishers, editors, and critics themselves ought to focus on the hazards and find ways of overcoming them to the extent possible. There frequently are solutions: the addition of a critic or perhaps making more extensive use of freelancers; providing additional travel funds and training and seeking other ways to upgrade the critics; paying greater heed to potential conflict of interest in the reporter-critic mix as well as in other areas ranging from problems involved in outside writing to personal relationships. Any or all of these approaches will go some way toward helping to achieve first-rate criticism of the arts in America.

7 ★ The Electronic Media

"How do I deal with two minutes and fifteen seconds? It is completely frustrating and I resign myself to the fact that that's the time limit and proceed from there." This is Joyce Kulhawik, movie and theater critic for WBZ-TV in Boston, talking about her job.

Kulhawick's words epitomize what can and must be said about live arts criticism (nearly entirely limited to theater) on television: the time limitation is enormously frustrating. Two minutes, give or take a few seconds, is the apparently immutable reality. The time limitations are as restrictive as they are nonnegotiable, largely because the television audience demands entertainment and is essentially antithetical to serious criticism. But even on public television, where the atmosphere might have been expected to be more hospitable to critiques, criticism of the arts, except for movies, is rarely encountered.

To talk about two and a quarter minutes of criticism is actually to exaggerate by half, because half of the time is usually devoted to filmed excerpts of the play or musical under review, bringing the actual time for commentary to about one minute. (In print, that would equal approximately 300–400 words. A critique in the daily newspaper is likely to be around 1,500 to 2,000 words.) The television critic usually appears at the end of the news program, just after sports and weather, when people tend to tune out.

As Kulhawik says, you proceed from there. But you do proceed, primarily because of the formidable power of television and its hold on the public. While there are very few surveys on the impact of any critics, print or television, most knowledgeable sources agree that the impact of television reviewing on the theater audience in New York is light-years below that of the impact of *The New York Times,* with other print media coming in second. Television comes in a distant third, followed by radio. The most influential of the New York television critics is generally considered to be Dennis Cunningham of CBS, with Pia Lindstrom of NBC following very closely.

George Wachtel, research director for The League of American Theatres and Producers, believes that the impact of television critics on theater is somewhat akin to word-of-mouth. They can be powerful agents in building audiences for a show, but Wachtel does not believe a bad television review is ever as damaging as one in the press. Wachtel points out that television advertisements for shows are highly effective and have become an increasingly important part of many productions' marketing budgets.

Critics on television are chosen for a variety of gifts, usually having relatively little to do with their understanding of theater and much to do with their ability to entertain. They appreciate the rule of survival—there must be no channel-switching during their two minutes on the tube.

But most television critics hardly consider their jobs frustrating. In fact, many theater and movie commentators are quite satisfied, especially since their salaries are usually considerably higher than their counterparts in the print media, ascending in some cases to six figures (in New York and a few other major cities). They bask in the kind of supermarket recognition visited upon nearly anyone who appears regularly on television, and they appear untroubled by any notions of the limited nature of their contribution to the arts. They enjoy their status right up to seeing their names under an excerpt from a review. They also have the satisfaction of knowing they sometimes focus attention on a work of artistic merit that deserves support.

Pia Lindstrom, theater and film critic for New York's WNBC-TV, does not trade in illusions about television and its relationship to the arts, about television and its audience, or about herself. Her firm tether to reality has helped her become one of the best-known television critics, and while she may be more forthright than most in discussing her role, she reflects widely held if not always widely acknowledged realities:

> I'm speaking to a mass of people who may not like theater. My job is to hold the audience, after sports . . . and to hand it over to the next person who comes on. I don't want them to turn me off the minute I come on because I start talking about translations of Molière. When I tried that . . . it was a mess, mainly because I

wanted to show off how smart I was . . . in a minute thirty you have to be concise and to the point.

In pinpointing the essential difference between television and newspaper reviewing, Lindstrom touches on a major limitation for all television criticism. The newspaper critics, she points out, are writing for people who are interested in reading them—or the reader can turn the page. She points out that with a newspaper "you have to specifically turn to the theater page and read what Rich[1] says. I am speaking to a person who might have turned on the television to hear sports or weather or crime, so I have to be interesting to somebody who's not turning to my 'page.' "

Lindstrom would advise television critics to go down to the Port Authority Terminal in New York City and photograph the first ten people who get off a bus, blow the picture to poster size, and look at the faces. Those people are your audience. "If I make what I say interesting and smart, bright, lively . . . maybe they'll be interested . . . we have a million people who watch, but they don't run to the box office . . . even if I say its great. . . . Most likely they can't buy a ticket and so I say this is what it's all about and this is what I personally thought. I have about three hundred and fifty words, one minute and thirty seconds [out of twenty-two minutes of news]. My obligation is to the viewers—should they buy a ticket." But Lindstrom knows very well, she says, that the people who go to the theater want to read the *Times*.

Lindstrom says that she can cover ballet or opera if she wants to, but that those are two areas not so well regarded by the management of most television stations. She explains:

> They feel that we are a popular medium and we shouldn't be aiming at an elitist audience. They feel that opera and ballet are elitist. They may be right, they may be wrong. But that's their opinion, and I follow what the party line is and that's what it is.

With variations, Lindstrom's assessment rings true for television critics around the country. Nearly all are aware of the realities and the limitations and know that in one way or another they must be entertainers—it is their personality as well as what they say that must hold their audience.

Making the point with a shade of exaggeration is Davey Marlin-Jones, who was critic for the Washington, D.C., CBS affiliate as well as for WDIV-TV in Detroit. To arrest the attention of his audience, he drew upon earlier aspects of his career as an actor, magician, comic, director, and writer in the theater. He favored eccentric dress for his show, always wearing a hat. He would speed up the rhythm of his presentation to finger-snapping exuberance, or use other vocal tricks to grab his audience. Utilizing tricks of television technology, for instance, he might appear to be floating in space. More passionate about theater perhaps than most of his colleagues, Marlin-Jones said he was determined to bring a sense of excitement and curiosity about the arts so "that we demand more of the arts and more of one's self as a perceiver of the arts." A new management at the Washington station, one said to be less interested in the arts, canceled his appearances.

At the NBC station in Washington (WRC-TV), Arch Campbell is also a performer, albeit a more subdued one. But he also equates being a critic on television with being an actor, for he believes television is a performance medium. He says he can speak about 120 words a minute, or 180 for the ninety seconds he has to talk. One rule he follows is to come to a definite conclusion: "Yes, go see that. No, don't go see that. Is it worth the money? I give ticket prices. Drives the theaters crazy."

Gary Franklin, KCBS-TV, Los Angeles, whose salary hovers around the $100,000 mark, is acutely aware of the restricted budgets of most of his viewers. Franklin estimates he has around a million listeners, and knows relatively few of them go to the theater. He says, "I'm not an instructor in drama at UCLA. I'm representing the average person out there. I'm merely an investment counselor, telling him if its worth the $100 or $150 he'll spend for an evening at the theater." In fact, however, Franklin also takes pride in getting people interested in theater, especially if a play has a social conscience. He remembers reviewing *Are You Now or Have You Ever Been* by Eric Bentley, a play about the House Committee on Un-American Activities, given at a small theater in Los Angeles. He found the play remarkably well performed, taped some scenes, and the day after his review went on the air the theater was sold out for three weeks.

Training

The major element in training for the job of television arts critic is a capability to use the medium effectively, developing a presentation that will hold the viewer to the station. Sally Quinn, writing of her experiences as a CBS news correspondent,[2] puts experience and training neatly into perspective—what really counts is ratings. The same, of course, is true for television critics. Quinn says:

> You can have the most horrible show in the world, but if the ratings are good you're there forever. You can have the best show in the world, but without ratings you're dead. Those who fail in television like to point out that taste, class and intelligence have nothing to do with ratings. But anybody who goes into television can never forget for a second that nothing else matters. ... The primary motivation in the world of television is fear.

For the critic the fear is that people will be bored and will switch channels. That means lower ratings and advertisers don't use shows that lose ratings.

Arthur Ballet, former television critic with KSTP-TV, an ABC affiliate in Minneapolis/St. Paul, and former professor of theater arts at the University of Minnesota and founder of its Center for Advanced Drama Research, was the director of the Theater Program of the National Endowment for the Arts. He believes that television can be used for effective criticism. He centered his critiques on three elements of a work—something about its content (always using some of the actual words from the play); something about the production; something about the performers. His comments on television were spare—there is no time to qualify matters —and his opinions were briefly stated.

Lucy Mohl, a theater and movie critic for Channel 5 in Seattle, got her training in theatergoing on forays to Manhattan from Princeton, where she was a student, and from trips to London. For Mohl, training is an ongoing matter. She takes two or three theatergoing trips a year to New York, knowing better than to ask for expenses. (Her salary is probably in the $40,000-plus range.) Ms. Mohl says she can put a lot into her two minutes and fifteen seconds by substituting for words the power of the images of filmed excerpts from the work under review.

Dennis Cunningham, arts and entertainment editor as well as theater and film critic of WCBS-TV, has somewhat unusual credentials in the industry. A former professor of drama with a Ph.D. in theater from Carnegie-Mellon University, Cunningham has acted and directed professionally. Six months after college he combined teaching with a weekly television program in his native Philadelphia. His appearances went from once a week to twice a week to a contract, and then a move to New York.

Cunningham finds both weaknesses and strengths in the medium. He gladly acknowledges he would kill to get an extra fifteen seconds—he is given between a minute and fifteen seconds and two minutes and fifteen seconds, the segment sandwiched between weather and sports. He estimates the print equivalent for most nights is about three short paragraphs. Even with what he calls a boffo Broadway hit he knows that 96 percent or 97 percent of his audience won't attend it. To keep his audience, he knows he has to be interesting: "Your face, your manner, everything. You have to have some sort of appeal. They say I have a passion for theater, and that even negative reviews are positive in the sense that I know how great the theater can be, I've seen it." But Cunningham, too, knows that among his audience the people who would know who Andrei Serban[3] is, for instance, are virtually nonexistent: "I have a whole theory of aesthetics which is clearly in every review, but it's never at the top level. The top level is a report that such a thing occurred, what it was about, and how successful it was."

Cunningham envies people in the print media because they don't have to show up at a studio for their review, and they don't have to depend on technology, while he is circumscribed in some important respects by the tape of the production he must show with his critique: "You have to come back from the theater, screen the footage that has been shot, and write a review that fits the picture." Under the present system, Cunningham finds that the films he is handed are ineffective 80 percent of the time, with the scenes all too frequently unrepresentative or dull. Producer Emanuel Azenberg won't let network camera crews shoot his shows, hiring his own videotape people and choosing the scenes, a process Cunningham finds much more effective: "I can't understand how Broadway spends hundreds of thousands of dollars on advertising on television, yet pays almost no attention to the video of a show which a reviewer is going to use. It's something approaching madness."

The stringent time limitations on the television critics, the mass audience overwhelmingly not interested in theater, the knowledge that if the audience is lost, so is the critic's job, all doubtless complicate the task of the managers of television stations in finding good people for the position of critic.

Of course, if there is a flawed, or virtually nonexistent, appreciation of the arts at the station to begin with, every problem is exacerbated. For instance, Peter Bannon, entertainment editor of the CBS affiliate in Atlanta, says the problem he has is with "welfare art," his description of art that is subsidized. He does not believe in subsidy and would therefore, presumably, throw out virtually all dance, classical music, and most of the theater performed throughout the country.

Who Makes the Decisions

With variations according to size, budget, and the way the television station operates, it is usually the general manager who decides whether or not the station will have a critic. Since virtually all arts critics on television are part of the news program, the line of command over the critic moves to the director of news and then to the news program's producers.

Carl Carey, vice president and general manager of New York's WNBC-TV, claims that in hiring a critic he looks for someone with as broad an experience throughout the arts as possible, even if theater and films are the staples of television commentary. He noted that Pia Lindstrom is on camera three times a day, five days a week because there are a lot of motion pictures coming out, and rarely does the station review the same thing twice on any one of its three daily news programs. Carey does not concede that time is the major problem with television arts coverage, but rather that so much of the so-called criticism is of poor quality, "very pop and not very meaningful," with the special problem in New York of candidly and honestly criticizing an institution—the theater—that is having a hard time staying alive. The allocation of time, Carey indicates, is commensurate with viewer interest in the arts. He notes that the CBS-sponsored television program on the arts was superb, but the audience response was dreadful and they had to drop it.

Ancil Payne, president of King Broadcasting in Seattle, an affiliate of both CBS and NBC, says he zealously abets programs of community interest, including the arts. Payne recognizes that most arts institutions are not self-supporting and need help. "We give free public service announcements to the symphonies, arts exhibits, and things like that."

Asked if the station ever would consider expanding its arts coverage, say, to an hour once a week on prime time, Payne said that they had done a thirty-minute program on the Seattle Symphony Orchestra and aired it three times, including "prime time . . . Sunday afternoon." That is not the 8:00 to 10:00 p.m. slot usually thought of as prime time, a slot that Payne said they'd probably never use for the arts because that would preempt network programs. He emphasized that the arts are of interest to "2 percent of the people . . . and I'm probably overestimating." Yet he also admits that the arts "are the heart of the city . . . that is what a city is about." He also sees problems within the arts community itself: "There is not enough unison and enough coherence inside the art community for them to be able to present to us, or for us to be able to put together, thirty minutes on a regular basis."

It is true that the arts communities in cities across the nation frequently disagree about how to serve their own interests, but even if they had a common program to obtain more coverage in the media, for example, how far they would get is questionable. Arts companies are in a highly vulnerable position, vis-à-vis the media, usually restricting complaints on coverage for fear of antagonizing the media. A leading group of theater representatives in New York City, for instance, arranged a meeting with television executives to urge that more and higher quality attention be given to the arts and got nowhere at all.

Looking at the stunted spectrum of television coverage of the arts, there is still one stunning omission. Public television does not have a single program on performing arts criticism or regular commentary on the arts save for film. This is even true for Channel 13 (WNET) in New York City, despite its often admirable presentations of opera, concert, dance, and theater, and its self-defined role of presenting programs that commercial television cannot or will not do.

According to WNET, there is "a sense" that so much criticism is available in the print or other media that no presentation need be made at Channel 13, save during a newspaper strike.

But public television could feature a discussion program on the arts with a diverse and informed group of critics or writers or other artists, something done successfully in England and, on occasion, in the United States. This interaction among critics and writers and artists could tellingly explore the ambivalences, diversities, strengths, and weaknesses of a play or opera or ballet and thereby give an audience another dimension of understanding and possibly create added interest and excitement in the arts themselves. It deserves a trial. Without that, public television is eschewing not only a major responsibility but a major opportunity.

National Public Radio has done better in its daily two-hour "Performance Today" program, which reaches over 100 cities, but not New York. A number of leading critics in the arts make periodic appearances. Architecture, art, dance, film, music, theater, and literature are covered, and this part of the program is financed by a grant from the National Endowment for the Humanities.

A last word on television theater criticism concerns the final "recap" by many anchors on news programs. They feel impelled to cap a critique, particularly a negative one, with some usually condescending or insulting remark meant to amuse ("Boy, will that make a great movie"), providing a demonstration of their lack of understanding, respect, and interest in the arts, as well as their essential lack of respect for their audience and the media.

And a final word on reviews in the medium of radio. With less impact than the print media or television, radio nevertheless reaches millions. A leading radio critic in New York is Leida Snow of WINS. With a background as a performer, dancer, singer, and actress, Snow understands the requirement of giving the essence of the work and her opinion within time restraints similar to those on television, and to present her critique so an audience "hears" her, since certain words are simply not "radio" words. Snow covers all Broadway and major Off-Broadway and Off-Off-Broadway productions. But "if it is a complex show, the time limitation is a heartbreaker," Snow says.

8 ★ Minority Performing Arts and Their Critics

Theater that is Asian-American, black, gay, Hispanic, women's, or otherwise identified with ethnic or special groups has proliferated rapidly and added immeasurably to the vitality of the American theater. Frequently if somewhat inaccurately referred to as minority theater, most of these groups do not believe they are given the kind of thoughtful and perceptive critical attention they merit. They note that the critics are nearly all white, male, or outside the experience and concerns of their particular theater. The complaints by the music and dance groups concerned are similar.

To what extent are the signals of distress justified, and if they are, what is an appropriate solution? Is it in assigning black critics to black plays, women critics to plays identified primarily with and about women, and other critics in accordance with the specialized nature of the production?

To begin with, note at the outset that the forces are drawn up unevenly when, for instance, coverage of black theater is being talked about (and the same situation obtains in the case of other "specialized" theater). In 1990, approximately 92 percent of all U.S. newsroom employees were white, about 4 percent were black, 2 percent were Hispanic, a bit over 1 percent were Asian-American, and about .026 percent were Native American, according to the American Society of Newspaper Editors. On a more hopeful note, the survey reported that "minorities account for nearly 20 percent of all new hires and almost one-third of all newsroom interns." (The survey also noted that, taken together, minority employment reached "4,500 of the 56,900 professionals working in the nation's newsrooms. . . . The findings are based on responses from 1,027 of 1,576 daily newspapers.")[1] The figures for women journalists are far less skewed, but there are far fewer women critics than men.

However significant, statistics don't provide the answer. The essential question centers on whether or not a qualified drama critic is any the less qualified when he or she is sent to an unfamiliar territory—be it black or Hispanic theater, French or Shakespearean, or a minority critic reviewing a piece outside that particular minority. All depends, of course, on the word "qualified."

Black Theater

Lloyd Richards,[2] the black director of many plays on Broadway and elsewhere, including the plays of August Wilson (most notably his Pulitzer Prize-winning and critically acclaimed *Fences* and *The Piano Lesson*), does not find the answer to the problems in instituting a system that would assign black critics to black shows, any more than Japanese or Italians should cover plays by their nationals. What he would insist on is that critics have a broad education —including the study of black literature, black theater, black culture. He says that too many critics cannot evaluate black works because their education has not covered these areas. "Some critics rationalize by saying, 'I represent the public . . . please don't blight my ignorance.' "

Attending a tribute to important new playwrights in the postwar theater, Woodie King, Jr., producer of New Federal Theater, a leading black organization in New York City, recalls a major newspaper writer speaking to the assemblage but not saying a word about Lorraine Hansberry. Her play, *A Raisin in the Sun*, was a major event in the American theater and an early signal of the importance and reach of black theater. King knew the speaker to be an honest writer and critic. Her failure to mention Hansberry seemed to King to be due to the fact that Hansberry was not important to the speaker's own history. From the speaker's point of view, King claimed, it was more important to deal with David Mamet or new European playwrights than with black authors, even if the author was a woman.

To King, the problem goes deeper. He claims that black playwrights like Steve Carter or Philip Hayes Dean or Leslie Lee, who have worked in both the white world and the black world and could write on any subject, are restricted to writing "black plays" by the color of their skin. Their plays, he says, should be widely performed across the United States, but are not—because of the largely white control of regional theater and the all-too-frequent perpetuation of this "European way of thinking"—namely, that blacks write for blacks and whites for whites. King wishes the critics saw their role here as challenging the "European way of thinking" rather than perpetuating it, returning to the "passion and fervor" that made them want to be critics in the first place.

King finds there are highly qualified black critics around, such as Clayton Reilly, George Goodman, and Gerald Fraser, all of whom have contributed at one time or another to *The New York Times,* or Earl Clague, who wrote for *The Atlanta Journal and Constitution,* and writers for the *New York Amsterdam News* such as Abiola St. Clair or Barbara Lewis, among others, or Stanley Crouch, who wrote for *The Village Voice.* But King emphasizes the importance both to them and to the black performing arts of having regular black critics with by-lines.

Playwright Philip Hayes Dean does not see much competence in either white or black critics of theater, but sees a great deal of racism among too many white critics who look for shorthand ways of dealing with black theater without understanding it—for example, "family plays," "symbolist plays." He sees a clue to this in the attitude of critics of black jazz. "One of the reasons is that jazz was thought of as primitive and there is still the holdover of wanting to think of blacks as primitive."

The chief theater critic for the city's leading black newspaper, the *New York Amsterdam News,* is Melvin S. Tapley, a graduate of Cooper Union, New York University, and Columbia University. He majored in art and English, and his first job was on the *New York Amsterdam News,* where he started as an artist on the editorial side, following the nearly traditional and therefore accidental path to becoming a critic. Because not much attention is given to a wide range of black arts, the *Amsterdam News* chooses to cover them extensively, going to performances often not covered by the white press.

Asked if he thought white critics could competently cover black events, Tapley replied that he hoped it could happen one day, but that sensibilities to black culture needed to be developed. He went outside the world of the arts for an example, to the settlement out of court for $3.1 million of a bias suit involving four black journalists with the *New York Daily News.* "The *News* did not even see it [the dismissal of the four journalists] as bias." In the trial, the *News* had claimed that the performance of the plaintiffs was not satisfactory. In looking at the broader problem of limited numbers of blacks and other minorities on newspapers and of their roles, Yanick Rice, president of the New York Association of Black Journalists, said that settlement of the suit will give other black journalists the strength and encouragement "to speak out on things they might have let go by."[3]

A leading theater in Atlanta, Jomandi Productions, is one of two black theater companies in that city; Marsha Jackson is its artistic co-director. The impact of the critics is substantial, Jackson says, and while she has good things to say about the critics, there is a leitmotif of concern in her remarks, paralleling those made in other black theaters: the problem is the extent to which white critics have the experience to plumb the black sensibility. Yet Jackson's hope is to present works of cross-cultural interest and to reach all audiences, all critics: "There are truths that cut across the strain of human experience, and if we're successful in elevating those ... both [blacks and whites] can appreciate that human strain, both can respond to it." Jackson continues: "These truths are not to be denied, not to be minimized. But there are cultural distinctions and references that enhance the life and truth of one work ... if you have just an average person and a botanist, both persons can appreciate the flower, but the botanist understands what has gone into the creation of that flower and its particular beauty—same as a black critic [for a black play]." Accordingly, Jackson does believe in the necessity of black critics and the necessity of providing them "with the avenue to reach our audiences, but they are not now allowed the same avenues to reach our audience."

August Wilson has written tellingly about these truths: "White American society is made up of various European ethnic groups which share a common history and sensibility. Black Americans . . . have a different way of responding to the world. We have different ideas about religion, different manners of social intercourse. We have different ideas about style, about language. We have different esthetics."[4]

Hispanic Theater

Even if Iberian ancestry gives Hispanic theater a common base, its diversity is great. Mexican-Americans make up some 60 percent of mainland Hispanics in the United States and they are joined by Puerto Ricans, Cuban-Americans, and populations of other diverse groups from Central and South America.[5] As in the black theater, there are distinct cultural differences from the white theater that require critics who have an understanding of these differences. There is an added complication in covering Hispanic theater—a certain amount of it is in Spanish and Spanish-speaking critics are required.

A leading Hispanic theater, the Bilingual Foundation of the Arts (BFA), in Los Angeles, started out performing all its plays in Spanish, making an attempt to present the theater literature of Spain, South America, and the Caribbean, and rarely got critics to come at all in its early days. One exception was Sylvie Drake of the *Los Angeles Times.* According to Carmen Zapata, BFA's producing director, a critic who is to cover Hispanic plays should be informed about the country of origin of the play and about the author, and should be familiar with Spanish-language classics. One basic problem, Zapata says, is that in our universities, Spanish literature is rarely taught. In most cases, critics don't speak Spanish, or a Spanish-speaking writer is sent who is not familiar with theater. The minimum requirement for acceptable criticism, Zapata says, is for newspapers to engage a critic who can function in Spanish and English and who has a broad perspective enabling him or her to encompass the complexities of Hispanic theater and culture. The critics on the *L.A. Weekly* are good critics, but the paper is not widely read compared to the major newspapers in Los Angeles. Zapata gives high marks to the Spanish-language newspapers, singling out *La Opinion* and noting that 70 percent of her theater's audience is Hispanic. One added reason for demanding competent critical coverage of the Hispanic theater, Zapata says, is the importance of enclosing critiques with grant applications.

Zapata was not sanguine over prospects for improving the situation. She reported that critics are contacted by her theater on an on-going basis to encourage them to attend performances (in the case of major newspapers you don't dare go to the top), yet it is a hard job to get them to actually come to a performance. Zapata has found no way of breaking the barrier between theater and newspaper. "Every so often a critic comes and is enchanted but then he gets lost," Zapata remarks with an air of resignation. Despite some encouraging examples of newspaper responsiveness to complaints of lack of coverage by performing arts groups, the success stories are rare.

The founder and director of the Ballet Hispanico in New York is Tina Ramirez. In a relatively few years she has made the company one of distinction both in New York and nationally. Her audience is varied, including a good proportion of Hispanics. She is acutely aware of the power of the critics—and disturbed by some of their limitations. "We keep deficits to a minimum, but the company still loses money. We also depend on government grants . . .

so if we don't get good notices our funding is finished. I'm not complaining, but that's the way of the ballgame."[6]

Despite her considerable success it pains Ramirez that so many critiques are written by those without a knowledge of the history, customs, and culture that are the source of the dances performed by her company. There is the all-too-frequent inability on the part of critics, for instance, to perceive the mystic relationships between realism and surrealism, which are so much a part of Hispanic culture and which are frequently reflected in her company's dances. She would be encouraged if more critics would read Federico Garcia Lorca and Jorge Luis Borges and study Hispanic history, society, and culture. "Then the language of my dance would speak more clearly and forcefully to them and they would be better able to interpret it to their readers who may not know it."

Critics and Women

"I sincerely believe it's about time we had a serious woman on the aisle."* It was less the novelty of the sentiment that commanded attention than its location—Liz Smith's column in the *New York Daily News*—and the heat of the blast which followed it. Smith was singling out sheeplike New Yorkers who, when it comes to print criticism, she says, indiscriminately follow the directions of *The New York Times* theater critics, male critics who are essentially male chauvinists used to condescending to women, and the town's leading cultural editors who are hit-goers but not theatergoers.[7]

Smith's column, sparked by the negative reviews of "the three big men on the aisle of New York newspaperdom" of *The Octette Bridge Club* by P. J. Barry—a play that never did succeed at the box office but had many enthusiasts—reflected the tides of women's liberation that have made themselves manifest on stage both in plays about women and by new women writers interested in exploring the role of women.

The Women's Project and Productions, a theater which began in 1978, is a leader in the presentation of women's work, operating in New York City with a national following. It started as a program of the American Place Theatre, to encourage both women playwrights and women directors, and today it is an independent pro-

---

*It should be noted that television and radio are not as discriminatory, with, among others, Leida Snow serving as critic for WINS in New York and Pia Lindstrom serving in the same capacity on NBC-TV. In addition, Linda Winer, who was critic for *USA Today*, currently is writing criticism for *Newsday*, and Edith Oliver and Mimi Kramer are *New Yorker* critics.

ducing organization under the artistic direction of Julia Miles, its founder.

"I think it would be better if there were more women reviewing," Miles says, "but I don't think they would give better reviews than a man. But there is such a thing as a woman with a feminist commitment, and I think such a woman could put her critique into the context of the woman writing the play . . . give a deeper review." Miles used as an example Rose Leiman Goldemberg's *Letters Home,* a play about Sylvia Plath and her mother. The play was demolished by Walter Kerr in *The New York Times* but has had productions in many places throughout the United States and throughout the world. Miles thinks that perhaps a woman reviewer might have understood it better. Maria Irene Fornes, a leading woman playwright, has been less understood by male reviewers than any other woman playwright, according to Miles. "She has a feminist point of view, but her plays are so layered, [have] so much to say, so complex, that it is very difficult for male reviewers."

Miles says her concerns over the ways women playwrights may be treated by male critics are transcended by far-reaching concerns over the impact of criticism on all playwrights. Miles finds criticism in theater much more personal than in dance or music. There have been playwrights who have been so devastated that they have stopped writing for years.

The American Place Theatre, under the artistic direction of Wynn Handman, early on did plays by black writers, and at one time, Miles, who was formerly associate director of the American Place Theatre, recalls the organization suggested to *The New York Times* that it have a black reviewer as well as its regular reviewer and print two reviews, as a fairer way of dealing with material that was then very new. Before the 1960s there had not been many black playwrights writing about black life. The *Times* would not follow this suggestion, Miles recalls, probably because to do so would have taken away from the power of the one review.

Miles also recalls that at the American Place Theatre writers could refuse to have critics cover their works, but that most chose to have their plays reviewed. "Playwrights say it's like the toss-of-the-dice it is so precarious, but I feel if you are going through the agony of having a play produced, the playwright should take the chance," Miles says.

Essentially, in discussing theater that serves a segment of society that doesn't usually get served, Miles calls for added emphasis on the training and knowledge that critics must bring to their jobs. Miles is skeptical about an argument she hears sometimes, that the critics must be responsible to the audience. "You can't just be responsible to the audience because you must also be responsible to the playwright, because in the end that is being responsible to the audience."

Gay Theater

Gay theater took a step toward the acceptance that it had long been denied with the production of Harvey Fierstein's *Torch Song Trilogy*. The original producer of that show was John Glines, founder and co-director of the Glines, a gay theater organization. When he began there was very little gay theater, Glines says, virtually no audience, and very few actors. Straight actors were afraid to play gay parts lest their careers founder, he recalls, and gay and lesbian actors feared they would be typecast from then on. Glines's fellow producers Off-Off-Broadway largely eschewed him and critics didn't want to come to his plays. In the case of *Gulp! A Gay Musical* in 1977, *The New York Times* refused even to run an advertisement because it did not use the word "gay." An offer to change the word to "homosexual" didn't change the paper's policy, Glines says. "Obviously, they saw it as pornography."

But it was the *Times,* too, that helped change all that with *Torch Song Trilogy*. This play of four and one-half hours about a Brooklyn Jewish drag queen adopting a child, with a scene of sex in the back room of a bar, did not do well at first. But by persuading Mel Gussow of the *Times* to cover the work for what turned out to be a favorable review, Glines obtained a lever with which to attract other major New York critics. Raves from the critics and capacity audiences followed. And then history was made again with Fierstein's musical adaptation of *La Cage Aux Folles*. Furthermore, Glines reports, the *Times* now accepts all his ads.

Glines says that today he does not have any problem with the major critics understanding gay plays. Nevertheless, he holds that there are plays written for "his community" only and he would not ask the critics, or expect them, to deal with such plays in the ordinary run of reviewing.

Fierstein was less fortunate with his next play about AIDS, *Safe Sex*. Prior to its opening, Fierstein pondered in a *New York Times*[8] interview whether or not the play could attract a mainstream audience (it couldn't). He noted that *La Cage* had "all those people from Westchester cheering wildly for two gay men on stage," and added that essentially he had no sense of foreboding about Broadway audiences—"only about Broadway critics."

The view is not so sanguine from the artistic director of a gay theater on the West Coast who did not wish to be identified, but who believes that some of the responses from major critics are homophobic, that the critics simply do not understand the gay community, that heterosexual people just do not respond to what hits gay people on a gut level. "Gay is a different sensibility, for them [gays] there are different realities—there is an oppression, a different humor, the different relationships. I think you must have a gay critic for a gay play."

On balance, looking at the spectrum of minority theater and the limited but instructive sampling of opinion here, there is evidence that too many works are reviewed by those not sufficiently familiar with the culture from which the works sprang to provide the most perceptive analysis or insights into them. Further, it is clear that a problem does exist in providing the important critical link to bring minority or ethnic plays to their audiences. This problem was put clearly by Brooks Atkinson a couple of decades ago.[9] Writing about *Fiddler on the Roof,* he said:

> The folk materials of Sholom Aleichem's stories are so full of nuances and religious subtleties that anyone who is not a Jew must be cautious about discussing them. Even in Maurice Samuel's *The World of Sholom Aleichem,* a notable work of illumination, it is not easy to understand the political and cultural relationships that created so lively and crotchety a civilization. Sholom Aleichem (Solomon Rabinowitz) was born in Kiev in 1859. He lived there until he came to America in 1906 along with hundreds of other immigrants after the Kissinoff pogroms. By experience as well as temperament he understood how this homogeneous unit of religious believers had survived in a nation that regarded them as infidels.

Yet there is no agreement on the oft-suggested possibility that a critic representing a particular culture or special constituency review each work that comes out of it. The fact is that such an undertaking is all but impossible, and certainly unrealistic save perhaps on special occasions. To implement that procedure would be an admission of cultural fractionalization that would essentially reject the centrality of cultural interchange and the communication of art. The hiring of multiple critics would be impractical to the point of chaos administratively and out of the question economically for a newspaper or other media.

But significant improvement is possible, starting with raising consciousness among publishers and editors on the requirement for high professionalism among critics (be the critic mainstream or minority), making use of freelancers on specially demanding occasions, and setting standards as high for critics as for the most competent writer in any other part of the publication. Specifically, this means selecting critics whose educational or experiential background has been broad and deep in literature, history, the arts, as well as in journalism, and with an added understanding that this training or the requisite acquired experience relates to a broad spectrum not only of literature but of social and cultural history as well. However demanding such standards may be, they need not be absolute, if it is kept in mind that education throughout a critic's career is a requisite; that he or she will not arrive perfect from the brow of Zeus, but rather, like the artist and the audience, the critic will undergo a lifetime of experiences. What is required is that the expectations for the critic must be high to match the responsibility.

A part of the job of criticism that emerges with particular force in writing about minority works—or for the minority critic writing about mainstream theater—is that of the critic's potential as educator, broadly speaking. Confronted with the works of artists exploring worlds not necessarily equally accessible to all audiences, the critic has the opportunity to be critic and guide and sage, bringing new insights to audiences and reminding audiences to accept more of the mysteries, the essences, and the ambivalencies that underlie art.

9 ★ Advice to the Critic from the Criticized

"If it hadn't been for Ken I don't think I, or Michael Billington, or [a number of others] would have thought of being critics. He made us believe it was something worth doing, and he taught us that there was a way of attacking the theater from a position of love." [1]

Sheridan Morley, arts editor and drama critic of *Punch*, was talking about the late Kenneth Tynan, one-time critic for *The Observer* and other London papers and for *The New Yorker*. His words capture one of the most often reiterated beliefs of the performing and creative artist: if the critic treats the theater—the arts —with love and respect, the criticism, be it negative or positive, will have a certain integrity.

True, it would be hard to guarantee that in the face of a bad notice, even by a critic who loves the theater, the artist would be so accepting, but many feel that relatively few critics genuinely love the theater or music or opera or dance. Tynan was among the enthusiasts: passionate, with a depth of knowledge and a respect for those who work in the theater. In the hands of such a critic, most artists believe that they will be spared the excesses of criticism —cruelties, caprices, and self-serving wit. Most artists profoundly hope that a critic will show respect for and knowledge of the art form he or she is involved with.

Nevertheless, a critic is not an artist, and a thoughtful artist who has spent a lifetime in his profession may possess insights that no one else can quite replicate. This chapter focuses on some of the recommendations creative and performing artists would give to the critic.

Playwright Rose Leiman Goldemberg rates a love of theater and caring for the efforts of those engaged in it as the essential underpinning of good criticism. She recalls reading Brooks Atkinson's reviews in *The New York Times* when she was young and learning from them. She found that when a critic looks at a play and writes about why something doesn't work, it's very useful. But, she says, if he writes:

> "Why did this abortion come to the theater, why did you bore me by putting me through it, why didn't you write it this way or that way?" you've been assaulted and hurt and that part of your-self which you try to keep fresh enough to keep writing gets damaged. . . . If the critics are not helping you, and I don't mean helping you by liking your play, but by noting where your play fell short, then there's an atmosphere in which you can't work.

If criticism drives out the people who have the normal, everyday desires of being appreciated for their work, of making a decent living and not wanting to take the excesses of personal punishment so often meted out by critics, then Goldemberg sees the theater as seriously diminished.

Theatrical agent Lois Berman has developed a strategy for what she considers the survival of a number of prominent playwrights she represents, including Sam Shepard. Berman advises her au-thors to have their works mounted in regional theaters first be-cause once a work gets a negative review in New York it is unlikely to be chosen for production elsewhere. She wishes more Broadway producers would see what is happening in the regional theater and not simply opt for London when setting forth from Broadway.

Actress Colleen Dewhurst believes we have lost track of what a critic is supposed to do:

> What disturbs me is to go to a play where, let's say, 50 percent of it works and the writer is obviously interesting and knows how to write . . . to come out of that and to kill it absolutely without ever giving a word of encouragement to that writer, to literally write him or her off the map for the dreadful work that they have done, or the dreadful evening they have put that critic through is to do a disservice to the theater.

Edward Villella, formerly a principal dancer with Balanchine's New York City Ballet and currently artistic director of the Miami City Ballet, would like to see a different tone in much criticism, one growing out of a more helpful stance. It is far more important, in Villella's view, to illuminate a problem that may not have been seen by an artist, a choreographer, or a composer than to condemn a work. A critic can simply point out that in his opinion a particular approach may not necessarily be artistically viable and give the reasons for such a judgment instead of taking backhand slaps. Villella recalls a negative review given him by John Martin in *The New York Times,* emphasizing that his performance was just not pleasing. Villella wishes Martin had said something which would have given him some direction, perhaps "'this is a young man who has an ability that is raw in its approach and it will be interesting to see how it develops, but right now this performance is physical more than artistic.' This would have been much more responsible."

Much of Villella's response to criticism, however, seems to have been inspired by the attitude of George Balanchine, who "was not directed by critics."

Of course, sometimes the artists expect too much. Edwin Denby, the highly respected dance critic who wrote for *The New York Herald Tribune* for some years during the 1940s, remembered a talk on criticism by Agnes de Mille:

> She spoke of the alternate confident and uncertain periods through which artists pass and how in his uncertainty the dancer longs for assistance and clarification. He is tempted then to turn to the critic to lead him out of his confusion by an authoritative estimate of his individual creative gifts. But Miss de Mille warned against relying on reviews in such moments of doubt. A good critic will tell the dancer which elements in a work get across and which do not. But that alone does not necessarily indicate the most productive, the most sincere direction for the dancer to take. An artist will find his own real strength not by listening to what is said about his work, but in the creative process itself. And it is safer for him to rely on himself to find his own identity for it is unlikely that anyone can find it for him.[2]

One thing a good critic will not do, according to Peter Martins, ballet master-in-chief of the New York City Ballet, is to suggest policies for ballet companies. Yet this is something critics frequently do. Martins says they will suggest, for instance, that a certain person should be invited to do a ballet. "It's none of their business. We know who's out there and who's not out there," Martins asserts. Nevertheless, Martins believes the critic must be very well informed. Classical ballet is a difficult art form to appreciate, he maintains, not easily accessible, requiring years and years of careful watching in order to appreciate it fully, to appreciate it to the point where one is able to dissect it, to understand what it means to be a choreographer and to create a dance. He explained:

I think critics are often much too quick to accept something as being great and new because of their own boredom. They see something slightly different and they think it's great. . . . There's nothing worse for a performer or for me when I choreograph than to read a review of myself and somebody says it's absolutely fantastic and then that same reviewer writes about something that anybody with a mind realizes is terrible—also being described as fantastic.

Creative and performing artists constantly reiterate their conviction that injustices are all too frequently done to them by inadequately trained or insufficiently informed critics.

Take the range of knowledge and experience required to write effectively about a single season (1986–87) at Washington's Arena Stage, whose productions included *The Marriage of Bette and Boo* by Christopher Durang, a contemporary writer of often witty, black absurdist comedy; Shakespeare's *Measure for Measure;* the nineteenth-century French farce *The Piggy Bank* by Eugene Labiche and A. Delacour; *Crime and Punishment,* Russian exile Yuri Lyubimov's interpretation of the Dostoyevsky classic; David Mamet's Pulitzer Prize-winning *Glengarry Glen Ross; Ourselves Alone,* a first play by Irish writer Anne Devlin, which won the Susan Smith Blackburn Prize for a distinguished work by a woman writer; George Bernard Shaw's *Heartbreak House;* and Arthur Miller's *The Crucible.* Without some reference points to the literature of the theater, to its history, to other productions of these works or the style of theater they represent, as well as an underpinning of insight into the complexities of staging, lighting, costume, and movement, any critiques of such a season are almost certain to be superficial.

The range of productions at the Arena is not unusual, and a comparable range obtains elsewhere for dance and music. Qualified professional presenters and artists, creative and performing, take the view that they are putting immense resources of experience, training, and commitment into these works, and they ask why they should expect any less from the critic whose words may have so much to do with their fate.

There are favorite devices that critics use which disturb both creative and performing artists, because they can be misleading. An example is comparisons to earlier works, to earlier performances, to earlier successes or failures. Such comparisons can be illustrative, but they can also be used to make a point without an exploration of the work itself.

144

For instance, Lloyd Richards, the Broadway director who has had particularly close associations with playwrights Athol Fugard and August Wilson, is highly suspicious of the extent to which comparisons are misused. Richards says:

> What I really hate is critics who put artists in competition with one another, putting the current event in competition with an earlier event, which has to do with memory, not with what he has seen [and is reviewing]. It is done because it gives a critic prestige, he has seen five or ten productions of the work, he is putting it in competition with what he has seen in other times under other circumstances and other conditions.

Richards sees the critic as not infrequently competing for center stage. His words have particular force because he is so convinced of the importance of the critic's role in setting standards for the artist.

David Mamet has expressed himself unequivocally on the low esteem in which he holds critics in general, but in detailing his admiration for a few exceptions he defines something of what he considers good criticism.

Among those critics he particularly favors are Michael Feingold, theater critic for *The Village Voice*. Feingold's erudition and historical perspective, as well as his ability to define what he considers the task and purpose of the theater, epitomize a good critic, according to Mamet. He admires the way Feingold meshes his responsibility to communicate with his readers with a consistent aesthetic, so that whether or not the reader agrees or disagrees, or even if Feingold himself occasionally changes an opinion, the basic philosophy remains. Such a stance removes Feingold's critiques from the "I liked it" or "I hated it" syndrome.

It is this development of an aesthetic, or a philosophy, that Mamet sees as distinguishing critics like Feingold from many others. Mamet believes that too often critics try to limit the artist if they are put off, for instance, by the artist's perceptions of reality, or if the artist challenges a complacent society and uses the stage as a testing place for new ideas, even for "socially subversive" ideas. Mamet himself is a playwright who is constantly challenging society through his vision of reality in works often coruscatingly astringent. In so doing he believes he is continually coming up against the "doormen"—both critics and audiences—who would deny him entry to the theater and prevent him from presenting his vision of reality, especially since his vision is often articulated in language they find offensive and violent. Mamet says:

> The critic has been elevated by a frightened society to a position supposedly of prominence. His task is to keep out that which is upsetting. . . . Society tries to create work for everyone. We create the welfare state not to help the poor but to help those who administer the welfare state. We create a medical profession not to help the people who are ill but to help the doctors. And the purpose of the critic is to be a flywheel dissipating a certain amount of energy, on the one hand giving the critics jobs but on the other hand ratifying the collective decision. Just in the same way the doorman at a disco is not hired to let in the best dancers but to let in the people who make the club look good. Similarly, the critic is making the club look a little bit more exclusive to the management of the newspaper and to the management of the theater. So his job is to ratify an inappropriate choice, to ratify a nontheatrical choice, to ratify the choice which says nothing much is going on here.

Mamet has had a large measure of popular success. He has won a Pulitizer Prize, has conquered Broadway, and has seen his works produced all over this country and abroad. Still, he views the theater as a reflection of a society terrified of its own thoughts and subconscious feelings. He believes that the theater, which used to be a place to exhibit and examine those feelings, has become the place where the feelings are in fact denied. He sees a serious diminution of theater in the parochial view critics all too often demand of "reality," and in the awards accorded that kind of sham reality. Mamet says:

> Of course, there are aberrations. I mean, for instance, in *The Gin Game*[3] and what's her name says "fuck" at the end of the second act and it brings the house down. Why? Because she doesn't mean it. You can say whatever you want in the theater so long as you don't mean it. If you mean it . . . it's a very violent play. You mean to tell me that a grown woman, obviously intelligent and not an unknowledgeable theatergoer, is going to get upset because somebody said "fuck" on the stage? . . . The theater . . . is to serve the same function in the collective conscious that dreams serve in our individual conscious, that is to address those problems which do not admit of a rational solution. . . . But as a group we feel that our problems are so overwhelming that rather than attempting to address them either mechanically or symboli-

cally we say they don't affect us. And [then we] say the theater is useless [because it] is used only to address [less important] rational problems.

The most important thing to me in dealing with a task in which feelings predominate [is] to learn to employ in moments of stress those things which [we] decided in moments of leisure are correct. . . . That is how one learns an art. The question is not whether or not this is good or bad but what criteria you arrive at in making that judgment. I think our critics in Chicago, each writing from a very different viewpoint, have been excellent critics over the years and have been responsible for the development of the Chicago theater, [especially] Glenna Syse on the *Chicago Sun-Times* and Dick Christiansen of the *Chicago Tribune.*

As mentioned earlier, playwright Arthur Miller believes that Brooks Atkinson was important to his success. Miller notes that Atkinson's reviews were structured in a constructive fashion, regardless of whether his opinion of the piece was negative or positive. For example, because of the tendency of readers to give up on any review that starts out negatively, there was some very real point in Atkinson's placing his conclusions at the end of his review.

Atkinson's practice reflected an approach to criticism sometimes attributed to Goethe[4] and frequently cited by critics. It calls for a critic to answer the following questions: What is the play about, what is the intention of the author, how well does the author succeed? While there is no right or wrong way to write a review, and while the finest critics have defined their own formulae, it seems incontestable that the more important the critic, either by the force of his own reputation or by the power of the publication he writes for, the stronger the case for writing a review in a way that enables the reader to make up his own mind. This does not call for the critic to subordinate his opinion of the work to any consideration other than its artistic merit. Tone, approach, philosophy, and structure matter.

Frank Rich's gifts as a writer enhance the power and influence of his reviews, which in any event are of major significance because they appear in *The New York Times.* Rich has the capacity to inform his critiques with both insight and balance. He also has the capacity to damn a work with one sentence and give neither reader nor production half a chance. (It must be kept in mind that *The New York Times* is a special case, frequently ordering the destiny of the shows it touches whether it wants that influence or not.)

Rich makes few concessions to restraint, often telegraphing his

147

opinion in the first paragraph of his critique, especially, it seems, if the news is really bad. He is frequently a first-paragraph killer, apparently adhering to a philosophy of getting the essential opinion to the reader as quickly as possible. Other critics prefer to let the reader first make up his own mind by providing the requisite information, then providing a direct opinion of the work.

Of a recent presentation, for instance, Rich wrote in the first paragraph:

> The lesson Public Theater audiences are likely to learn at *Largo Desolato,* the new play by Czechoslovak dissident writer Vaclav Havel, is not necessarily the one its author intends. . . . This evening tells us less about the suffering of writers in a police state than it does about the self-indulgence of American directors who plaster their egos over playwrights' words.

Or:

> The hero of *The Count of Monte Cristo* . . . spends 18 years locked away unjustly in the dungeons of the Chateau d'If. After watching the director Peter Sellars' stage version of Alexander Dumas's 1844 warhorse, an audience will know just how Dantes felt.

Or in a review of *I'm Not Rappaport:*

> No one can accuse Herb Gardner of betraying his convictions to keep up with changing times. Almost 25 years after his first Broadway success, *A Thousand Clowns,* he is still writing roughly the same play.

Admittedly, using only a few lines of a review such as these creates the danger of misrepresenting the overall review. In some of these cases, Rich has gone on to give a modicum of praise to some element of a production he essentially dislikes. Nor do these examples attempt to comment on the validity of his opinion; in fact, for some of the works cited above there were highly negative reviews from other critics as well. The point is to show how and when the critic uses a negative statement.

Many artists yearn for good reviews, but good for what they consider the right reasons. Artists want informed critiques, including praise for what they believe they have accomplished (and they may be quite wrong) or done best, or for the work's particular distinction or originality.

Composer Ellen Taaffe Zwilich wants her compositions to be

reviewed for what she wrote and not for the piece the critics may have wanted her to write, or thought she should have written.

> I really like it when someone reviews a work of mine and I feel they like it for the right reasons and understood it. By that I mean understanding what your goals are and the way in which you've approached them.

Zwilich said she "respects a person who, writing about a piece that might need more than one hearing, incorporates that idea [into a review]. . . . Very often critics will ask to see the music if it's a first performance—the *Times* does as a matter of course."

Zwilich shares a concern with some critics and many in the music world over the need to understand that music is a living art that must constantly be replenished with new performers, new composers, new pieces. She views that understanding as the critics' central role, as opposed to dealing with the "glamorous" past and established figures:

> A critic needs a range of interests, and should be able to review Milton Babbitt or Philip Glass or Beethoven or Debussy. . . . [John] Rockwell (of *The New York Times*) is interested in music as a living art [and therefore] covers a lot of new music. People can criticize him for doing too much by going into rock and pop but he does have that commitment, and I think that's very important.

Audience Reaction—A Legitimate Concern of the Critic?

Time and again there are shows that audiences seem to be delighted with, where audiences react during previews in ways which canny managements, often but not always experienced in judging the capricious currents of public approval, quite correctly interpret as enthusiasm. Then come bad reviews, and the show falters and closes. There is not infrequently a feeling that if only the critic had reported on the enthusiasm of the audience, even if he did not like the show, the outcome would have been different. Composer Ezra Laderman is unequivocal in his belief that reporting on the event itself is part of the job of the critic, and it is therefore incumbent on the critic to describe the audience and report on how it liked the work.

Some critics do take audience reaction into account. Dance critic Edwin Denby, writing about a ballet opening, noted:

The enthusiasm of the house was the really gala aspect of Ballet Theatre's opening Sunday night at the Metropolitan. The company as a whole has given and no doubt will give more brilliant performances. Sunday night the ensemble was tired and many had not been able to find hotel rooms. But the fans were rapturous at having them back and applauded everything with welcoming abandon.[5]

But most critics take the position that they have been hired for their informed opinion, not for that of the rest of the audience. They argue that the audience is not necessarily the best judge of a work from an artistic standpoint, whether they liked it or not. In a day when television-saturated audiences are so used to demonstrations of euphoria for game-show hostesses that they appear to give a standing ovation to any performer who can remember his lines, the critics have a point.

In music, the focus of critical comment is often on the performer, or the interpretation, or the conductor's body language— a fact that troubles some in the music world. Libby Larsen, composer-in-residence of the Minnesota Orchestra, would like to see less emphasis by critics on performance technique and comparisons of one performer with another and more emphasis on critics' own evaluations and knowledge as they relate to the work itself. Larsen would challenge critics to convey the spirit of the music, its texture and color, as well as the experience of hearing it in the concert hall. "I'm worried," Larsen says," that we are developing a generation of people who are not listening to the music, they are listening to the performance of the music."

Particularly discouraging to the artist is to be acting or singing or composing or writing or dancing in a city or town in which there is no critic with the requisite expertise. While the chances of the artist's work being underappreciated or misunderstood may be great, there is also the chance that the work will be praised out of all relation to its merits. A number of artists regard undisciplined acceptance as the death of artistic standards, and frustrating to their own development.

In the long run, critiques either unjustifiably harsh or unjustifiably indulgent are inimical to the best interest of the artist or the arts. Artists in those environments want better, more qualified critics. Their claim is that if such were the case, they could rejoice more fully in a good critique and be more philosophical in accepting a bad one.

A composer-conductor in a city of 400,000, and a playwright in a somewhat smaller community, both believe their local newspapers are doing the arts a disservice through the inadequacy of their critics. Requesting anonymity, the composer-conductor said the major fault of the criticism was not the harshness of the commentary but the kindness: "The critics are afraid to delve into interpretation, preferring to look at entertainment value not substance, catering to what the paper thinks the public wants." The playwright claimed that theater and the readers of the newspaper were being done a disservice by the sheer inadequacy of the critics, by their lack of grasp of theater literature, of production values, or of the roles of producer, director, writer, and actor in shaping the production. He feels the very personal interest the critics took in the theater companies and their members skewed their critical responses. Most important, though, he believes that while some of the local theaters had achieved a rather high artistic level, they were deprived of the cutting edge of good criticism that could have raised them even higher: "If the critics were more acute in identifying excellence, it would encourage excellent work, theaters would try harder. When the critics say they like something or not, they don't say why and the reason they don't say why is because they don't know why."

The Case for a Second Look

Launching a career, a play, an opera, or a dance piece is all too frequently a gamble, depending on the review of a single critic or maybe two. This can be most devastatingly true of theater in New York, but in varying degrees it is true across the range of performing arts and across the country. The result can be instant success or instant failure. There is usually little in between, and rarely a second chance, a second review after more time for reflection.

Stephen Sondheim, who today stands among the leading, and certainly the most adventuresome, composer-lyricists in the American musical theater, believes his works have frequently suffered because the system dictates a single look that can seal their fate one way or the other. By virtue of Sondheim's courage to take artistic risks with virtually each new show, he has made himself painfully vulnerable. These gifts of originality and innovation have penalized him, he believes, when it comes to the first-night evaluation. The very fact that *Sweeney Todd* is light years from *Pacific Overtures* in composition, concept, and style, or *Follies* from *Sunday in the*

Park with George, or *A Little Night Music* from *A Funny Thing Happened on the Way to the Forum* has, he believes, worked to their disadvantage. According to Sondheim:

> When a critic goes into a show that he feels he may not understand because it may be different and offer different ways of going at things, he's tense, and if a critic knows that he's going to write about the show in two and a half hours, he doesn't go to relax and enjoy it. He's thinking, "How can I explain this?" and right away his defenses are up, and it is so much easier to write about what is wrong than what is right. It makes his job easier.

Sondheim recalls one exception when Howard Kissel, a man with an impressive dedication to theater, gave a highly unfavorable review to *Sunday in the Park with George* (lyrics and music by Sondheim; book by James Lapine) when Kissel was the critic for New York's *Women's Wear Daily* prior to his becoming critic for the *Daily News*. In a move highly unusual among critics, Kissel gave the show a second, highly favorable review, and was willing to acknowledge a reversal of opinion. The change came about because Kissel felt obliged to see the show again before voting in the annual awards of the New York Drama Critics Circle. The second time he thought it was terrific.

Sondheim came across this second review by happenstance, prompting him to read the first, which he had missed. Reading the two reviews in combination gave him, he believes, two insights into improving criticism. First is the inestimable value of taking a second look, and second is the ability to watch a performance without pressure. Sondheim said:

> I suddenly thought, "Why did he change his mind?" and then I knew, and it never occurred to me in all my years in the theater. The second time Howard Kissel went he didn't have to write about it. . . . He could go to the show and . . . relax. Relaxing, he was able to get into it and this was the kind of show you have to get into. You cannot go and stay on the outside and in any way enjoy it . . . in certain kinds of tits and feathers shows you can do that, [but not for] a strange or avant-garde or peculiar play. If you and I went tonight, we could say to each other after the show, "Well, I didn't understand it but I really loved it," and you could say, "I thought it was the worst piece of shit I ever saw in my life," and then we'd go off and have dinner. We wouldn't

have to defend our opinions. We wouldn't have to articulate them.

The point is that the critics are sitting there thinking, "I've got to write about this damned thing."

In the case of one prominent critic, Sondheim says, half of his review of *Pacific Overtures* (book by John Weidman) was the history of the Kabuki theater rather than a review of the play. Why? Sondheim believes that "the poor man went so panicky he probably thought, 'It's one of those Sondheim shows I'm not going to understand, so what am I going to write about?' As a result [the history], which he wrote in the afternoon, before he got there, I know. He was so tense he never had a chance to have a good time." Another critic who reviewed *Pacific Overtures* on opening night already had seen it in preview and was able to write that he had originally considered the musical pretentious trash and was glad he had seen it that second time because he found it to be a masterpiece.

Reviewing a show a second time is not usually a possibility when there is a full season of presentations requiring nearly daily reviews, nor would editors be inclined to give space for a second critique. The competition is already fierce among the many departments fighting for their share of newspaper space.

But Stephen Sondheim's experience is indicative of how important it is for the competent critic to have a depth of background in theater, in literature, and in the arts generally to deal effectively with what is new and innovative.

Some critics disagree on the value of a second viewing, and David Richards of *The New York Times* is one: "Never have I found a second viewing has really changed [anything for me]. I may understand more why I liked a play or didn't. I haven't found myself reversing original instincts."

A special concern, too, of composers such as Sondheim is that theater critics do not necessarily have the training to deal with the music in a musical. For some musicals he would like to see a second review on opening night by a music critic, something that very seldom occurs. He cites the former critic for the *New York Daily News,* Douglas Watt, as an exception among theater critics for his ability to deal with the music in a show.

Composer Jerry Herman reflected Sondheim's concerns and makes a case for a change in the critical approach to musicals. In an article in *Variety*[6] marking his becoming the first composer-lyricist to have three musicals to run on Broadway for over 1,500 performances each (*Hello, Dolly!, Mame,* and *La Cage Aux Folles*), he is quoted as saying that he did not think it was possible to get more than a general impression of a score on a single hearing. Herman believes it takes several hearings to analyze a complicated score: "God gave me a fabulous ear to be able to retain musical phrases, and I can't assimilate a new score in one hearing."

There is another problem in reviewing musicals, according to Peter Stone, author of plays, musicals, screenplays, and television scripts. Most theater critics don't understand the importance of the book of a musical to the success of the work. How often, he wonders, has he read that it's

> "a good musical but the book is poor." It's impossible to say that . . . they don't understand what the book is . . . it's the structure and energy of the whole show, defines its musical character, tells where the dances go, it is the structure that makes the musical; you have to write a musical so it takes half the time of a play because you need the time for the songs, for the dances.

Composers, conductors, and others in the world of music are concerned about the critic's musical ear. Conductor Gerard Schwarz notes that music critics don't take hearing tests before being assigned to their jobs, and there are numerous critics whose ear is not sufficiently acute or well trained to do justice to the subtleties, nuances, and tones of the music they are called upon to evaluate. According to Schwarz:

> We want critics with an open ear. Very many critics do not hear so well. They have to hear the way the conductor hears. He has to hear what's going on. The critic's job is the same. I've gotten reviews that may say things were wonderful that weren't, or weren't wonderful when they were. Very often, the critics just aren't listening. I'm talking about a good ear. I think they ask at newspapers about writing skills but rarely about "good ears." I read the reviews of Bernheimer and almost always agree when I've been to the same concert. When something isn't exactly right at a concert of mine, he catches it and when things are very positive and exciting he writes about that in the same way.

Critics, as judges of quality, have an obligation to be demanding. Artists, as the ones being judged, have a right to expect competent critics. Ernest Fleischmann, general director of the Los Angeles Philharmonic, is unequivocal on the point:

154

Either you [the critic] know your material properly or you get out of the bloody thing. There are no compromises in the arts. You take risks but you don't compromise. If somebody is going to sit in judgment, he must know as much, if not more, than those he judges. In the same way if a conductor gets up in front of an orchestra and tells them how to play a piece, he must know as much or more about that piece as any of the musicians he is telling how to play the damn thing. Otherwise, if he has any conscience . . . he shouldn't be able to face himself.

PART III

The Philosophy of Criticism

Toward the Best of All Worlds

★ CRITICISM'S ACTUAL and potential power for influencing the arts, for better or worse, is formidable. While that power is sometimes wielded brilliantly, it too often fails the arts. The reasons for this are varied. The critic simply may not have the requisite knowledge and training; he or she may have the will and potential to develop critical skills but is not given the opportunity; or arts coverage on the newspaper or publication may not be held in sufficiently high esteem by an editor or publisher to ensure a well-qualified critic adequate compensation, sufficient space for writing, and the opportunity to travel to other centers of the arts, which are important for maintaining standards of criticism.

Fortunately, there is much that can be done to elevate the state of criticism. This section deals with some of the possibilities as well as the underpinnings for effective criticism.

10 ★ The Critic: The End in View

"Criticism . . . must always profess an end in view, which, roughly speaking, appears to be the elucidation of works of art and the correction of taste."[1] These few words of T. S. Eliot may make critics who are bent on perfecting their craft wonder at the beauty and simplicity with which the task has been formulated and tremble at the demands and responsibilities it imposes.

Having an end in view requires starting with a philosophy: what does a critic see as the purpose of criticism, as its goal? There are many considerations in, and many ways of, arriving at a point of view. Whether the end in view emerges through scholarship, experience, or inspiration, it will be based on a highly personal sensibility. But there is no formula, and the best critic is highly idiosyncratic. Former *New York Times* music critic Harold Schonberg claims that critics who profess to work according to set, immutable aesthetic and technical laws are fooling themselves. In the end there are no immutable laws. "There is only the critic himself: his background, his taste and intuition, his ideals, his literary ability."[2]

But the case for a philosophy is strongly made by the very fact that those critics we accord the most respect have nearly without exception informed their criticism with some animating force and direction, some end in view, *supported by a profound knowledge of the art with which they are involved.*

The need for a philosophy of criticism is confirmed by the work of those critics who do not write with a point of view, those innocent of any animating philosophy or perhaps burdened by a limited competence that leaves them to settle for only the most simplistic goals, often not criticism at all. There are, for instance, those who are essentially consumer counselors, providing little more than advice on buying a "product"; or those who claim to be simply surrogates for the audience, eschewing the knowledge and development of a discerning eye and ear required by the professional; or those who view themselves as perhaps the self-appointed adviser to the creative or performing artist. There are the drumbeaters, who critic Richard Gilman says do nobody any good because they don't give the theater any sense of where it may be going wrong. While such praise may in the short run get more people into the theater, the truth is that, as the late theater critic George Jean Nathan said, "The drama critic has the duty of telling the truth at the risk of bankrupting every box office in the country."

Among the kinds of critics identified with an end in view is the critic as "gatekeeper to the arts"—one who believes criticism's primary importance is in maintaining high standards. To a greater or lesser extent all good critics have something of this about them. There is also the "critic militant"—another form of gatekeeper, but one who guards the territory with a set of often rigidly defined or passionately held ideas about the arts and will do battle for them. There is the "critic as historian," who sees his work as providing the indispensable record for the future upon which the arts themselves may build. There is the "critic polemicist," regarding his position as a pulpit to forward one view of the arts—or of life or society—or another. There is the "critic activist," often associated with politics, who sees the arts most importantly as a vehicle for forwarding social or political issues. There are the critics who see their role as mainly educational, although reading the reviews of any good critic who brings insight to his critique is bound in some way to be an educational experience.

Standing virtually by himself is Richard Hummler, theater editor and critic for *Variety,* read throughout the arts and entertainment fields from coast to coast. His approach is from a commercial point of view. Will the show sell? If not, why not? But Hummler, a highly experienced critic, does not neglect writing on the quality and texture of a work regardless of its commercial possibilities.

While critics may tend toward any of these types, these categories are essentially a matter of emphasis, not a framework a critic is bound by. In fact, there are few critics who do not combine several of these roles at different times.

The End in View for Kenneth Tynan

The late Kenneth Tynan, one of the small number of preeminent critics of his time, was also one of the most influential critics on either side of the Atlantic. When he died in 1980, he had been variously critic for London's *Evening Standard* and *Observer* as well as for *The New Yorker*. Later he served as literary manager for Britain's National Theatre under Laurence Olivier. His passionate interests reached every corner of theater. He championed the formation of a national theater, and he championed individual artists as well as theater companies that caught his attention. He often expressed his passions militantly: "Rouse tempers, goad and lacerate, raise whirlwinds" were words above his desk.[3]

Like many passionate critics, he could be most wrathful where those he most admired fell below the standards he held for them, or that he felt they should have held for themselves. His admiration for the English Stage Company at the Royal Court Theatre is a case in point. But when taken to task for giving one of the Royal Court's productions a negative review and for not supporting the promising young troop, he tersely replied that he was not a salesman.[4]

Perhaps his advocacy of new playwrights, prominent among them John Osborne and others whose early works first appeared at the Royal Court Theatre, was his most fervent enthusiasm and an area where he was highly influential. His passion seemed to stem from his deeply held convictions about British society, about which he sensed a

> swelling suspicion on the part of British youth that their country is culturally out of touch, somehow shrunken and inhibited, desperately behind the times. . . . A place where novelists were expected to have the right accent and a proper disdain for the lower orders.[5]

Tynan went on to identify fear of America, fear of the advent of commercial television, fear of criticism, and the repressive effects of censorship by film censors and of theater by the Lord Chamberlain as further eroding the cultural life of the nation.

Hilton Kramer deftly fixed Tynan in his age: "From time to time a critic emerges who may truly be said to personify a period —to embody in his person as well as his writings the spirit of a certain historical moment." Kramer went on to find that Tynan had "driving ambition, demonic energy, literary talent, journalistic flair, critical acumen, and a ferocious appetite for work: to all these were added, in Tynan's case, an indispensable gift for making himself as much of a personality as the great performers he wrote about with so much admiration."[6] These latter attributes may tell us little of the critic's philosophy but do tell us something more about Tynan. They remind us that some critics can generate an excitement and create a following, and that their words are often endowed with a formidable power.

Among the many determinants of animating philosophies or points of view can be a disenchantment with theater, a dissatisfaction that leads to the determination to exhort the theater troops to gain higher ground or to take other tacks. Robert Brustein, artistic director of the American Repertory Theatre and theater critic for *The New Republic,* is the critic militant. In his book *Seasons of Discontent,* he says:

> A drama critic working in a journalistic capacity, unwilling to lower his standards, and continually confronted with the spurious, the mediocre, and the false, can become a social philosopher like Bernard Shaw, an aesthetician of the stage like Stark Young, or an analyst of dramatic technique like Eric Bentley. If he works for a mass magazine, he is more likely to become an entertaining stylist like Kenneth Tynan. But he establishes his claim to serious criticism when discussing a genuine work of art, bringing his whole experience and expertise into the service of analysis, illumination, and interpretation. And this is why I bite with such obvious relish into the occasional masterpieces that come my way and why, lacking these, I often choose to belabor [my readers] with extra-critical lectures on the dismal state of our culture, our theater and our national spirit. For if the critic is the humble servant of genuine art, he is the implacable enemy of pseudo art, waging war on all the conditions which produce it, including the writer's cynicism, the producer's greed, the actor's ambition, and the spectator's spiritual emptiness.[7]

The daily reviewer for a newspaper, of course, would find his tenure brief if he waited for the "occasional masterpiece." A daily newspaper critic has a responsibility to a wider audience that is not imposed on the critics for more specialized publications. But this does not relieve the daily critic of the need for an animating philosophy and a set of standards. And there have been more than enough daily critics who have written with distinction for us to know that it can be done.

The daily newspaper critic who defines the arts for the vast majority of those who go to theater, music, and dance performances exerts the greatest impact on the immediate destiny of any given work. This is not to say that the daily critic is more important than the critic on a specialized publication who can bring a unique depth of analysis and insight to the arts, but by reaching more people more quickly, and often more decisively than others, the daily critic is especially important in the pursuit of excellence, in shaping the arts.

The Critic as Educator

John Von Rhein, music critic of the *Chicago Tribune,* sees for himself a role encompassing both education and the maintenance of standards:

> We want to build a constituency, an awareness. Basically we are trying to create a consciousness out there in which music can thrive. That is the thrust of all the things we do ... to make people a little more aware of the problems that beset the performer and the composer.

Effective criticism is educational in that it opens up to readers new ways of appreciation, of understanding, or of entry into the arts. From Aristotle to Addison to Shaw to a number of today's critics, the educational aspect of criticism has been central.

The Critic as Historian

The critic is unlikely to do his most discerning work if he consciously writes *for* history, but what the critic writes *is* history whether he wills it or not. An awareness of that fact commands the best that the critic can give, and validates in another compelling way the need for a point of view. Critiques serve as history with their commentaries on how the arts reflect the society, politics, manners, and mores of a generation; they reflect the aesthetic history of their times; they are often the only history to inform the artists themselves as they go back to earlier forms or look to earlier styles and achievements in the creation of new forms.

Village Voice critic Gordon Rogoff, upon his receiving the George Jean Nathan Award for Dramatic Criticism in 1987, said:

> Characteristically, Shaw made a serious joke about why he should be heeded, if not honored: "Some day they will reprint my articles," Shaw said, "and then what will all your puffs and long

163

runs and photographs and papered houses and cheap successes avail you, O lovely leading ladies and well tailored actor-managers? The twentieth century, if it concerns itself about either of us, will see you as I see you. Therefore study my tastes, flatter me, bribe me and see that your actor-managers are conscious of my existence and impressed with my importance."

Each generation needs educator-critics to accompany the emergence of creative and performing artists. The capability of critics to interpret new and sometimes bewildering voices and to help them gain access, if not always acceptability, to audiences has been an integral part of the process of change and growth in the arts. The critic must be in the forefront of those who can differentiate new and artistically significant work from that which is merely masquerading as such. The critic's instinct, knowledge, perception, and insight all come into play here.

One explosion in theater took place when the so-called Theater of the Absurd burst upon the stages of the English-speaking world in the 1960s, albeit its genesis was much earlier. (Theater of the Absurd is used here to describe many experimental forms which emerged as a challenge to traditional theater.) However identified, these forms intrigued, bewildered, sometimes repelled. But a number of discerning critics became the champions of such authors as Beckett, Artaud, Adamov, and Ionesco, and such theater innovators as Peter Brook, Julian Beck, and Judith Malina. Maps of the initially bewildering terrain of the Theater of the Absurd were supplied by critics reviewing regularly as well as by such writers and critics as Margaret Croyden in her book, *Lunatics, Lovers and Poets.*[8]

Martin Esslin is a British critic for plays who teaches at Stanford and has written extensively on theater. He was in that band of critics who championed the Theater of the Absurd and wrote an essay for the *Tulane Drama Review* that was considered highly influential. It is an instructive example of the critic's function of elucidating the new:

> At first sight these plays ... confront their public with a bewildering experience, a veritable barrage of wildly irrational, often nonsensical goings-on that seem to go counter to all accepted standards of stage convention.... The characters hardly have any individuality and often even lack a name; moreover, halfway through the action they tend to change their nature completely. ... The laws of probability as well as those of physics are suspended.... As a result, it is often unclear whether the action is

meant to represent a dream world of nightmares or real happenings . . . the dialogue tends to get out of hand so that at times the words seem to go counter to the actions of the characters on the stage . . . everything that happens seems to be beyond rational motivation, happening at random or through the demented caprice of an unaccountable idiot fate. Yet, these wildly extravagant tragic farces and farcical tragedies, although they have suffered their share of protests and scandals, do arouse interest and are received with laughter and thoughtful respect.[9]

Since all critics are likely to be faced with works that are novel or experimental, their background should prepare them to deal with such works. Ideally their familiarity with theater, from its earliest days to the present, with the whole spectrum of literature, and with other branches of the performing arts must be profound. Without such a background the critic is particularly vulnerable to being taken in by what is merely diverting, shocking, or hollow, alive at all perhaps only because of its trappings. Similarly, the critic may require this foundation in order to hold to his position, either positively or negatively, in the face of fashion, trendiness, or their conservative opposites.

Robert Wilson is among the most celebrated innovators in theater, causing enthusiastic audience response, especially in Europe. He has often been hailed by discerning critics for the experiences he has created through arresting combinations of music, stage design, and words.

But Bonnie Marranca, who with her husband Gautam Dasgupta edits and publishes *Performing Arts Journal* and PAJ Publications, and together are among the most consistent and experienced critics of the avant-garde in the country, challenges the quality of some of the critiques of Wilson's works. In writing about the Robert Wilson–Philip Glass opera, *Einstein on the Beach,* which had capacity-attendance productions at the Metropolitan Opera House and the Brooklyn Academy of Music, Marranca noted that *Einstein* was one of the most eagerly anticipated theatrical events of the season, having already been presented throughout Europe. Discussing the work's critical reception in New York, and drawing wide implications for criticism in general, she wrote:

Several people who have written about *Einstein* expressed the belief, good intentioned to be sure, that one could only experience the work, that analysis of it is either "inadequate" or "irrelevant," as if the simple act of coming to terms with the quality of the experience, or its nature, might somehow spoil its integrity as a Work of Art.

Such mindlessness on the part of critics, whose writings help shape the audience's attitude toward the arts, smacks of faddishness and ultimately creates an unhealthy situation in any attempt at prolonged discourse on the arts. This attitude makes the critics the cultural lackeys of artists in vogue, champions of a theater they do not understand but feel they must praise because everybody is talking about it. Or worse, it turns critics into glorified press agents.

What we are witnessing in a certain segment of avant-garde circles is the development of critics and audiences conditioned to relate to works of art on a purely personal, impressionistic level, as if the work had no relation to historical, social, economic, and aesthetic forces surrounding or preceding it. This . . . has virtually reduced any discussion of performance to the simple level of description.[10]

Allan Ulrich, dance critic for the *San Francisco Examiner,* considers it his mission to find, then bring to the attention of the public, the most important new creative minds. This has put him on his guard against fashion in criticism, which he sees as a particular danger in New York:

There is an A and a B list of the people who have achieved the Pantheon. How it comes about I don't know . . . Merce [Cunningham] is God . . . [Maurice] Béjart out. Balanchine is God . . . anything that descends from him necessarily good . . . holy. . . . Peter Martins's inflated reputation as choreographer at New York City Ballet is another example.

Village Voice theater critic Julius Novick makes a distinction between the polemic critic who believes that some kinds of theater are essentially good and some essentially bad, and who believes that his sacred duty is to fight for the former against the latter, and the eclectic critic who finds value (though not necessarily equal value) in virtually all theater and wants to show that everything can be done well or badly. Novick includes among the eclectic critics Max Beerbohm and Harold Clurman, and among the polemicists George Bernard Shaw, Kenneth Tynan, Eric Bentley, Walter Kerr, and Robert Brustein. Novick says: "Essentially the theater matters to [Brustein] because of its relationship to society. It matters because it is a moral force, or damn well ought to be. It matters because it is the chosen battlefield on which he fights the Good Fight."

Novick, in an article for *American Theatre,* wrote:

> The kind of theatre I advocate is . . . a theatre allied to a collective ideal, associated with training, organic in nature, continuous in operation, permanent in status. It is theatre that connects itself to the soul, mind, emotions of the audience, to the public and private life of the polity. It is a theatre that has as its goal not profits and deals but artistic fulfillment, not the advancement of careers but of talent, to be the springboard not for opportunism but for spiritual development and growth. It is a theatre of danger, dreams, surprise, adventure, a theatre of the unexpected and the unknown.[11]

It is a substantial loss to the theater that the very effort to retain high standards of criticism and to invest in a well-considered philosophic stance has turned some of our most gifted critics away from a theater they do not think merits their serious attention. Richard Gilman, Elizabeth Hardwick, Eric Bentley, Susan Sontag, Stanley Kauffmann, among others, have all largely stopped writing theater criticism, as had the late Mary McCarthy. In the case of Sontag, she has become suspicious of criticism's role of interpretation, characterizing it as the revenge of the intellect upon art.[12]

It is one thing to develop a philosophy that will encompass a set of standards; it is another to adhere to that philosophy when publishers, editors, and advertising or circulation departments do not provide a hospitable setting for dissent and possibly "unpopular" controversy. Unless the critic is able to join a publication that will prove congenial, the job can be a frustrating one, and can lead thoughtful critics to defect.

Richard Gilman, speaking of former *New York Times* theater critic Stanley Kauffmann, says that he " was essentially fired from the *Times* because he was too critical, too tough. They got tremendous complaints from the producers. There were threats in the advertising area, all kinds of things. Papers don't want negative critics; nor do they want someone who is forever praising everything." Of the late critic Brooks Atkinson, Gilman says:

> I had very little respect for him—a nice man I'm sure, but no kind of style and dull. You know, good humanist, praising nice humanistic works, vaguely aware of changes, but for forty years he wrote this deadly dull column essentially supporting the the-

ater . . . I think [Frank] Rich has to show from time to time that he is tough.

Standards . . . the Subtleties of Flexibility

Perhaps paramount among the multitude of considerations that inform a philosophic stance is the definition of standards. Some critics believe absolute standards are the responsibility of those who love the arts. Others argue that flexibility is the key, and that standards are not immutable.

The critic is called upon to judge a vast range of artistic effort— that put forward by the established and highly professional company, by the company with limited resources, by the new company, by the beginning artist, by writers or composers or choreographers on their maiden voyages. Extended to a wide range of performing and creative artists, the question of absolutism and flexibility has much to do with George Bernard Shaw's warning, "If you want to enjoy masterly acting twenty years hence, you must be very tender to the apprentices and journeymen of today."

A work that frequently challenges a critic's definition of standards is one with modest aims that may not have any high artistic merit, in fact may be flawed, but obviously has the capacity to please audiences and is an honorable entry involving competent, sometimes even gifted professionals at every level. But it is still not a major work. The dilemma for the critic is whether or not to bring out the howitzer to kill a mosquito, or, if the work is only fair but entertaining, even to bring out a few modestly encouraging adjectives.

One example of that situation was apparent in the 1987 import from England, *Stepping Out,* a play with music and dancing by Richard Harris. It had been doing very well in London for some years when it was brought to New York. The play was about a group of people who come together in the evenings in a London church hall to learn to dance in a chorus line for a show they will put on in the church hall, hoping to give their somewhat drab or troubled lives a fillip. Their strengths and weaknesses, their dreams and their secrets are exposed in the play as they get to know each other, and they proceed from nearly hopeless clods at dancing to a triumphant finale, which leaves many members of the audience as exuberant as the performers. The play is superficial but quite obviously delighted audiences. How to deal with it on a critical level? An amiable nod or full exposure of its frailties? The differing ways a number of New York critics treated the play are instructive in the question of formulating standards.

Frank Rich reviewed *Stepping Out* by telling his readers early on that they must wait two hours for the finale to receive ten sustained minutes of fun, and wondered in the last sentence if those ten minutes of a showstopper could be called a showstopper when there wasn't a show to stop?

Edwin Wilson, in *The Wall Street Journal,* found it not difficult to uncover both flaws and virtues in A. R. Gurney, Jr.'s *Sweet Sue* and *Stepping Out,* which he reviewed together:

> In the former, for example, the role of the young man is under-written, and in the latter too much time is spent on the characters' personal traumas, but overall, both productions provide a full measure of entertainment. They are what people in the trade refer to as "audience shows": The critics point out their faults but audiences enjoy themselves thoroughly.

Variety, which attempts to assess the commercial potential of the shows it reviews, ran a critique by Richard Hummler which noted that "glitzy staging by Tommy Tune doesn't camouflage the deficiencies of *Stepping Out,* a West End longrunner which will not ditto on Broadway."

Brendan Gill's *New Yorker* review resorted to a parable:

> Stepping Out . . . puts me in mind of an anecdote about the Spanish writer Jose Ortega y Gasset, who at a tea party in Madrid in the nineteen-twenties had his first encounter with that newly fashionable article, a pleated skirt. In wonderment and delight he exclaimed "The things that could be more and are contented to be less!" The attractiveness of *Stepping Out* lies precisely in its being contented with the modesty of its scale; if it had attempted to penetrate even as much as a millimeter below the amiable surface of its wind-up, wind-down little plot, it would have destroyed itself.

Gill claims the author had mastered the art which is indispensable to the commercial theater—that of pleasing the large segment of the public which asks, "Isn't there misery enough without our having to spend good money watching it onstage?"

Stepping Out and a comedy by John Bishop, *The Musical Comedy Murders of 1940,* both of which he favored, moved John Simon to write an essay on what the typical theatergoer expects of a critic and how Simon himself differentiates between a type of commercial play that he regards as harmless fun not to be trampled on by critics and another sort of commercial product that he considers ersatz and therefore grist for the critical mill ("though critics can do very little against it once it has received the imprimatur of the *Times* and the raves of the Word-of-Mouth"). Simon wrote:

> There is . . . the show with little or no pretension to truth, depth, social significance, or artistic quality; the show content to enter-tain on a level of craft just above standard television fare. Such a show—if it is charming, skillful, unassuming—should be patted on the back by the critic. Not too firmly, mind you, lest it collapse but just enough to propel it into the world, where it will do no great good or harm, but spread some guiltless contentment.

In *The Village Voice* Michael Feingold resolutely spurned *Stepping Out:* "Richard Harris's script is a third-rate specimen even of Broadway or West End seriousness."

For the most part, the critics modified their standards for *Stepping Out* and apparently still achieved what they wanted to achieve. They were able to evaluate the piece according to their experience and at least in some instances according to a philosophy, however informal, of what they conceive their role to be.

Many years ago Brooks Atkinson gave a critical boost to an author at an important point early in his career. Today, when insecurity has too often led critics to assert their tough-minded competence by lambasting first, Atkinson's words stand out. He said of Eugene O'Neill's *The Great God Brown:*

> What Mr. O'Neill has succeeded in doing . . . is obviously more important than what he has not succeeded in doing. He has not made himself clear. But he has placed within the reach of the stage finer shades of beauty, more delicate nuances of truth and more passionate qualities of emotion than we can discover in any other single modern play.[13]

Throughout the years, then, many discerning critics have called for high standards while applying shadings to their scale of values, taking into consideration the ambitions and purposes of a work, always trying to ensure that they do not adversely affect the vitality of the arts.

A Formula to Defuse Confusion

Clive Barnes believes that there is confusion over the role of the critic. He would adhere to a very direct formula: What was the artist trying to do? How well did he do it? Was it worth doing? Barnes notes that the last point calls for the totally subjective view of the critic. The confusion arises, Barnes holds, in overelaborating the rational function of the critic as a kind of traffic cop to the arts, a censor, or a dispenser of the Good Housekeeping seal of approval. Nor, Barnes insists, should critics be in the business of giving playwrights lessons in playwriting:

> I couldn't. I am not an artist. I am not in a position to give lessons to artists . . . how to dance, how to write . . . critics are writing for the audience not for the artist. I've never encountered an artist who said, "I've learned something from you." They only learn how to suffer from critics . . . to a sensitive artist, even the breath of an adverse criticism is going to seem like a deadly insult. As a critic I've been criticized more harshly than almost anyone I have criticized. But I can't complain, nor can I say I don't read it, nor can I say it doesn't hurt.

(In particular, Barnes has been accused of sleeping through productions, but aside from dropping off from boredom on occasion, he says, he can hardly sleep for long in view of the detailed critiques he writes.)

Howard Kissel of the *New York Daily News* also favors the direct-approach formula but prefaces his opinion by stating that the person he is writing for is essentially himself. His aim is to describe the play, to evaluate its intention, to determine whether or not the production fulfills that intention, and then to write the review in an amusing way. And he wants to tell the reader whether or not the time spent in the theater was worthwhile, even if he, as critic, is paid to be there. For certain works, Kissel's aims expand: "If I see a work I particularly love, then I feel I am writing also for the people who did it. I can give something back." A letter he received from a reader expressed the view that even though the reader was perfectly aware that Kissel did not like a particular play, he described it in such a way that the reader wanted to see it. "The reader could decide for himself," Kissel said. "If I can do that enough times, while giving my opinion, I feel I will have succeeded."

Discord on the Music Page

In the exploration of philosophic underpinning for criticism, each of the performing arts must be seen in a different focus, depending on its unique nature. Music, for example, unlike theater or dance, relies much more heavily on classics than on new works. There is a move (not widespread but significant) in music criticism to jar musicians and presenters of musical events, as well as the audience, out of their nearly single-minded dedication to music of the past. This move represents another kind of end in view for critics, a philosophy representing a strong voice for change.

Music criticism in the United States is a fraud, according to *Time* magazine music critic Michael Walsh, because it is not music criticism but performance criticism. This conviction, Walsh says, influences his writing:

> Music criticism generally plays into the hands of the music biz people who use the critics and the mass media as instruments of their own publicity and for the box office. It's not dispassionate criticism; it's not even talking about the art. It's talking about a certain number of marketable performers . . . this is not necessarily the critic's fault, but many of them play into it by becoming tame dogs and exclusively performance critics. They confuse the artist with the art.

Underlying the problem, Walsh claims, is the fact that music is the "deadest" of the arts, and that a critic can make a respectable career of doing nothing but reviewing performers playing dead music:

> A music critic today in the United States is not forced to look for new art. He's not forced by his readers, he's not forced by his editors, he's not forced by his own conscience because he has been playing the publicity game, perhaps unwittingly, all his life. I would like to see the music business, a deplorable phrase by the way, conducted more along the lines of theater or art in the sense that there is a premium on the new. . . . I would, in the best of all possible worlds, like to see a moratorium on works of the nineteenth and eighteenth century for some long period of time, not to deprive . . . listeners of their favorite bedtime story which they insist on hearing over and over again, but to put these works back into some kind of fresh perspective. . . . The argument that there is no good new music to play is purely specious, and it is based on a confusion of art with religion. The canonical repertory . . . is not a religion. . . . I think that many symphony managers, and people who really love music . . . fear that to change things radically would lose them their audiences

and would lose them, ultimately, their livelihoods. Perhaps it would lose me my livelihood also.

There is another point to be made here. To some extent Walsh's philosophic independence is a luxury. He can indulge in it in ways that would be difficult for most critics on dailies who must cover virtually every local music event of any importance and certainly every opera, concert, or presentation of the local music organizations. These critics are in some ways circumscribed by their readers, who will stand for only a certain amount of rebellion. In this respect, critics on weeklies have some special advantages in the selectivity they are frequently permitted.

Pointing up the difficulties critics face in taking iconoclastic or highly independent stands, Walsh also cited the limitations imposed by the status of the newspaper itself:

> If you've talked with Frank Rich, or if you've talked to anybody at the *Times* regarding theater, you know how closely concerned they are with not damaging the economic health of the large institutions. The *Times* is a large institution, as we are, and large institutions tend to be solicitous of one another's good health and the *Times* has replaced drama critics who they felt were not in the best interests of Broadway. They don't seem to take quite the same mercantilistic view of the music columns.

Harold Schonberg, himself sometimes accused of not having been hospitable to new composers, acknowledges that indeed he was tabbed as the ultraconservative critic in the United States. Composers kept on saying that the audience had to be exposed to new music, that there was a cultural lag:

> The fact remains that in thirty years of this kind of composition . . . I can't think of more than two or three kinds of works, if that many, that have entered the international repertory. . . . Composers today are no longer writing what they call totally organized music. Now, where do I stand in all this? You have to come around in fifty years and ask me. The point is this. If Boulez, Babbitt, and Stockhausen are an integral part of the repertory by then, I was dead wrong. But if they are what I suspect they are, sort of footnotes to history, I was dead right. As a matter of fact, I think I was dead right, because their music still isn't played . . . except in special concerts. My job as a critic is not to be a propagandist.

And as his own footnote to history, Schonberg adds that regardless of how things turn out, musicians he may not have favored could look to his counterpart, the late Virgil Thomson, who he claims was very hospitable to modern American music: "So my views and his views sort of balanced each other off, didn't they?"

Politics and Criticism

The end in view for the critic can be either enhanced or skewed by political considerations. Today the arts, perhaps as much as they have ever been in the past, are laden with political content. Artists in almost every medium are directly addressing ethnic, sexual, and other social issues from overtly political points of view. Contemporary audiences as well are often primed to approach a particular work with political expectations as much as aesthetic criteria. To the extent this is the case, it imposes a difficult but crucial burden on the critic to separate out the differing elements in a work and evaluate them for what they are and what they intend.

Inevitably the critic will also have political perspectives and convictions. The extent to which these are allowed to affect the judgment of a work with high political content is a constant hazard to which every responsible critic must remain alert. A strongly political work may be successful in conveying a message to an audience that wants to hear it, but may also be of mediocre or inferior artistic quality. The responsible critic must be able to distinguish and describe the difference, irrespective of whether he is or is not sympathetic to the political stance the work reflects. A critic who is unaware of or uninformed about the social content the artist is addressing will not be competent to write an informed and discerning critique.

With traditional aesthetic criteria being increasingly challenged, it has perhaps never been more difficult for the critic to sort out the varying elements in a work and to emerge with a rigorous evaluation of artistic success or failure that will stand the test of time. For even the most knowledgeable and sophisticated critic, it is a high-wire act. The critic's ability to describe the content of the work with its fullest implications, his informed and fast hold on standards of quality, and his rigorous evaluation of the work's artistic success or failure will best serve the causes of art.

Hilton Kramer, making a case for political involvement, claims that criticism that pretends to ignore political elements in our society is not to be trusted.

It's one of the givens of the arts in our time that they encompass a great many political elements, and criticism that pretends to ignore those political elements, I think, is simply not to be trusted. What we set out to do in *The New Criterion,* in this respect, was basically two things: one was to identify the political components where we felt they existed and where they were exerting a role both in the creation of the art form and in the reception of the art form; two, was . . . to defend the arts against excessive politicization and try to separate as much as possible questions of artistic quality from ideological conformity. . . . In a sense, of course, you cannot be free of politics if you are trying to defend art from excessive politicization, but that is really one of our functions.

Deborah Jowitt, the influential dance critic for *The Village Voice,* finds that some dance provokes moral or ethical or political considerations that one can't ignore. Jowitt points out that such considerations were not as evident when she first started writing about dance, and so she was able to concentrate on what was very pure in dance. Today she is more eager to encompass dance in all its implications, all its relationships to history and the world: "I still have the feeling of wanting to confront the work directly, but I also do not want to close myself off to all of the ramifications of the work."

Philosophy and Funding

The question of funding surfaces occasionally when a critic, usually in the course of a negative review of the quality of a production that has been underwritten by a foundation, corporation, or government agency—the means of funding for most of dance, music, and theater across the country—questions the justification for spending public or tax-exempt funds to help support the work in question.

Grants from the National Endowment for the Arts, or foundation or corporate grants, all come within the purview of any writer on the arts, but for the critic the expression of such concerns is properly left to any columns he may write from time to time rather than within the context of a critique. To evaluate the appropriateness of the grant process on the basis of a single production whose quality is under consideration is to become involved in complex questions of program support that go far beyond the work under scrutiny. Granting agencies are usually looking not just at a single production, as is the critic, but at the development of an institution or an art form or the stimulation of creativity and myriad other questions, usually of a long-term nature and usually involving risk and the possibility of failure.

For a critic to pass on the appropriateness of funding also means superimposing a single opinion on the lifeline of an arts institution, and the more powerful the paper involved the more adverse the impact it may have—for example, the funding agency may decide to substitute caution for initiative. Furthermore, dealing with the question of support distorts or corrupts the critical argument.

A Sense of the Experience

Important as philosophy is, perhaps transcending all else is the critic's ability to engage the reader with a sense of his own experience—conveying what he underwent at the event under review. Eric Bentley puts it this way:

> Criticism may often be in a parlous state but it has never yet been rescued from that state by a philosophy of aesthetics, nor yet by semantic judgements. . . . Nothing a critic has can open your eyes except his own eye: he says, look! and you look. . . . A good critic will get you to do so.[14]

Arlene Croce similarly stresses the importance of re-creating an experience: "That's the responsibility of the critic and it's very hard to do."

Frank Rich, speaking at a public forum on criticism, said:

> For me, passing judgment on a play is absolutely the least interesting part of the job. . . . The creative part of the job, the reason I enjoy doing it, is to try to re-create for the reader the experience of what it was like to be in the theater and see a particular play. If you do that, you increase the understanding of theatergoers who don't have the inclination or time to devote all their energies to thinking about theater. That's why I feel one test of an effective critic is that he or she can get you excited or interested or driven to go see something based on a negative review.[15]

There are many in the theater who would argue that while some critics may inspire such understanding, Rich all too often presents his negative reviews so strongly that he rather convinces readers to abandon all hope of having a worthwhile experience by attending a given play.

Deborah Jowitt professes that she does not like to sit in judgment over others. John Lahr, once of *The Village Voice* and now writing in London, sees judgments as the end of criticism: "The function of criticism isn't to be right. There is no right. . . . A critic's only job is to debate a play; to engage it with the world."

In all of this, the reader, too, has a responsibility if criticism at its best is to succeed. No aspirations of a critic will matter if there are no readers to take the critic seriously or to demand more from him than consumer advice. The critic's role in developing such readers is of major importance, according to Hilton Kramer, who insists that if the critic will take himself seriously he will be taken seriously. "The real readership for criticism is anyone who realizes that there are real issues in what critics are writing about," Kramer said. "When I came to *The New York Times* you were supposed to be lighthearted, untaxing—so I told my readers, 'If you are interested in artistic issues, you'll find them with me [although] others may be more entertaining.' Readers are as serious as the critic requires them to be."

11 ★ Inside the Critique: The Underpinnings of Criticism

Without an effective philosophy, however arrived at, criticism can be neither steady nor in the final analysis valid. But a philosophy does not define the elements that go into critiques of dance, music, or theater. This chapter attempts to set forth some of these elements, with the awareness that there are no aspects that either *must* be included in a critique or that *should not* be there. There are, however, some guidelines that have been found useful by discerning critics: some generalities that are distilled from informed if highly personal visions.

Among them is the importance for the critic to take himself and his audience seriously; to oppose the not infrequently held newspaper managerial position that the arts are peripheral or are a merely entertaining diversion; to oppose any editorial efforts to downplay the readership.

Another key aspect of criticism concerns the love, or at least the respect, a critic brings to the arts in general and to the art form under review in particular. Without that, it is hard for a critic to maintain that enthusiasm which will enable him or her to persevere through countless nights of the familiar or the mediocre or worse, or to triumph when works of artistic merit or even genius come along.

David Richards of *The New York Times,* as noted earlier, puts theater right after water and bread, has a passion for it, and says he'd fight for it with his dying breath—or against those he views as misusing it. Robert Brustein caught the importance of finding this balance between enthusiasm and rigor in a review he wrote of Kathleen Tynan's biography of her husband, British critic Kenneth Tynan: "Tynan's affinity for performers occasionally turned into fan notes and love letters. But he never lost his gift for formulating the exact verbal equivalent of the visual events he had witnessed, as if he were not just an observer but a dancer joining the dance."[1] If Tynan had joined the dancers and been seduced by them, he would have invalidated the premise. But he did not. His enthusiasm was companion to rigorous judgment.

Knowledge May Not Be All, but . . .

Still another requirement is for a formidable background in the arts in order for the critic to place a work under discussion in its context within the arts, to weigh and evaluate it in relation to a wider spectrum of achievements, and to make sense of the enormous variety of presentations he may be called upon to review. These will range from the classical to the modern to avant-garde leaps of imagination to encounters with the bizarre. But knowledge without that critical sense, without that analytic power and a capability to write, is to little avail. As Michael Walsh, music critic for *Time,* says: "It's nice to look for the critic's musical degree, and he should have one; but in the case of music, it's even more important to know that he understands what the hell it's all about."

The director Peter Brook, one of the most innovative forces in the contemporary theater, is head of the International Centre of Theatre Research in Paris. He warns against a critic holding too structured a view of the elements of theater. Rather, he makes the case for the critic's involvement in the work itself. Speaking of his production of the Indian epic *The Mahabharata,* Brook argues that if the critic comes with his own set of notions on religion, be it Christianity or Hinduism, he is likely to spend his time debating the theoretical approach for something that can't be limited to the theatrical level. The work must be entered, Brook says. "You cannot come to analyze, dissent, pigeonhole, compare."[2] While there are certainly theater works that demand an intellectual response, Brook warns against that response taking over at the cost of missing the play.

Some Underpinnings for the Practice of Theater Criticism

A man of epic enthusiasm for the theater, for the arts, for life itself, the late Harold Clurman, for many years theater critic for *The Nation,* was a man of formidable knowledge as well. He had been a founder of the Group Theatre and directed many notable Broadway presentations. Clurman was eclectic in his tastes. As the first selector of plays to receive subsidy from the Theatre Development Fund, he steadily maintained that if only the funds would permit, he would subsidize every play of serious intent that came his way, believing that all voices should be heard. Nevertheless, he was among the theater's most discerning critics and no matter how exuberant, argumentive, or even didactic he could be in conversation, he was a gentle but rigorous critic, and one who adhered to consistent standards. Clurman set forth what he considered the requirements for effective criticism:

The Compleat Critic's Qualifications

Besides having cultivated taste, feeling, and a talent for clear observation of people:

1. The critic should know the greater part of classic and contemporary drama as written and played. Added to this, he must be conversant with general literature: novels, poetry, essays of wide scope.

2. He should know the history of the theater from its origin to the present.

3. He should have a long and broad play-going experience —of native and foreign productions.

4. He should possess an interest in and a familiarity with the arts: painting, music, architecture, and the dance.

5. He should have worked in the theater in some capacity (apart from criticism).

6. He should know the history of his country and world history: the social thinking of past and present.

7. He should have something like a philosophy, an attitude toward life.

8. He should write lucidly and, if possible, gracefully.

9. He should respect his readers by upholding high standards and encourage his readers to cultivate the same.

10. He should be aware of his prejudices and blind spots.

11. He should err on the side of generosity rather than display an opposite zeal.

12. He should seek to enlighten rather than carp or puff.[3]

Arthur Friedman of *The Cambridge Express* has also made a list that he calls his Ten Commandments for Serious Theater Critics. Among other things, he urges critics to justify any adjectives they use, to be polite to publicity people but to keep their distance, and to keep in mind that being well liked doesn't come with the critic's territory. He warns them never to think of themselves as representing the average playgoer. "That's for hacks," he says. The serious critic must know more.

Not all critics have had practical experience in the art that they write about—in fact, some determinedly avoid it—but virtually all who have been personally involved agree the experience has helped them in their writings. Australian theater critic and publisher Katherine Brisbane, speaking at the National Playwrights Conference of the Eugene O'Neill Memorial Theatre Center in 1984, said she had never understood the bias among so many critics against knowing the rudiments of theater, against working in the theater. "No other element of the writing-journalist world operates under this system—quite to the contrary. Unless you know what's under the hood you don't write about autos." It is Brisbane's contention that practical experience in the theater, along with a knowledge of its history and literature, is the best preparation for becoming a critic.

Playwright David Mamet wants critics to ask the right questions and not what he considers "impossible" ones. The questions a critic might logically ask of a play he is going to review, Mamet holds, include: What is the line of the play? What is its structure? What is the structure of the incidents in the play; for example, why does the second act end here rather than there? Is there an extraneous scene? Do you consider that the ending was the inevitable outcome of the forces set in motion at the beginning of the play?

These questions are within the realm of the possible because a critic can answer them. Mamet does not include in that realm comments on a play's theme. He says:

A playwright does not concern himself with the theme. The theme is an illusion. As all things must have qualities, it is the quality which the finished work has that is perceived by the audience. The question, "What were you trying to say?" is an insulting question because what the playwright was trying to say was the play. . . . "Where do you get your ideas?" is not an insulting question but a baffling one, because the playwright gets his ideas from the same place anybody gets his ideas. He thinks of them. . . . What happens after that is not with him. It's with the gods. The idea that you can control someone else's action is a heresy. You can't do it. No one can do it, not even the critics.

Some Underpinnings for Music Criticism

An essential for the practice of music criticism is a musical background that includes the study of music, either formal or informal, the ability to read scores and to play at least one instrument, and exposure to a wide range of music. Hearing a Beethoven symphony once may be enchanting; hearing it for the hundredth time may put a critic on the road to understanding its nuances. The requirement for a critic to have this intensive knowledge is undeniable; how to achieve it is very much in question. Conservatory courses in musicology have often been an effective route, but as Martin Bernheimer says, taking the right courses doesn't assure critics of being good at their craft. There are self-taught musicians who are very good critics, "who have good ears and good eyes." Bernheimer himself professes to being a "card-carrying musicologist, for whatever that means." In his case, it means a B.A. with honors in music from Brown University, study at the Munich Conservatory, and an M.A. in music from New York University. He studied voice, piano, and violin—"never to perform, but to understand music . . . the technical problems. I do it all very badly. I sing in the shower." And no amount of training, Bernheimer notes, will do any good without writing skills or the proper selection process: "I think one of the great flaws in music criticism today is that anyone can be a critic. All you need is an editor dumb enough to pay your salary and zap! You're a music critic."

Troubling to some critics is the emphasis on so-called performance criticism, where the performer or performance takes precedence over the music itself. Michael Walsh does not have to cover every concert in town, and, he can pretty well select what he will cover. He is an advocate for new music; he says that the music itself has always been his primary interest, the performer secondary:

> I didn't come at music as a fan of a performer, or of performance itself, but rather I tried to listen to the music. Of course, the performance is what brings you the music, and I don't discount its importance, but not in the way that some critics are specific fans of the trappings of music rather than of the art, of the thing itself.

182

Among the practices that some critics can get entangled in and other critics decry is monitoring every note that may be missed. According to critics who decry the practice, a great many gifted performers *will* miss a note or two or three. But the test must be the overall performance, the fidelity to the spirit of the music, and the general attention to the composer's intentions. There must be a balanced analysis.

Gerard Schwarz, the peripatetic conductor and music director, covers vast territory geographically as well as professionally. He has reflected a good deal on the role of the critic—and on the continuing dilemma: To what extent can training for the music critic be accomplished through listening to records? There are evident and important reasons for using recordings, and also pitfalls.

Schwarz finds that critics who rely too heavily on records are vulnerable in interpreting the values of a live concert. A recording is a very different performing medium, Schwarz notes, it is a document of one performance; there is none of the spontaneity and excitement of a concert. When a live program is put together, major considerations include how a piece is going to be affected by what comes before and after it; for a recording the main concern is usually with mistakes. Mistakes in a concert are not that important in an otherwise fine performance, but Schwarz claims the critic trained on records won't know this. He is so used to a certain way of hearing a particular work on the recording he's been listening to that he has difficulty hearing it any other way.

Schwarz believes music critics should essentially play three roles: 1. to criticize the event and report on it; 2. to do think pieces and analyses—on the direction of new music, on the state of subsidy for music, and so on; 3. to create an awareness of the arts, an excitement about the arts they're writing about. Noting the power of the critics on *The New York Times,* Schwarz points out that some of the *Times* critics are very good; its chief music critic, Donal Henahan, is very fair and thoughtful; but Schwarz is distressed by some of the others. What he finds is a lack of imaginative writing, too great a reliance on what's promoted by public relations efforts rather than a reliance on the critics' own minds. He would like to see the critics take the initiative—or be given it—to write about subjects of particular interest to them, to do think pieces.

Richard S. Ginell, the young music critic for the Los Angeles *Daily News,* is a fanatical record collector; in fact, he started his music reviewing by doing critiques of records. His collection consists mostly of classical music and jazz but includes rock-and-roll, folk, rhythm, blues. If he listens to a record as preparation for a work he will review, he tries to find one that is as objective as possible, something that takes experience to determine. His preferred way of preparation is to read the score, especially in the case of opera. In any musical event, what Ginell finds most important is answering the question,

> Does this turn me on, does this move me?... I don't go to concerts with my knives sharpened . . . Artur Rubenstein missed notes. Simply unimportant. I'm looking for outlook, style, how does this performer see his work, does he see a Beethoven symphony, for example, as a leap forward into the nineteenth century or does he see it as a holdover from the classicism of the eighteenth century. In the best performances you can hear a give and take between soloist and conductor as if they were carrying on a dialogue.

Classical music critic Robert Marsh of the Chicago *Sun-Times* also warns against the Wrong Note or Missed Note Syndrome and is particularly vehement about record-dependence. Over the years, Marsh said, he discovered music for himself, defined himself musically, and then was able to ask two important questions: 1. Is the music in the range of an accurate, faithful realization of the composer's intentions? 2. How well was it played? Wrong notes, according to Marsh, are not so bad, "but if you are not hearing what the composer wrote, then that is no good."

In the process of developing as a critic Marsh believes it absolutely necessary to attend rehearsals with gifted conductors. Part of his learning process, for instance, was to go to a rehearsal of the Cleveland Symphony Orchestra under George Szell and try to determine why he had stopped the orchestra, to try to listen to the music as a conductor would, to learn why in the Beethoven Fifth, for instance, the oboe entrances were never just right. He understood that errors weren't serious if the cumulative effect of the playing of the piece was nonetheless powerful. And finally, Marsh says he keeps in mind the words of pianist and composer Artur Schnabel: "Music is better than it ever can be played."

Does the Opera Multiple Critic Exist?

Beverly Sills believes as many as eight different critics are ideally needed to adequately cover one opera. Her multi-critic fantasy places the requirements of opera criticism in the context of all its complexity:

> We are looking at one person who is supposed to be qualified to judge a performance by a singer, an instrumentalist, a conductor, a stage designer, a costume designer, a stage director, actors, and be fluent in at least three languages—otherwise how could a critic say who is a good actor without knowing what the actor is saying? Having made that statement, I realize . . . it's an unrealistic approach because you cannot expect a newspaper to hire eight different critics who specialize in one particular area.

Realistically, Sills still believes a critic must have a workable knowledge of two languages other than English; must have had a dozen singing lessons that will familiarize the critic with techniques of singing—the various causes of flatness in singing, pitch deviation, what's involved in the discipline. It would help the critic to read some rudimentary books on the art of lighting, and to do as many interviews as possible with scenic designers to see why things are done as they are. "What I'm really saying," she added, "is that there should be involvement in the art form other than sitting in one's seat as a spectator . . . and can we hire people who at least know how to write?"

Some Underpinnings for Dance Criticism

No organization of critics—and one exists for each of the performing arts—appears to be more active or enterprising than the Dance Critics Association. It addresses the problems of dance criticism assiduously. Each performing art has its problems in criticism. Among those in dance is conveying the experience of motion—the form, shape, and rhythm of the body in motion.

Deborah Jowitt believes that the dance critic's job of analysis and evocative description is difficult because dance is more ephemeral than the other arts. Jowitt says she has continuously made an effort to find words to convey something about the quality of different dances, and to experiment with ways in which the rhythm of the sentences she writes has some kind of structural analogy to the dancing, knowing that her aspiration is a very ambitious one. If she is writing about a rather blunt, everyday kind of dance, her language is likely to be terse and blunt, while it is likely to be more gracious and expansive when describing the ballets of Balanchine. "It is quite fascinating to try to work with language," she says, "to

185

make it do as good a job as it can of evoking something about the work."

Edward Villella says there are two kinds of critics, one of insight and understanding, the other writing for himself or herself. In his view, the two greatest dance critics have been the late Edwin Denby and now Arlene Croce because of "their incredible integrity." He deplores the critics who will lambaste a work, drawing attention to their writing with witty, clever put-downs, all those "attractive" elements that are used to capture readers with tricks of style and flamboyance, often bordering on the sensational.

The major responsibility of critics, Villella says, is to make us understand, to give us an insight into what the performance was, into what makes a good, a mediocre, or a poor performance:

> When you look at the dance it isn't just your ability to identify the good dancer and the good choreographer, it is how all of those elements come together to make a unity, some kind of harmony that then translates into art. . . . We have the choreographer who chooses the piece of music and the approach to that piece, and who is aware enough musically to indicate to the conductor his or her pleasure. That's the first level whereby a critic can identify all of the specific elements and how they function together—"network"—or whether they indeed do function successfully together. Then critics must get into the primary elements . . . the actual articulation of the choreography by the dancer and the level of expertise, competence, invention and creativity that the choreographer has provided. One would look for the relationship between steps and music. . . . What we expect finally from a choreographer is a satisfactory physicalization of the music . . . the relationship between dance and the music is key.

The critic, Villella says, must have knowledge of the techniques involved in dance in order to understand whether the technical demands have been met and whether the performance has been successfully rendered; a critic has to give us his understanding of theatricality from the moment the curtain rises until it descends:

> I would have to say that my responsibility (were I a critic) would be to be an expert in terms of the physicality, in terms of performance. I'm almost positive Denby danced. Arlene Croce, on the other hand, I don't think danced. . . . You absorb over time, over

years, through observation, experience. So while primary experience [as a dancer] may not be necessary, I think it is helpful.

Charles Reinhart, director of the American Dance Festival at Duke University, has set down some guidelines for the dance critic that reflect Villella's concerns:

A critic should take dance classes, gain an understanding of kinesthesia [the sensation of movement or strain in muscles, tendons, and joints] and of the body in relationship to space and time. A critic must understand technique. He must know the history of dance to know if a movement is from Isadora Duncan or a brand new movement—in modern dance originality counts.

A critic must have a knowledge of ethnic dance. If you don't know classic Indian dance, how can you review it or know how ethnic dances have influenced modern or contemporary choreographers?

A critic can't intellectualize too much, must get into the kinesthetic response; the unique gesture. Baryishnikov can do a double tour in air and land on one knee and his technique is clean and he will bring the audience to its feet. That's the easy part for a critic. But when Paul Taylor does *Runes*—I get this incredible feeling of going back thousands of years. That's what he gives me—something tribal, prehistoric. How did he do it? Movement can be very simple . . . a body moving in form and shape to invoke in audience the prehistoric. . . .

And you must get people who can write.

Dance critic Donald F. McDonagh, who is author of *The Complete Guide to Modern Dance* and *How to Enjoy Ballet,* took two years of ballet classes to find out how dance worked. But he does not believe discussion of technique has much place in reviewing. McDonagh says:

The most boring thing in reviews is discussion of technicalities. I have never felt in writing about art that I had to be able to paint a picture or attack a piece of marble. There can be endless discussion about technique, the precise placement of the limbs to other parts of the body, these things teachers ought to talk about, but I don't think that it's of any great benefit to the public. I shy away from using technical terms. The basic job of the critic is to perceive the artistic intent of the choreographer.

Arlene Croce said that among the most important things she learned from the dance critic she most admired, Edwin Denby, was to go to the dance with an openness of responses and to transfer that openness to print.

Dance Intelligence

Edwin Denby was able to inspire and give direction to dance writing. His descriptions of what he calls dance intelligence, and of motion itself, serve to illuminate the essentials of dance criticism:

> Expression in dancing is what really interests everybody, and everybody recognizes it as a sign of intelligence in the dancer. But dancing is physical motion, it doesn't involve words at all. And so it is an error to suppose that dance intelligence is the same as other sorts of intelligence which involve, on the contrary, words only and no physical movement whatever. What is expressive in a dance is not the dancer's opinion, psychological, political or moral. It isn't even what she thinks about episodes in her private life. What is expressive in dancing is the way she moves about the stage, the way she exhibits her body in motion. A dancer's intelligence isn't shown by what intellectual allusions she can make in costume or pantomime, or, if she is a choreographer, in her subject matter. It is shown by how interesting to look at she can make her body the whole time she is on the stage.[4]

Denby said that, apart from the question of choreography, of importance was the variety of visual emphases, such as the shifts in the pacing of a sequence, the points where the dancer hurries or delays, the decision to attack either sharply or mildly a step or arm gesture. He noted that the variation of these movements drew the eye to one phase of motion rather than another, to one line of the body rather than another, or to the dancer's partner. These are some of the physical characteristics of dance expression, and "the brilliant use of them to arouse our interest, to thrill and to satisfy us, a proof of an artist's exceptional dance intelligence."

Among the most important conclusions that can be drawn from serious critics in dance, music, and theater on the underpinnings of criticism are the need to re-create the event for the reader and the need for the critic to be informed by a profound knowledge and to be animated by a viewpoint and a philosophy that combines humanism with a tough-minded commitment to the art. A critic must be passionate in his belief that criticism must never, never be casual.

12 ★ Conclusions

Criticism of the performing arts in the United States has to be given mixed notices. It is inadequate to its potentially important role in the cultural life of the nation, all too often neither doing justice to the highest achievements in the arts nor identifying the worst offenses. There are a relatively small number of critics who bring distinction to the profession; they can be found in many parts of the nation and on newspapers and other publications both large and small. The bad or merely inadequate critics are also widely dispersed. There is a widespread failure of accountability, of standards, of philosophy, and of insight.

The critics that audiences, artists, and managers pay most attention to are the daily newspaper critics, who have the most immediate and often the greatest long-range effects as well. They are responsible to their editors—usually a features editor or an arts editor—who, in turn, are responsible to managing editors. The publisher is the final authority.

The publisher's interest in arts coverage—usually reflecting general reader interests—is frequently peripheral, and here resides a fundamental problem in raising standards of criticism. The arts have not traditionally been considered top priorities for newspaper coverage, a fact that translates into limited budgets, space, and attention. This attitude affects adversely every consideration relating to criticism: standards, appointments of critics, and opportunities for development, including travel and compensation.

Budgetary concerns arise not only from the differing perceptions of the importance of the arts by publishers and editors but also from the unyielding realities of the newspaper business—the need to raise circulation to attract advertisers, and the need to allocate sometimes scarce resources where they will bring the greatest return. For the best newspapers there is often a conflict between commerce and journalistic responsibility that need not always be decided in favor of commerce, yet a newspaper's responsibility is to stay in business. Budgetary concerns can torpedo the most enlightened plans for bolstering the quality of criticism—be they for bringing on a qualified dance critic, say, rather than insisting on coverage of music and dance by one critic who may not have the qualifications for both tasks. But even here, perceptions about the role of the arts in a publication's coverage come into play, as when critical excellence takes second place to what both the business and editorial sides of a publication see as the advantages of a critic who will be controversial rather than profound.

The few organizations or institutions that are involved in raising the standards of criticism have not made any fundamental difference, however useful a role they play. Critics' groups within the performing arts do not have membership requirements that focus on raising standards in any rigorous way, although some have provided courses and seminars and meetings toward that goal. But neither sufficient time nor sufficient money appears to be available.

The arts themselves—the music, dance, and theater companies and organizations as well as the individual artists—those with the greatest stakes in the critical sweepstakes, are not in a strong position to pressure publications to improve criticism. Such efforts will either be perceived (sometimes correctly) as self-interest or else will put the arts in a very vulnerable and awkward position. A certain restraint is necessary in approaching the media in such delicate areas.

While news industry economic factors will inevitably mandate certain limitations, improving the state of criticism is likely to be very difficult because of a much wider problem—the failure to recognize the arts themselves as an important element in the national life.

The arts are hardly accepted in our country as a major element in the life of a free and advanced society. Arts institutions are obliged to justify their existence year by year to find the support they need from government agencies, corporate and private foundations, and private patrons; the arts institutions and the artists all too often live precariously from request to request. Moreover, as we enter the 1990s, funding for the arts has come under increasing attack from those who, having little understanding of the role of the artist in a free society, are so fearful of the results of constitutional guarantees of freedom of expression that they are increasingly willing to impose narrow interpretations of human behavior on creativity. Their politically adroit campaigns carry dolorous implications for the entire range of funding for the arts unless the arts themselves can mobilize with matching force, intensity, and skill. In any event, without adjustment, the system of support will only continue to work uncertainly and capriciously, doing justice to neither the arts nor the public.

Our history provides generous clues to our attitudes toward the arts as they have developed over the two centuries of our existence. Writing early in the nineteenth century, a French visitor to the young republic, Alexis de Tocqueville,[1] claimed that the religion professed by the first immigrants, and bequeathed by them to their descendants—"simple in its forms, austere and almost harsh in its principle, and hostile to external symbols and to ceremonial pomp —is naturally unfavorable to the fine arts. . . . The spirit of gain is always on the stretch, and the human mind, constantly diverted from the pleasures of imagination and the labors of the intellect, is there swayed by no impulse but the pursuit of wealth."

Today, another observer, Riccardo Muti, a conductor with a notable career in his native Italy as music director of Milan's La Scala and now music director of the Philadelphia Orchestra, reflects de Tocqueville's own observations:

> In America you have many more universities, certainly, than any other country. You also have many orchestras and many musicians. Yet from my experience, I have the feeling that America is the country where music and most of the other arts have the least connection to the general society. . . . In fact, when I first came here I was shocked, not in a judgmental way, but just because I did not understand how a culture could function this way.
>
> People here seemed to think I was somebody who conducted symphonies for the pleasure of a few thousand people, and that was it. But I come from Italy, where music and the arts are part of the daily organization of society. The newspapers cover musical events like other news. In fact, they treat the opening of La Scala every year in December the way your newspapers treat the Super Bowl. They pay attention to composers, to new works, in much the same way as to an election debate, a court decision, or a scientific discovery.[2]

Recognizing, then, historic and economic forces behind the limitations on arts coverage as well as the realities of reader interest, is it still not reasonable to call on publishers and editors to treat criticism in newspapers and periodicals with the same sense of responsibility and professionalism accorded virtually all other elements of the news in the better newspapers? Without such changes, the publishers and editors will fall short of the standards of excellence and professionalism that they profess; without them, the critics themselves, who too often fail to take their profession seriously, remain merely consumer guides or entertaining commentators on the arts.

Apart from the general state of criticism, there is a specific aspect that demands attention in any analysis of criticism because it exerts so stunning an influence on the world of the arts in the United States. That unique factor is *The New York Times.* This phenomenon can be approached through a story of parsnips. Elizabeth I. McCann, one of New York's shrewdest Broadway producers and managers, set out one Saturday morning on a somewhat unaccustomed errand, at the request of a friend, to buy parsnips. After visiting at least seven stores in her neighborhood and finding none, she finally asked a grocer, didn't *anyone* carry parsnips? The reply was, "Didn't you read the *Times* this morning? There was a recipe calling for parsnips." Hardly a stranger to the impact of the *Times,* since the destiny of her shows is frequently in its hands, McCann says that the affair of the parsnips brought the matter home in a curiously impressive way.

As noted, a critique in *The New York Times* can often make or break a Broadway play, although there are enough exceptions to disprove the rule. But in the case of a seriously negative review there is virtually no reprieve. A rave can send a new playwright to dizzying heights of success, its opposite possibly deny him a future. The paper's verdict is the Grand Reality. A *Times* review even influences the *Times:* if the work is reviewed positively, the play and playwright and actors and director and others are likely to be the subject of numerous feature articles; if negatively, the *Times* has an Orwellian capability to erase every trace of the work from its pages. Even if the same work is touted all over town, not much good will ensue. The opinion of the critic on the *Times* is the key. Perhaps with not the same finality, a *Times* review can be of the most consequential influence for opera, music, and dance, affecting importantly the future of the performing and creative artists as well as the institutions that present them.

But there is more, for it is not alone New York that is under the spell of the *Times*. The Sunday Arts and Leisure section is read all around the nation—and attention is paid. The young pianist who has given his first recital in New York and is favorably reviewed may get engagements all over the country.

It is hard to gauge the influence of the *Times* on the choice of plays a producer will consider mounting on Broadway. But with the escalating costs of Broadway productions the question of whether or not the *Times* is likely to approve a play inevitably arises. Gerald Schoenfeld, chairman of the Shubert Organization, the major producing and theater-owning entity in New York, puts it this way:

> I don't believe that anyone says I'll batten down the hatches, but you would feel more encouraged to work with something the *Times* found favorable in its subject matter. . . . I don't mean we won't put a play on, but we will take into consideration what we perceive to be a predisposition of a critic not to like a certain genre of play or musical.

It also works the other way: a favorable review by Frank Rich of a play at a regional theater can speed it to Broadway, according to Richard Hummler of *Variety:* "It helps with financing, casting, everything." But if Rich pans a play in a nonprofit theater, even if it's under option, "It's good-bye New York." Hummler, incidentally, considers Rich a wonder with words but very limited as a critic.

The *Times*'s influence extends abroad as well. Depending on the nature of a *Times* review by Frank Rich of an English production, a London play's chance of being brought to Broadway can likely be increased or diminished, although such a factor is far less important, if operative at all, in the case of musicals. The real problem is one of having the chief critic of the *Times* review a London play.

The scope and quality of the *Times*'s news coverage in general and its coverage of the arts in particular endow it with power. While variable, to be sure, arts reporting and features in the *Times* set an example admired across the nation. In addition to direct coverage of events, the newspaper pays serious attention to a wide range of concerns in the arts (for example, policy or economics) that are rarely addressed elsewhere. A few newspapers around the nation do cover the arts with distinction, but if more newspapers lavished the same attention and space and energy on arts coverage as the *Times*, the arts in this country would be in a stronger position and the public better served.

The *Times* also goes to considerable lengths in choosing most of its critics, making extensive searches beyond its own staff, looking with care at the background and experience of candidates and then paying them relatively well. This practice has raised the odds of obtaining excellent coverage although it certainly has been no guarantee.

It should be emphasized that the *Times* has not asked for the formidable power its critics often have but that to a dismaying extent its readers have given them the power. Indeed, its readers all too often follow its critics virtually unquestioningly. Certainly the dizzying rise in ticket prices has made audiences more wary and more determined to make their money count by going to only the well-pretested presentations. For help in making these decisions, they seek guidance. New York lacks a substantial dedicated theatergoing audience, independent, informed, and determined to go to performances to make up their own minds. In dance and music the audience is more consistently supportive, often exerting considerable independence and discrimination. For this audience, critical opinion is less important than for theatergoers.

But the power of the *Times* in the arts, more particularly its influence on theater, is not healthy. In one of the largest cities in the world, in what some consider the cultural capital of the country, this single critical voice dominates. There is virtually no diversity of opinion to do justice to the diversity of the arts. And there is no court of appeal once an opinion is given.

A. R. Gurney, Jr., a major playwright (author of *The Dining Room* and *The Cocktail Hour* among many other plays), believes that because of the power of the *Times* there is a kind of tyranny in theater criticism which is different from the other arts. He sees opera, for instance, with certain built-in guarantees of continuity, possibly in the form of a Pavarotti or a Sutherland or simply in mounting that invariably sold-out *Traviata*. There are parallels throughout the music world and in dance, but not in theater, which does not have the classic favorites that guarantee continuity.

"Frank Rich is a good critic," Gurney says. "I wouldn't be sitting here talking to you without him. But *The New York Times* is continually reminding us about democratic tradition and the abuse of power, yet in theater *The New York Times* abuses power by allowing only one critic." If he doesn't like a play, Gurney points out, and if it survives by hook or by crook, the work won't even be mentioned in feature or news articles, while plays that the *Times* has praised often have multiple follow-up stories. That system is arbitrary and unfair.

Various attempts have been made by professional groups within the theater in meetings with *Times* executives to put forward suggestions aimed at ameliorating the situation from the theater's point of view. But the system remains essentially unchanged. One suggestion was to provide a brief compendium of critical comment that had appeared in other publications or on the electronic media about each new show; another was to be evenhanded on the matter of follow-up articles, whether the show had won the *Times*'s praise or not, and to discontinue reviews of London works by the critic who would review them when they came to the United States, a possible form of prior censorship in view of the likely disastrous economic consequences bad reviews carry. (Indeed, there seems no question that to avoid even the appearance of precensorship, the *Times*'s chief theater critic should not review plays in London being considered for a New York production, although carrying news stories about them, accounts of local reviews, or even reviews by *Times* critics who would not review the work when it arrived in New York would not be a problem.)

Composer William Schuman relays a suggestion, admittedly impractical, but worth putting forward nevertheless, he says; for the sake of fairness, the *Times* should have a guest reviewer along with its regular reviewer for every important performing event. (Although that has not happened, the *Times* has, as noted previously, reinstituted an earlier practice of having a regular Sunday critic in order presumably to provide a counterpoint of opinion.) Katharine Hepburn recalled the days when New York had seven or eight newspapers and seven or eight critics. She would consider it fairer if the *Times* at least could have two voices for each production. And she can't believe that the present arrangement isn't tough on the critic, who probably doesn't like the idea of drowning an effort that is "honest and decent and certainly hasn't meant harm even if it doesn't succeed."

Richard Hummler is critical of the *Times*'s practice of doing feature stories on productions to which it has given good reviews and paying no attention to those it has not liked. "I can only construe this as a desire to maintain that influence they officially decry," Hummler says.

Max Frankel, executive editor of *The New York Times,* addressing some of these suggestions, says first of all that he believes the power of the *Times* is much overstated.

As for the idea of two daily critics, Frankel says, "Absurd. What if both critics don't like something . . . 90 percent of the time they'd probably agree. Maybe I could be persuaded we need a play critic and a musical theater critic." As for reprinting the comments of critics from other newspapers, Frankel replied that people could buy the other newspapers and that the producers take out advertisements with the blurbs of other critics anyway.

"To the extent we are influential, I like to think we earn it. It is true of everything in the *Times*. . . . It has earned a very special trust," Frankel says. In response to the notion that the *Times* has a special responsibility to the arts by wielding such power, he replies, "Do we have a social responsibility to theater or to our readers? We believe it is in favor of our readers. We are not going to compromise our good faith obligations."

It is worth noting that *The Village Voice* occasionally will have two of its critics review the same work when a difference of opinion has surfaced within the staff. This is true for theater particularly, and on occasion the same play may end up being reviewed both extremely negatively and positively. The practice, along with the *Voice*'s generally informal and irreverent stance, lends its pages a considerable vitality. Diversity of opinion is encouraged to the advantage of both the readers and the theater.

Attempting to compensate for a bad review in *The New York Times* by placing an advertisement with favorable quotes from other critics can be done, but at a nearly prohibitive expense for most theater managements—more than $40,000 per page on Sundays. Of daily and universal distress in the theater community is the *Times*'s advertising policy as it relates to daily theater listings for Broadway and Off-Broadway known as the ABCs. These listings are virtually indispensable for the theater, virtual necessities for New Yorkers and out-of-towners alike. A small box, permitting perhaps one short quote—often from the *Times*—along with the bare facts a theatergoer needs, costs around $175. Some of the most profitable pastimes known to modern civilization are publicized in the *Times* for free—baseball games are listed, as are TV schedules.

The phenomenon of the *Times*'s power is not new. Brooks Atkinson wrote in 1962, in a parody of *The New Yorker's* famous feature, the Cliché Expert:

Q: "What is it that drama critics have too much of?" Answer: "They have too much power. They have the power of life and death over plays. They kill shows. They throw actors out of work to satisfy their egos. They keep the public from seeing plays it wants to see. They bankrupt producers."

And for good measure Atkinson added:

> [Critics] are disappointed playwrights. They are former sports writers. They are the butchers of Broadway. They are the aisle-sitters, the play tasters, the arbiters, the hired theatre-goers. They are too old, too jaded, too bored, too drunk. . . . They destroy the work of many sincere theatre people and the life savings of indigent backers for the sake of a wisecrack. They write to impress one another. In a half hour they undo the work of months.[3]

Plus ça change . . . the *Times* continues to endow with instantaneous power any critic it appoints. The situation demands the *Times*'s attention in reconsidering the ways in which it can foster some diversity of opinion. Bringing the ad rates down for theater could make a quick and highly justifiable start by enabling the inclusion of more quotes from a diversity of critics. But it is the editorial side that requires the most innovative approaches.

Raising the level of criticism around the country is no easy matter considering entrenched attitudes that fail to take into account the importance of the arts in a free society.

In many ways the arts have failed to make the best case for themselves to the public as well as to the media, to publishers, and to editors. That effort must encompass an understanding of the multiple responsibility of newspapers to provide the news, to fulfill their community and public service obligations, and to make money.

Despite the vulnerability of arts companies where the media are concerned, they must attempt to persuade media management of the importance of the arts. Their influential board members should be involved in this effort. A high-level, rigorously planned, national effort has never been made. The time is past due.

The annual meetings of the American Newspaper Publishers Association and the American Society of Newspaper Editors (ASNE) are key factors in reaching the print media. Only at one meeting of the ASNE were the arts a major focus of attention.

One possible way of dealing with budgetary strictures which editors say inhibit them from providing high-quality arts coverage would be the more extensive and imaginative use of freelance critics. Good critics are never easy to find, but a modest investment to provide the freelancers with courses of study at one of the critics' workshops might well pay dividends. (Here is a place where foundations could help with direct grants to the critics and improvement of the courses themselves.) Part of the resistance to using freelancers—and/or paying them a sum commensurate with their capabilities—is the claim that Newspaper Guild labor contracts prevent the practice. The Guild claims managers are using the Guild as an excuse not to take on freelance critics. This situation needs to be talked over, argued over, and perhaps fought over.

Another possibility which might be explored is for a consortium of newspapers in a particular region to jointly hire a critic or critics if "going it alone" is considered financially impossible. Newspapers traditionally guard their independence jealously and are not given to sharing staff. Problems of allocation of time, of supervision, and of pay scales are evident drawbacks to such a plan. Nevertheless, newspapers do share wire services for the very same reason—the indispensable requirement to have access to news or features for which editors do not have the staff.

The Associated Press, the largest American press association, has a theater critic who operates out of New York City and whose critiques of Broadway are available throughout the country. But what if the AP added dance, music, and theater critics in its regional bureaus—perhaps the cost to be covered by the AP itself and a special levy from the newspapers involved? This would be one way of upgrading coverage throughout the country. Inasmuch as the job would be of a roving nature, it would tend not to be in conflict with that of local critics, and the additional attention to criticism could benefit all.

Louis Boccardi, president and general manager of the Associated Press, responded to the suggestion of extended AP coverage through regional critics as an idea worth considering but did not seem particularly sanguine over the realities of such an innovation coming into existence. Boccardi noted that, in addition to theater from New York, the AP does provide movie and television criticism as well as some music and dance criticism—from country music to Lincoln Center—and that AP bureaus all over the country cover the arts on occasion. He thought it would be possible to write criticism out of the regional bureau but pointed out that the AP does not generally write columns of opinion of any kind, for which other newspaper services might be more likely candidates.

Budgetary restrictions in relation to AP priorities are compelling, as articulated by Boccardi:

If I were suddenly to be given the resources in six regional headquarters to add three people in each, which comes to eighteen, I am not quite sure that a critic would rank among them. From my perspective arts are important. Whether that is the most important thing for us to do if more resources would become available is more than an academic question, it's at the heart of what you are talking about. . . . A few years ago the AP made an investment of additional resources of people and the three areas were business news coverage . . . graphic artists to expand the staff of those preparing all kinds of charts and visual materials, and six regional news reporters. Those decisions represented our judgment as to where we felt we needed to do more and there were many other things we might have done . . . but if 1,300 people [the number of AP newspaper members] were at my door saying, "We need a first rate music critic," that's a voice we would hear, that's when a music critic would fit into the list of priorities. No one sat in the chair you are in and suggested more for the arts.

And that is a parable for the world of criticism. Unless the newspapers are activated by forces from the outside it is unlikely that much will be done to improve the situation—either by providing greater opportunities for those who are writing criticism, or by finding critics of a higher level of experience or promise. Editors are unlikely to set higher standards and goals for arts coverage unless there is a call for them, placing considerable responsibility on the arts themselves for practical ways in which the process can be forwarded. There is more than ample evidence that higher professional standards by critics across the nation can have an effect on raising the regard in which criticism is held, as well as on raising the estate of the arts. If readers of criticism, artists, arts managers, and all those who have a commitment to the arts demand serious criticism, the prospects for change will be greatly enhanced.

APPENDIX

PERSONS INTERVIEWED

This list contains the names of those persons who were interviewed for this work, including those quoted in the book as well as others whose information and insights contributed to the author's analyses and conclusions. The vast majority of those listed were interviewed in person, a few by telephone. The names of three or four persons who asked for anonymity are not included, and in a very limited number of cases remarks were made off the record. The interviews took place during the period 1985–89. Affiliations are correct for the time the interviews were held and do not necessarily correspond to present affiliations, mobility in the worlds of the arts and journalism being quite as fluid as in other areas of American life.

Atlanta

Anthony, Vince, director, Puppet Theatre

Bacchetti, J. Thomas, executive vice president and general manager, Atlanta Symphony Orchestra

Bannon, Peter, entertainment editor, critic, WAGA-TV

Boeker, Tom, theater editor, *Creative Loafing*

Chappell, Fred, artistic director, Alliance Theatre/Atlanta Children's Theatre

Crouch, Paula, theater critic, *Journal and Constitution*

Culver, Kevin Alden, composer, conductor

Eason, Deborah, editor and publisher, *Creative Loafing*

Fraser, Jack, director of News, WAGA-TV

Head, David, producing director, Theatrical Outfit, actor

Hertz, Kenneth, executive director, Atlanta Ballet

Hume, Ann, formerly director, Public Relations, Atlanta Symphony Orchestra

Jackson, Marsha, co-artistic director, Jomandi Productions

Lerner, Ruby, director, Alternate Roots (organization of theaters of the South)

McGhee, Joanne, executive director, Dancer's Collective Theatre

Osier, David, assistant managing editor, *Journal and Constitution*

Peck, Jim, playwright

Ratka, Frank, director, Georgia Council for the Arts

Schneider, John, interim music critic (formerly critic), *Journal and Constitution*

Sears, Edward, managing editor, *Journal and Constitution*

Sherbert, Linda, assistant theater critic, *Journal and Constitution*

Smith, Helen C., cultural affairs writer, theater and dance critic, *Journal and Constitution*

West, Sharon, arts and entertainment editor, WSB-AM

Williams, Walt, program manager, WSB-AM

Wittow, Frank, Academy Theatre

Boston

Altman, Peter, producing director, Huntington Theatre Company

Eder, Richard, book critic, *Los Angeles Times,* formerly theater critic, *The New York Times*

Friedman, Arthur, theater critic, *Boston Herald* (also freelance)

Koch, John, arts editor, *Boston Globe*

Kulhawik, Joyce, arts and entertainment reporter, film and theater critic, WBZ-TV

Murray, Lawrence, executive director, ARTS/Boston

Pilavachi, Costa, artistic administrator, Boston Symphony Orchestra

Chicago

Christiansen, Richard, entertainment editor, *Chicago Tribune*

Dischon, Colleen, associate editor, *Chicago Tribune*

Economos, Diane G., League of Chicago Theatres

Falls, Robert, artistic director, Wisdom Bridge Theatre

Finney, David R., director, Programs, WMAQ-TV

Henry, Patrick, artistic director, Free Street Theatre

Kleinfeld, Lenny, columnist on theater for *Chicago* magazine and, under name of Bury St. Edmund, critic for *The Reader*

Krainik, Ardis, general manager, Chicago Lyric Opera

Lobo, Richard M., vice president and general manager, WMAQ-TV

Marks, Diana, executive director, Chicago City Ballet

Marsh, Robert C., classical music critic, *Chicago Sun-Times*

Mejia, Paul, co-artistic director, Chicago City Ballet

Ollendorff, Lucille, president and general manager, Music of the Baroque Concert Series

Perry, Jeff, actor and artistic management, Steppenwolf Theatre Company

Powers, Scott, deputy features editor, Arts and Entertainment, *Chicago Sun-Times*

Radis, Jackie S., artistic director, Moming Dance and Arts Center

Scorca, Marc, managing director, Chicago Opera Theatre

Sloan, Larry, associate director, acting artistic director, Goodman Theatre

Syse, Glenna, theater critic, *Chicago Sun-Times*

Towers, Kenneth D., managing editor, *Chicago Sun-Times*

Von Rhein, John, music critic, *Chicago Tribune*

Los Angeles

Amari, Jane, features editor, *Los Angeles Daily News*

Bernheimer, Martin, music critic, *Los Angeles Times*

Champlin, Charles, arts editor, *Los Angeles Times*

Davidson, Gordon, artistic director, Mark Taper Forum

Eitner, Don, artistic director and founder, American Conservatory Arts Theater

Fleischmann, Ernest, general director, Los Angeles Philharmonic

Franklin, Gary, theater and film critic, KCBS-TV

Fryer, Robert, artistic director, Ahmanson Theatre

Ginell, Richard S., music critic, *Daily News*

Lewitzky, Bella, artistic director and principal choreographer, Bella Lewitzky Dance Company

Sullivan, Dan, theater critic, *Los Angeles Times*

Taylor, Jean Sharley, associate editor, *Los Angeles Times*

Viertel, Jack, theater critic, *Los Angeles Herald Examiner*

Zapata, Carmen, producing director, Bilingual Foundation of the Arts

Minneapolis

Anthony, Michael, music critic, *Minneapolis Star and Tribune*

Ballet, Arthur, entertainment specialist and theater critic, KSTP-TV

Berg, Daniel L., development director, Minnesota Opera Co.

Collins, Robert, theater critic, *City Pages* and Minnesota Public Radio

Corn, Edward, general director, Minnesota Opera Co.

Cranney, Jon, artistic director, The Children's Theatre Co. and School

Davis, Kathy, public relations and marketing director, Minnesota Opera Co.

Hage, George, former professor of journalism, University of Minnesota

Handberg, Ron, vice president and general manager, WCCO-TV

Kramer, Joel, managing editor, *Minneapolis Star and Tribune*

Larsen, Libby, composer-in-residence, Minnesota Orchestra

Mirus, Judith, freelance arts administrator, formerly executive director, Minnesota Independent Choreographers Alliance

203

Parkinson, Roger, publisher, *Minneapolis Star and Tribune*

Picone, Linda, assistant managing editor for features, *Minneapolis Star and Tribune*

Schoenbaum, Donald, managing director, The Guthrie Theater

Smith, Kevin, general manager, Minnesota Opera Co.

Stearns, Robert, director, Performing Arts, Walker Arts Center

Steele, Mike, dance and theater critic, *Minneapolis Star and Tribune*

New York City

Anderson, Jack, dance critic, *The New York Times*

Armstrong, Tom, director, Whitney Museum of American Art

Ashdown, Marie M., lecturer and writer on opera

Banes, Sally, dance critic, author, contributor to *The Village Voice*

Barnes, Clive, theater and dance critic, *New York Post*

Barr, Richard (deceased), theater producer, president, League of American Theatres and Producers

Berman, Lois, writers' agent

Bingham, Susan H., composer

Bishop, Andre, artistic director, Playwrights Horizons

Boccardi, Louis, president and general manager, the Associated Press

Brisbane, Katherine, theater critic, managing editor Currency Press, Sydney, Australia

Carey, Carl, vice president and general manager, WNBC-TV

Chapin, Schuyler, dean, School of the Arts, Columbia University

Clarke, Martha, performance art conceptualizer and director

Cohen, Alexander, theater producer

Crawford, Bruce, general manager, Metropolitan Opera Company

Croce, Arlene, dance critic, *The New Yorker*

Cunningham, Dennis, arts and entertainment editor, critic, WCBS-TV

Dasgupta, Gautam, co-editor, *Performing Arts Journal*

Dean, Philip Hayes, playwright, actor

de Mille, Agnes, choreographer, author

Dewhurst, Colleen, actress

Duff, James Allen, playwright

Feingold, Michael, theater critic, *The Village Voice*

Feld, Eliot, artistic director, choreographer, Feld Ballet

Frankel, Max, executive editor, *The New York Times*

Gale, William K., theater and dance critic, *The Journal and the Bulletin*, Providence

Gerard, Jeremy, Broadway reporter, *The New York Times*

Gilman, Richard, critic, author, professor, Yale University School of Drama

Glines, John, founder and co-director, The Glines, a theater company

Goldemberg, Rose Leiman, playwright

Goldsby, Robert, theater director, formerly artistic director, producer, Berkeley Stage Company, Calif.

Gurney, A. R., Jr., playwright

Gussow, Mel, theater critic, *The New York Times*

Hayes, Mary, executive director, New York State Council on the Arts

Henahan, Donal, chief music critic, *The New York Times*

Henry, William III, associate editor, theater critic, *Time*

Hepburn, Katharine, actress

Hewes, Henry, writer, critic, former president, American Association of Theatre Critics

Honan, William, culture editor, *The New York Times*

Hummler, Richard, theater editor and critic, *Variety*

Jacobs, Bernard B., president, The Shubert Organization

Jowitt, Deborah, chief dance critic, *The Village Voice*

King, Woodie, Jr., director, New Federal Theater

Kirstein, Lincoln, president, New York City Ballet

Kissel, Howard, drama critic, *New York Daily News*

Kisselgoff, Anna, chief dance critic, *The New York Times*

Kotlowitz, Robert, vice president, Production Center, WNET-TV

Kramer, Hilton, editor, *The New Criterion*

Kroll, Jack, theater and film critic, *Newsweek*

Laderman, Ezra, composer

Lichtenstein, Harvey, president, Brooklyn Academy of Music

Lindstrom, Pia, film and theater critic, WNBC-TV

Lipman, Samuel, publisher and music critic, *The New Criterion*

Mamet, David, playwright

Marx, Robert, former director for theatre programs, New York State Council on the Arts and National Endowment for the Arts

Maranca, Bonnie, co-editor, *Performing Arts Journal*

Martins, Peter, ballet master in chief, New York City Ballet

McCann, Elizabeth I., theater producer

McDonagh, Donald F., dance critic, author

Miles, Julia, artistic director, The Womens Project and Productions

Miller, Arthur, playwright

Moss, Jane S., executive director, The Alliance of Resident Theatres

Munk, Erika, theater editor, *The Village Voice*

Nachman, Jerry, news director, News 4 New York, NBC-TV

Page, Tim, music critic, *The New York Times*

Papp, Joseph, president, The New York Shakespeare Festival

Paton, Angela, actress, formerly artistic director, Berkeley Stage Company

Piser, Joan, writer on music, biographer of Pierre Boulez and Leonard Bernstein

Polisi, Joseph, president, The Julliard School

Prince, Harold, theater producer

Ramirez, Tina, founder and director, Ballet Hispanico

Reinhart, Charles, director, American Dance Festival, Duke University

Rich, Frank, chief drama critic, *The New York Times*

Richards, David, theater critic, Arts and Leisure Section, *The New York Times*

Richards, Lloyd, dean, Yale School of Drama, artistic director, Yale Repertory Theatre

Rockwell, John, music critic, *The New York Times*

Rothstein, Edward, music critic, *The New Republic*

Schaap, Richard, sports reporter, correspondent, World News Tonight, ABC-TV

Schoenfeld, Gerald, chairman, The Shubert Organization

Schonberg, Harold, former chief music critic, *The New York Times*

Schubart, Mark, director, Lincoln Center Institute

Schuman, William, composer

Schwarz, Gerard, principal conductor, Seattle Symphony Orchestra, music director, Mostly Mozart, Lincoln Center

Segal, Martin, chairman, Lincoln Center for the Performing Arts

Sills, Beverly, general director, New York City Opera

Simon, John, theater critic, *New York* magazine

Snow, Leida, theater critic, WINS Radio

Sondheim, Stephen, composer, lyricist

Stasio, Marilyn, contributing critic, *New York Post*

Stone, Peter, playwright, scenarist, president, The Dramatist Guild

Tapley, Melvin S., arts and entertainment editor, New York *Amsterdam News*

Tcherkassky, Marianna A., principal dancer, American Ballet Theatre

Thomson, Virgil (deceased), composer, music critic

Villella, Edward, artistic director, Miami City Ballet, former principal dancer, New York City Ballet

Wachtel, George, director of research, The League of American Theatres and Producers

Walsh, Michael, associate editor, music critic, *Time*

Wasserman, Steve, news director, WCBS-TV

Wilson, Edwin, theater critic, *The Wall Street Journal*

Winship, Tom, senior fellow, Gannett Center for Media Studies, formerly editor, *Boston Globe,* 1965–85

Wolf, Matt, cultural correspondent, The Associated Press, London, freelance theater critic

Zeckendorf, Nancy, former dancer, member of the board, American Ballet Theatre

Zeisler, Peter, director, Theatre Communications Group

Zollo, Frederick, theater producer

Zwilich, Ellen Taaffe, composer

St. Paul

Close, Roy, music critic, *St. Paul Pioneer Press-Dispatch*
Finnegan, John, vice president/editor, *St. Paul Pioneer Press-Dispatch*
Hage, George, president of board, Actors Theatre of St. Paul
Hawley, David, drama critic, *St. Paul Pioneer Press-Dispatch*
Henry, John, publisher, *St. Paul Pioneer Press-Dispatch*
Koelsch, Patrice Clark, director, Center for Arts Criticism
Solotaroff, Sarah, general manager, The St. Paul Chamber Orchestra

San Francisco

Adler, Kurt Herbert, former general director, San Francisco Opera
Berson, Misha, director, Theater Communications Center Bay Area, theater critic, *San Francisco Bay Guardian*
Commanday, Robert, music and dance critic, *San Francisco Chronicle*
Corsaro, Kim, editor, *Coming Up*
Duggan, Charles H., manager, co-producer, Marine Memorial Theatre
Esslin, Martin, professor of drama, Stanford University, member Arts Council Great Britain, writer and critic for *Play* (London), and author
Guillermo, Emil, entertainment specialist, critic, KRON-TV
Holden, Joan, resident playwright, San Francisco Mime Troupe
Hurwitt, Robert, theater critic, *The Express* and *California* magazine, editor, *West Coast Plays*
LeBlond, Richard, director, San Francisco Ballet
Littlejohn, David, professor of journalism, University of California, Berkeley
MacDougall, Robert M., composer, actor, theater director
Moore, Benjamin, managing director, ACT theater company
Pastreich, A. Peter, executive director, San Francisco Symphony
Scott, Nancy, theater critic, *San Francisco Examiner*
Taylor, Robert, drama and film critic, *The Tribune* (Oakland)
Ulrich, Allan, dance critic, *San Francisco Examiner*
Weiner, Bernard, theater critic and columnist, *The Chronicle*

Santa Fe

Riolo, Anthony, executive director, The Santa Fe Opera

Seattle

Adcock, Joe, theater critic, *Seattle Post-Intelligencer*
Bargreen, Melinda L., music critic, *The Seattle Times*
Brewster, David, publisher and editor, *Seattle Weekly*

Campbell, Richard M., music and dance critic, *Seattle Post-Intelligencer*
Donelly, Peter, producing director, Seattle Repertory Theatre
Downey, Roger, arts columnist, *Seattle Weekly*
Fancher, Michael, managing editor, *The Seattle Times*
Fassio, Virgil, publisher, *Seattle Post-Intelligencer*
Fry, Donn, arts and entertainment editor, *The Seattle Times*
Gelles, George, music critic, *Seattle Weekly*
Gray, Maxine Cushing, editor/publisher, *Northwest Arts*
Hanna, Barbara, entertainment editor, *Bellevue Journal American*
Jenkins, Speight, general director, Seattle Opera former music critic, *New York Post*
Johnson, Wayne, drama critic, *The Seattle Times*
Meagher, Cyndi, assistant managing editor/Sunday, *The Seattle Times*
Mohl, Lucy, arts and entertainment editor, King-TV
Payne, Ancil, president, King Broadcasting Company
Stowell, Kent, artistic director, Pacific Northwest Ballet
Sullivan, Daniel, artistic director, Seattle Repertory Theatre
Walker, M. Burke, founding artistic director, Empty Space Theatre
Wetzel, Frank, editor, *Bellevue Journal American*

Washington, D.C.

Bartow, Arthur, artistic director, New Playwrights theatre
Bradlee, Ben, executive editor, *The Washington Post*
Campbell, Arch, critic-at-large, WRC-TV
Feinstein, Martin, director, Washington Opera
Fichandler, Thomas, executive director, Arena Stage
Fogel, Henry, executive director, National Symphony Orchestra
Kriegsman, Alan, dance editor and critic, *The Washington Post*
Marlin-Jones, Davey, arts critic for CBS affiliate and Post Newsweek TV in Detroit
McLellan, Joseph D., music critic, *The Washington Post*
Stevens, Roger L., chairman, John F. Kennedy Center for the Performing Arts
Teter, Harry, Jr., general manager, National Theatre

Waterford, Conn.

(National Critics Institute of the Eugene O'Neill Memorial Theater Center)

FACULTY

Bednar, Rudy, producer/director, ABC-TV
Cook, Joe, writer, ABC-TV
DeVine, Lawrence, theater critic, *The Detroit Free Press*
Hill, Holly, New York Theater correspondent for *The Times* of London

Schier, Ernest, director of the Institute and over many years theater and film critic for *The Philadelphia Bulletin*

Siegel, Joel, theater and film critic, ABC-TV

Waites, James, drama critic for *The National Times,* Sydney, Australia

CRITIC FELLOWS

DeVries, Hilary S., covers theater and film for *The Christian Science Monitor*

Havel, O'Dette Pauline, theater and film reviews for the *El Paso Times*

Phillips, Michael, freelance theater critic for the *St. Paul Pioneer Press*

Stoner, Patrick, theater and film critic for WHYY-TV, Philadelphia

Winston-Salem

Amidon, Stephen, theater critic, *The Spectator*

Goodman, Joe, managing editor, *Winston-Salem Journal and the Sentinel*

Hamlin, Larry Leon, executive and aristic director, North Carolina Black Repertory Theatre

Hanes, Philip, arts partron and activist

Hickock, Robert, dean, school of music, North Carolina School of the Arts

Howard, Roseanne, theater critic, *Winston-Salem Journal and the Sentinel*

Lindgren, Robert A., dean, school of dance, North Carolina School of the Arts

Lindsley, Clyde, manager, Roger Stevens Center

Mashburn, Rick, associate editor, *The Spectator*

Mixter, Perry, manager, Winston-Salem Symphony Orchestra

Morrison, Malcolm, dean, school of drama, North Carolina School of the Arts, and director, The North Carolina Shakespeare Festival

Perret, Peter, conductor, Winston-Salem Symphony Orchestra

Schertzer, Jim, staff arts reporter and performing arts critic, *Winston-Salem Journal and the Sentinel*

NOTES

Chapter 1. The Impact on the Performing and Creative Artist

1. "From the Phantom, with Love," *The New York Times,* October 12, 1988.

2. George Bernard Shaw, *Advice to a Young Critic and Other Letters* (New York: Crown Publishers, Inc., 1955).

3. Clifton Fadiman, ed., *The Little, Brown Book of Anecdotes* (Boston: Little, Brown and Company, 1985).

4. Interview with Isaac Stern by Harold Schonberg, music critic, *The New York Times,* December 4, 1984.

5. *The New York Times,* April 5, 1987.

6. Dorothy Parker (1893–1967), a major American writer, humorist and satirist, short-story writer, screenwriter.

7. George Plimpton, ed., *The Paris Review Interviews,* Third Series (New York: Penguin Books, 1977).

8. Gordon Rogoff, in remarks upon his receiving the George Jean Nathan Award for Dramatic Criticism, *The Village Voice,* June 16, 1987.

9. New York Drama Critics Award, 1948.

Chapter 2. The Impact on Performing Arts Companies: Theater

1. *Variety,* June 20, 1984.

2. These three critics, writing at various times from the thirties through the sixties (all are now deceased), had an impact on theater: Harold Clurman, theater critic for *The Nation;* Brooks Atkinson, for *The New York Times;* and Kenneth Tynan, for *The Observer* and *The New Yorker,* among other publications.

3. Dan Sullivan is theater critic for the *Los Angeles Times.*

Chapter 3. The Impact on Performing Arts Companies: Music and Dance

1. Jean-Pierre Ponnelle died in August 1988.

2. Leonard Bernstein, the composer and conductor; the late Otto

Klemperer, conductor of many prominent symphony orchestras and opera companies.

3. Mehta submitted his resignation to the New York Philharmonic Orchestra in 1988 to be effective in 1991.

Chapter 4. Profile of the Critic: The Accidental Route

1. George Bernard Shaw, *Advice to a Young Critic and Other Letters* (New York: Crown Publishers, Inc., 1955). Shaw was dramatic critic for *The Saturday Review,* London, 1895–98. Earlier he had been a music critic, first for the *Star* (1888–90) and then for the *World* (1890–94).

2. Shaw, *Advice to a Young Critic and Other Letters.*

3. As noted earlier, these materials are available from the publisher.

4. Theatre Development Fund is a New York City nonprofit organization for the development and stimulation of a wide range of theater, with many programs, among them one for providing a margin of subsidy for works of artistic merit in theater through the purchase of tickets to these works prior to opening night with the tickets subsequently resold at low prices to students and others.

5. *The Physicists* by Friedrich Duerrenmatt.

6. A speculative figure, the author not having been able to find any authoritative overall listings.

7. Beatrice Handel, ed., *The National Directory for the Performing Arts/ Educational,* 3d ed. (New York: Handel & Sons, Inc., and John Wiley & Sons, 1978).

8. Richard Gilman, *Common and Uncommon Masks: Writings on Theatre 1961–70* (New York: Random House, 1971).

Chapter 5. Publishers and Editors

1. *1986 Editor and Publisher Yearbook.*

2. Census Bureau, New York Regional Office.

3. Meeting of the American Society of Newspaper Editors, Washington, D.C., April 13, 1985, reported in *The New York Times* of April 14, 1985, p. 11.

4. *Halls Magazine Reports,* December 1985, and National Advertising Bureau's 1984 Report.

5. Arts Coverage Survey, May 1985, from the National Endowment for the Arts.

6. National Advertising Bureau's 1984 Report.

7. Foreword, by Frank Hodsoll, chairman, National Endowment for the Arts, for the 1965–86 Chronology of Federal Involvement in the Arts.

8. For Roger Stevens, see Chapter 2.

9. *1989 Editor and Publisher Yearbook.*

Chapter 6. The Critic's Career: The Hazards and the Perils

1. *Port de bras*—the carriage of the upper torso.
2. *The New Yorker*, April 7, 1986.
3. *American Theatre*, May 1987, published by Theatre Communications Group, New York.
4. *Mr. Chow v. Ste. Jour Azur*, Second Circuit (see *New York Law Journal*, April 8, 1985).
5. *The Guardian*, London, December 20, 1985.
6. Kathleen Tynan, *The Life of Kenneth Tynan* (New York: William Morrow and Company, 1987).
7. Diana Rigg, *No Turn Unstoned* (London: Arrow Books Limited, 1983); Nicolas Slonimsky, *Lexicon of Musical Invective* (Seattle: University of Washington Press, 1953); and Bill Henderson, *Rotten Reviews: A Literary Companion* (New York: Penguin Books, 1987).

Chapter 7. The Electronic Media

1. Frank Rich, chief drama critic for *The New York Times*.
2. Sally Quinn, *We're Going to Make You a Star* (New York: Simon & Schuster, 1975).
3. Andrei Serban, a teacher and theater director, widely known, for instance, for his startlingly innovative productions of Greek classics at New York's La Mama Theater and Anton Chekhov's *The Cherry Orchard* at Lincoln Center's Vivian Beaumont Theater.

Chapter 8. Minority Performing Arts and Their Critics

1. American Society of Newspaper Editors, annual survey.
2. Lloyd Richards is dean of the Yale School of Drama; artistic director of the Yale Repertory Theatre; and artistic director of the National Playwrights Conference of the Eugene O'Neill Theater Center.
3. *The New York Times*, June 11, 1987.
4. *The New York Times*, September 26, 1990.
5. "Hispanic Theater in the United States and Puerto Rico," by Joanne Pottlitzer, Report to the Ford Foundation, New York, 1988.
6. Article by Dan Cox, *Dancemagazine*, November 1985.
7. Liz Smith, *New York Daily News*, March 10, 1985.
8. *The New York Times*, April 5, 1987.
9. Brooks Atkinson, *Brief Chronicles* (New York: Coward-McCann, 1966).

Chapter 9. Advice to the Critic from the Criticized

1. Sheridan Morley, quoted in Kathleen Tynan, *The Life of Kenneth Tynan* (New York: William Morrow and Company, 1987). Michael Billington is theater critic for *The Guardian.*

2. From *The New York Herald Tribune,* April 2, 1944, as excerpted in Edwin Denby, *Dance Writings,* ed. Robert Cornfield and William Mackay (New York: Alfred A. Knopf, 1986).

3. *The Gin Game* by D. L. Coburn.

4. Although the approach has frequently been attributed to Goethe, the author has been unable to find reference to it in the writings of Goethe.

5. *The New York Herald Tribune,* October 9, 1944.

6. *Variety,* March 25, 1987.

Chapter 10. The Critic: The End in View

1. "The Function of Criticism," 1923, reprinted in *Selected Prose of T. S. Eliot,* ed. Frank Kermode (New York: Harcourt Brace Jovanovich, Farrar, Straus and Giroux, 1975). (First published in *Criterion,* 1923.)

2. Harold Schonberg, *Facing the Music* (New York: Summit Books, 1985).

3. From the jacket of Kathleen Tynan, *The Life of Kenneth Tynan* (New York: William Morrow and Company, 1987).

4. From an article in *The Atlantic Monthly,* November 1954, quoted in *The Life of Kenneth Tynan.*

5. From *The Atlantic,* November 1954, as summarized in *The Life of Kenneth Tynan.*

6. *The New Criterion,* October 1987.

7. Robert Brustein, *Seasons of Discontent: Dramatic Opinions 1959–1965* (New York: Simon & Schuster, 1987).

8. Margaret Croyden, *Lunatics, Lovers and Poets* (New York: McGraw-Hill Book Company, 1974).

9. Martin Esslin, "Theater of the Absurd," *Tulane Drama Review,* May 1960.

10. Bonnie Marranca, *Theatre Writings* (New York: Performing Arts Journal Publications, 1984).

11. From *Crying in the Wilderness* by Julius Novick, a theater critic for *The Village Voice,* in an article in *American Theatre,* January 1988.

12. Susan Sontag, *Against Interpretation* (New York: Delta Books, 1961).

13. Arthur and Barbara Gelb, *O'Neill* (New York: Harper and Brothers, 1960).

14. An essay by Eric Bentley in Stark Young, *Theatre* (New York: Limelight Editions, 1986).

15. Remarks made by Frank Rich at the New York City 92d Street YMHA Critics on Criticism Series headed by Jane Moss.

Chapter 11. *Inside the Critique: The Underpinnings of Criticism*

1. Robert Brustein, *American Theatre,* January 1988.
2. Peter Brook, remarks at the Drama Desk, 1987.
3. Harold Clurman, *Dramatists Guild Quarterly,* Spring 1984.
4. Edwin Denby, *Dance Writings,* ed. Robert Cornfield and William Mackay (New York: Alfred A. Knopf, 1986).

Chapter 12. *Conclusions*

1. Alexis de Tocqueville, *Democracy in America,* ed. and abridged by Richard D. Hefner (New York: New American Library, 1956).
2. From a commencement address by Riccardo Muti at the University of Pennsylvania, 1987. Printed in *Keynote Magazine* (New York: Copyright GAF Broadcasting Co., 1987).
3. From Brooks Atkinson, *Tuesdays and Fridays* (New York: Random House, 1960).

INDEX